Mentalization-Based Tr
for Adolescents

Mentalization-Based Treatment for Adolescents (MBT-A) is a practical guide for child and adolescent mental health professionals to help enhance their knowledge, skills and practice.

The book focuses on describing MBT work with adolescents in a practical way that reflects everyday clinical practice. With chapters authored by international experts, it elucidates how to work within a mentalization-based framework with adolescents in individual, family and group settings. Following an initial theoretical orientation embedded in adolescent development, the second part of the book illuminates the MBT stance and technique when working with young people, as well as the supervisory structures employed to sustain the MBT-A therapist. The third part describes applications of MBT-A therapies to support adolescents with a range of presentations.

This book will appeal to therapists working with adolescents who wish to develop their expertise in MBT as well as other child and adolescent mental health professionals.

Trudie Rossouw, MD, is a Consultant Child and Adolescent Psychiatrist, fully registered with the General Medical Council. She has over 20 years of experience treating the full range of child and adolescent mental health conditions. Dr Rossouw currently works as a consultant child and adolescent psychiatrist at the Priory Hospital, North London and in her own child and adolescent mental health service, the Stepping Stones Clinic in London.

Maria Wiwe, MA, is a Clinical Psychologist and Psychotherapist and qualified MBT-A therapist, supervisor and trainer as well as a certified MBT-F practitioner. Together with Trudie Rossouw, Maria is training and assessing new MBT-A supervisors at the Anna Freud National Centre for Children and Families. She is an experienced lecturer and supervisor in MBT-A and has written several books on the subject in Swedish.

Ioanna Vrouva, PhD, DClinPsy, is a Clinical Psychologist, MBT-A therapist and supervisor, and an Honorary Research Associate at UCL. She works in North London in a CAMHS team for the National Health Service and in private practice.

Mentalization-Based Treatment for Adolescents

A Practical Treatment Guide

Edited by Trudie Rossouw,
Maria Wiwe, and
Ioanna Vrouva

Routledge
Taylor & Francis Group

LONDON AND NEW YORK

First published 2021
by Routledge
2 Park Square, Milton Park, Abingdon, Oxon OX14 4RN

and by Routledge
52 Vanderbilt Avenue, New York, NY 10017

Routledge is an imprint of the Taylor & Francis Group, an informa business

British Library Cataloguing-in-Publication Data
A catalogue record for this book is available from the British Library

Library of Congress Cataloging-in-Publication Data
A catalog record has been requested for this book

ISBN: 978-0-367-34101-5 (hbk)
ISBN: 978-0-367-34103-9 (pbk)
ISBN: 978-0-429-32392-8 (ebk)

Typeset in Bembo
by MPS Limited, Dehradun

Contents

Contributors

Dickon Bevington, MBBS, MRCPsych, is Medical Director at the Anna Freud National Centre for Children and Families, where he develops and leads training in AMBIT and other MBT approaches and is a member of the Mentalization-based Treatment for Families (MBT-F) team. Dr Bevington is also a Consultant Child and Adolescent Psychiatrist in Cambridgeshire and Peterborough NHS FT, where he leads CASUS, an outreach service for complex substance-using youth, and he is also a Fellow of the Cambridge and Peterborough CLARHC, a collaboration based in Cambridge University dedicated to developing leadership and research in health and social care.

Mark Dangerfield, PhD, is a Clinical Psychologist, Psychotherapist (member of the EFPP and EuroPsy) and Psychoanalyst (member of the Spanish Psychoanalytical Society and the International Psychoanalytical Association). He is a Professor at the University Institute of Mental Health (Ramon Llull University, Barcelona), an AMBIT Trainer at the Anna Freud National Centre for Children and Families and an MBT-A Supervisor. He has worked for over 25 years in paediatric hospitals and mental health services in Barcelona, specialising in working with adolescents and adults. He is the Director of the ECID project (Home Intervention Clinical Teams) of the Vidal and Barraquer Foundation, a pioneering project in Spain, where community outreach mental health teams work with non-help-seeking young people with high psychopathological risk and high risk of social exclusion, based on the AMBIT model of the Anna Freud National Centre for Children and Families.

Holly Dwyer Hall is a Child and Adolescent Psychoanalytic Psychotherapist, Arts Therapist and an accredited MBT Practitioner with Adults, Families and Adolescents and an MBT-A Supervisor and MBT- F Supervisor and Trainer for the Anna Freud National Centre for Children and Families. She has worked in the UK's National Health Service in Child and Adolescent Mental Health Services and as part of an Arts Psychotherapies Team providing group and individual Mentalization-based Arts Therapy for adults with a diagnosis of borderline personality disorder. Holly was a lead trainer and clinical supervisor with ICAPT, the International Centre for Arts Psychotherapies at the CNWL NHS Foundation Trust and has lectured and presented for Arts Therapies Courses and conferences in the UK and internationally.

Peter Fonagy is Director of the Division of Psychology and Language Sciences at UCL; Chief Executive of the Anna Freud National Centre for Children and Families, London; is Senior Clinical Advisor in NHS England on Children and Young People's Mental Health; and holds visiting professorships at Yale and Harvard Medical Schools. His clinical interests centre on issues of early attachment relationships, social cognition, borderline personality disorder and violence.

Sophie Hauschild is a Clinical Psychologist, MBT-A therapist in training and research assistant at the Institute of Psychosocial Prevention, University Hospital Heidelberg. Her research focuses on mentalization-based therapy and mentalization-based training, conduct disorder and borderline personality disorder.

Haiko Jessurun, MSc, is a Clinical Psychologist and Child and Adolescent Psychotherapist in the Netherlands. Over the past 35 years, he has held different positions in mental health care, as a therapist, team leader, and manager. He is a Senior Lecturer on the Child and Adolescent Psychotherapy training course and teaches MBT-A at the post-graduate course for Clinical Psychologists. Furthermore, he is a PhD student at the University of Technology, Eindhoven, researching the effects of chronic relative underperformance. He completed MBT-A, MBT-F, AMBIT and MBT-P training at the Anna Freud National Centre for Children and Families in London, and he is an AFC recognised MBT-A supervisor. In the Netherlands, he is actively involved in the expansion of AMBIT.

Patrick Luyten, PhD, is Professor of Clinical Psychology at the Faculty of Psychology and Educational Sciences, University of Leuven (Belgium) and Professor of Psychodynamic Psychology at the Research Department of Clinical, Educational, and Health Psychology, University College London (UK). His main research interests are disorders from the affective spectrum (i.e., depression and stress- and pain-related disorders), and personality disorders. In both areas, he is involved in basic research and interventional research.

Saskia Malcorps is a Clinical Psychologist and PhD student at the faculty of Psychology and Educational Sciences at the University of Leuven (Belgium). Her research focuses on the role of mentalizing in the development of children and adolescents at risk of psychopathology.

Jason Maldonado-Page is a Senior Family and Systemic Psychotherapist, Clinical Social Worker and Lecturer in the NHS and privately. He has held specialist and senior clinical posts at several internationally renowned London institutions and is an experienced lecturer in both social work and systemic practice. Jason is particularly drawn to the use of self and how we each make meaning from our lived experiences.

Nicole Muller is a Child and Adolescent Psychotherapist and Family Therapist based at the Jutters, Child and Adolescent Mental Health Service, part of the Parnassia Group in the Netherlands. She originally trained as a Cognitive Behavioural Therapist and worked extensively with Guided Affective Imagery before becoming interested in MBT, which she has now used for many years in her work with children and adolescents with attachment disorder, trauma, or emerging personality disorder, and their families. She has co-written with an international team the book "Mentalization-Based Treatment for Children: a time-limited approach" an MBT treatment guide for work with children aged 5-12 years. She is trainer and supervisor for MBT-C, MBT-A and MBT-F in the Netherlands and London at the Anna Freud National Centre for Children and Families.

Trudie Rossouw MD is a Consultant Child and Adolescent Psychiatrist, fully registered with the General Medical Council. She has over 20 years of experience treating the full range of child and adolescent mental health conditions. Dr Rossouw currently works as a consultant child and adolescent psychiatrist at the Priory Hospital, North London and in her own child and adolescent mental health service, the Stepping Stones Clinic in London. She is also a Psychoanalyst and qualified MBT-A therapist, supervisor, trainer and course leader and an honorary senior lecturer at University College London. Together with Peter Fonagy, she is the founder of the MBT-A model. She has published the RCT on MBT-A (Rossouw & Fonagy, 2012), and written extensively on self-harm and MBT-A.

Svenja Taubner is Professor for Psychosocial Prevention at the University Hospital in Heidelberg, Germany and Head of the Institute for Psychosocial Prevention. She is a Clinical Psychologist, Psychoanalyst and MBT-A supervisor and trainer. Her research focuses on conduct disorder, borderline personality disorder, psychotherapy research and competence development in mental health professionals. She was editor in chief of Mental Health & Prevention, is editor of Praxis der Kinderpsychologie & Kinderpsychiatrie and Psychotherapeut, and is President of the European Chapter of the Society for Psychotherapy Research (SPR). She is setting up MBT services in Germany.

Ioanna Vrouva, PhD, DClinPsy, is a Clinical Psychologist, MBT-A therapist and supervisor, and an Honorary Research Associate at UCL. She works in North London in a CAMHS team for the National Health Service, and in private practice. She has co-edited the book "Minding the Child: Mentalization- Based Interventions with Children, Young People, and their Families".

Maria Wiwe, MA, is a Clinical Psychologist and Psychotherapist and qualified MBT-A therapist, supervisor and trainer as well as a certified MBT-F practitioner. Together with Trudie Rossouw, Maria is training and assessing new MBT-A supervisors at the Anna Freud National Centre for Children and Families. She is an experienced lecturer and supervisor in MBT-A and has written several books on the subject in Swedish.

Foreword

Peter Fonagy

Something dramatic, unacceptable and hard to understand is happening. The scale and burden of the mental health problems experienced by our young people represent a public health crisis. In the UK, we now have relatively comprehensive and reliable information about the breadth and depth of mental health difficulties experienced by children and young people (Sadler et al., 2018). Overall, the prevalence of childhood mental disorder might have increased from one in ten to one in eight over fifteen years. When segregated by age, we find that in young women aged 17 to 19, this rate has increased to 24%. The adult morbidity survey (McManus, Bebbington, Jenkins, & Brugha, 2016), now six years old, similarly shows a substantial increase in the prevalence of anxiety and depression in particular amongst the 18 to 25-year-old cohort. Although less systematic, but impressive in terms of panel size, the UCL Covid-19 community survey has revealed an even more disturbing picture (Fancourt, Bu, Mak, & Steptoe, 2020). Week after week, tens of thousands of UK residents were surveyed in relation to their experiences during the national lockdown. The survey included two widely used and highly reliable measures of depression (PHQ-9) and anxiety (GAD-7). The overall level of mental health problems revealed a relatively reassuring picture. However, focusing on the 18–29-year-old sample, the many thousands of young people completing the survey showed mean levels of 10 and 8 on the PHQ-9 and the GAD-7 respectively. The mean clinical cut-off for these instruments are 10 and 8, respectively. Even adjusting for the abnormality of the distribution of underlying scores in both these instruments, the prevalence of anxiety and depression in this large panel survey would appear to be above 40%.

I do not believe that anyone fully understands the reason why mental health problems are so clearly focused in a young age group. There are many explanations offered. The emergence and dominance of social media in the lives of young people may be an important factor. Much has also been written about disproportionality concerning gender. There is no doubt that social pressures on young women are far greater (or have been at least until most recently) with conflicting roles of educational and professional success and an effectively unchanged value system surrounding sexual roles in our society. Of course, there is likely to be intersectionality amongst these risk factors. Gender may have implications for social media use and women are far more vulnerable in relation to the visually dominated social media most present in youth culture than males.

Many of the general vulnerabilities associated with adolescence are brilliantly reviewed in the first part of this book. But of course, understanding development at both psychosocial and neurobiological levels does not explain why, in England at least, the number of young people presenting with mental health problems in 2019 alone increased by 15%. It doesn't explain why 50% of the young women who experienced diagnosable mental health problems have self-harmed or made a suicide attempt. It doesn't explain why suicide rates are rising in this age group. This shift takes on a catastrophic flavour if we fully recognise just how important adolescence is as the period which defines people's subsequent career, health and well-being trajectories. If 75% of mental health difficulties manifest by the age of 18, as some research suggests (Murphy & Fonagy, 2013), it is obvious that nothing short of a radical transformation is needed, working across disciplines and approaches to mental health to bring the best and most readily adapted evidence-based intervention to our communities, to young people and their families.

And this is where the wonderful collection of chapters in this book comes in. The editors are to be warmly congratulated for providing a comprehensive introduction to a common language which may be readily adopted by clinicians, regardless of their orientation or primary training, by families attempting to provide the best support to young people regardless of the specific problem, by young people trying to find their way through their increasingly complex social network and by the broader systems of schools, communities and social institutions which are so evidently failing in mitigating depression and anxiety in our young people.

This book proposes a generic, atheoretical and potentially extremely helpful conceptual framework that is simple and obvious that it is hard to understand why the clinical world of child and adolescent mental health services has been relatively slow in adopting it. It is in keeping with a paradigm shift in the world of psychosocial treatments that a number of us have noted (e.g., Fonagy & Luyten, 2019). This shift is characterised by a decreasing emphasis on *named therapies* defined by a set of technologies addressed to a particular clearly defined group of patients. Difficulties in scientifically validating these groups have contributed to this decline. Similarly, the idea of *schools of psychotherapy* has also lost some currency. It used to be enough to say that a therapist was psychodynamically or cognitive behaviourally trained and this would be a kind of passport both in terms of accreditation but also defining their "therapeutic nationality".

Meanwhile, balancing these declines, we can observe a rise in *testable models of intervention*. In the first trial of mentalization-based treatments for adolescents (Rossouw & Fonagy, 2012), we measured both a capacity for mentalizing and security of attachment as possible mediators of treatment effects. Assuming that mentalizing matters, enhancing this psychological capacity provides an experimental framework for placing MBT under a microscope. There should be and there will be more *mediation and moderation studies*. As several chapters in this book clearly identify, the conceptual frame of mentalizing provides a new form of diagnosis based on a kind of *mechanistic functional analysis*. Different forms of mentalizing failure may lead to different manifestations of mental disorder rooted in a common core of dysfunction of social cognition associated with patterns of adaptation in types of child–caregiver relationships. Mentalizing also represents an approach, in common with other orientations such as ACT (Hayes, 2015) and compassion focused therapy (Gilbert, 2019), where we may discern a *move from nomothetic to idiographic* approaches. We need more than an effect size coefficient associated with mean differences between two groups that differ principally in the treatment to which they were exposed. We know that beneath the group mean in a treatment trial are substantially different trajectories that correspond to individual paths often reflecting deteriorations alongside the recovery even when overall improvement predominates. All this opens the door to a kind of 'personalized medicine' approach to psychological therapies with elements of therapy being used in combination configured to best fit an individual's presenting difficulties, creating an approach that integrates, or perhaps bridges, different treatment orientations, settings and even cultures.

Does the approach presented in this book provide a key to understanding the mental health problems our young people face? Mentalizing is rooted deep in our evolutionary history when becoming bipedal drove our species towards social living that in turn, required greater cognitive capacity (Dunbar & Sosis, 2018). Human babies are born markedly more immature than other primates. Birth itself is painful and dangerous and requires social support from kin (Hrdy, 2013). Our species require long periods of essential safeguarding and care and intense and protracted learning before the young human is ready to join the community of approximately 150 individuals engaged primarily in foraging with familiarity and reciprocal relationships between members of the group (Dunbar & Sosis, 2018). Everyone within the group, not just close relatives, has responsibility for protecting young humans. Relatives and other group members are present all the time and children can roam freely seeking contact, comfort, and play from whoever they choose.

Human sociality is explained by the unique capacity to share mental states with and of others (Tomasello, 2019). When people are poised to interact, they achieve interpersonal awareness through a meeting of minds. Mental states are assumed by individuals within a social system to be joined or shared by everyone. Philosophers of mind have named this category of mental events "jointly seeing to it" (Tuomela, 2005). This feeling of we-ness underpins social collaboration. Being part of a set of thoughts and feelings that are beyond one's own is the essence of humanity. Thinking together in this way creates a collective form of social cognition called the "we-mode". This we-mode provides the context in infancy in which mentalizing develops. This is the context that spurs mentalizing on in toddlerhood and moves play from a solitary activity to social collaboration. This is the context in which peer relationships of middle childhood are formed and families acquire their unique systemic properties. We-ness permeates the social bonds of adolescence and the essential social support which peer groups provide young people transitioning from dependence to selfhood. This is also the core idea that runs through the therapeutic models and techniques described in this collection of excellent reviews. We-ness is the distillation of the mentalization-based approach to psychotherapy. Perhaps it goes beyond MBT and motivates other therapeutic approaches such as DBT or ACT as well.

But what of the increased prevalence of adolescent mental disorder? Our environment of biological adaptation, the social environment of the hunter-gatherer, where we acquired the capacity to jointly see to something and share our mutual understanding of mental states, is ecologically threatened in much the same way as the thinning of the ozone layer threatens vital facets of our physical environment. Mentalizing, according to this formulation, evolved in and for adaptation to a community rather than one on one relationships. In some ways, attachment theory may not have helped here. This theory, and our early writings on mentalizing, emphasised a model of parent/caregiver interaction that was essentially dyadic (Bowlby, 1969, 1973; Fonagy, Gergely, Jurist, & Target, 2002). Drawing on attachment research, we emphasised the dyadic: turn-taking, smooth completed interactions between infant and caregiver, the reflection in the caregiver's face of the child's emerging affect, etc. as the essential components or foundation stones upon which mentalizing was built. In other words, we supported a cultural ideal of the infant as an agent sensitised to use parental qualities and attributes as the primary referent of their actions. In this account, when infants recognised the mother's representation of them as the central agent, this generated the sense of self-recognition which was assumed to be at the heart of self-development not just in infancy but perhaps also through adolescence and of adulthood. There is little doubt about the reality of this, but it is a partial story. This dyadic experience might best be understood as a part of a broader category of we-mode: perhaps self-focused dyadic interaction is one special way of generating a sense of belonging and a sense of self? Perhaps among hunter-gatherers, different forms of we-mode were emphasised in developing these aspects of identity, and perhaps they still are in many non-Western societies. In societies more like hunter-gatherers' and different from ours, children and caregivers are engaged in multiple simultaneous ongoing activities and very rarely in dyadic interactions (Keller, 2018). These support a cultural ideal that is quite different from the one which prioritises the infant or child as the central agent, the focus of the caregivers' attention. In this broader, multiply layered, constantly preoccupied interaction, the child is sensitised to attend to others' mental states, their wishes and their interests. It is the mental states of others, the social group, rather than their own, which can be used by the child as the primary referent for actions. It is the recognition of belonging, finding oneself similar to the central tendency of the group that creates and validates identity.

What is suggested here is that mentalizing is a product of social adaptation to collaboration in groups. As a result, it may be risky for this idea to be hijacked into a framework that emphasises the self as the central agent. We have for many years, cautioned against excessive self-reflection as a therapeutic approach for individuals whose sense of self is poorly formed. Perhaps we did not quite recognise the importance of our recommendation, rooted as it was in clinical experience rather than theoretical considerations. If we see mentalizing as essentially a signal of belonging, then one way of seeing difficulties in mentalizing is as an experience of loss of social cohesion and social belonging. I wonder if we should not see the increased prevalence of adolescent mental health difficulties as a limitation of resilience rooted in a vulnerability that arises out of a partial failure of social connectedness. I am not suggesting that social connectedness between young people is less intense now than it was in the past. I do think, however, that there is evidence to suggest that intergenerational contact has been on the wane since the Second World War and young people have in many respects become their own socialising agents. While the importance of peer groups for development is clear, I do believe that we have arrived at a human evolutionary mismatch in the way we have reconstructed adolescence in the late 20th and early 21st-centuries.

Humans now live in environments diverging rapidly from those in which they evolved – the so-called *environment of biological adaptation*, the contexts where certain functions fulfilled a selective advantage. The discrepancy between the current environment and the environment where the selective advantage was clear is referred to as an *evolutionary mismatch*. The mismatch is due to the *adaptive lag* that occurs because the environment that called forth a capacity or function with selection advantage changes more rapidly than the time needed for the evolved function to adapt to change. An evolutionary mechanism such as a preference for sweet things makes perfect sense in the context of scarce resources where sucrose will lead to a preference for fruits and honey that yield calories and vitamins. In the context where manufactured foods replaced those found in nature, this built-in preference for sweet things can lead to a preference for foods with little nutritional value and high-calorie content leading to an epidemic of childhood obesity. For 99% of human history, people lived as hunter-gatherers in small kin-based groups. The evolutionary mismatch for we-ness started perhaps 10,000 years ago when agriculture arose but the mismatch became worse again with the industrial revolution. We-ness, *jointly seeing to it* makes sense in the environment of hunter-gatherers. The viability of mutual understanding is increasingly tested with the increasing complexity of social structures, particularly social hierarchies and the psychological complexities these bring with them.

I think that modern education has generated a similar adaptive lag by removing key features of the environment of biological adaptation. The environment of biological adaptation for adolescent development included supportive, vertically (intergenerationally) integrated groups. An evolutionary mismatch occurred when, for the best of social reasons, education was prolonged beyond puberty into late adolescence and young adulthood. The mismatch is rooted in the relative absence of adults within the groups where adolescent upbringing takes place. Adolescents spend less time with adult role models now than was the case when apprenticeships dominated the educational model. Adolescence is a period when we are biologically programmed to seek independence from our caregivers. The drive for independence should not preclude non-kin adults with an educational function. Yet socialising adults are remote in the large classes of most secondary schools. Young people do not feel they are known about as individuals. In modern adolescence, parts of our biological heritage are retained, such as the drive to take increased responsibility for one's actions; at the same time components designed to support enhanced responsibility, namely increased agency, have been compromised. Responsibility without agency is never a helpful combination. Having been brought up in a culture where self-agency is king, the lack of agency creates incoherence and a gap between the actual and ideal self that many cannot cope with. It is right that adolescents should push against parental involvement in their lives, but it is challenging that the current social structure also makes them excessively dependent at least financially on parental input. Social media may indeed bear some responsibility for increasing stress. But it is an underlying compromise of an intergenerational social network that may have additional significance.

Why are we in this situation where young people may rightly feel inadequately supported by the previous generation, while simultaneously being apparently overprotected from taking on the markers of adulthood responsibility? The driver for the modern prolongation of adolescence is the changed environment – the demands placed upon learning by the increased complexity of the human knowledge base. The increased complexity of tools we now use require longer learning and the adequate transmission of cultural knowledge simply takes more time. To counter the impact of the demands of this changed environment, we need to create natural protective adaptations which promote processes that enable connections, enhance agency and strengthen the social network. This is the touchstone of we-ness and a mentalizing informed approach.

The increased impulsivity, risk-taking and the prioritisation of peer group interactions in adolescence represent an adaptation to facilitate moving away from reliance on caregivers towards becoming an individual that in turn necessitates complete reconfiguration of self-structures to encompass physical and sexual maturation. The task of adolescence is to integrate a vastly changed body, to manage increased sexuality, to accommodate enhanced emotional intensity and to deal with a greater capacity for symbolic and abstract thinking in organising a sense of oneself and one's relationships at the same time as being equal to the massive pressures that the sometimes intensely competitive nature of peer relationships impose with additional psychosocial demands for creating separation and autonomy and developing a distinct adult sense of self. How can we expect young people to achieve this on their own? Within the historical context of hunter-gatherer socialisation, the function of the community around the individual was to manage the 'perfect storm' of adolescence: the neurodevelopmental progression of mentalizing brain circuits that are undergoing pruning and may therefore be less able to modulate arousal and emotion and respond to the demands of the limbic system. This, in turn, generates increasingly intense emotional experiences linked to a desire for novelty and stimulation. In brief, the adolescent without adult support may often be inadequate to the tasks that we require of them. Perhaps the hypermentalizing (Sharp et al., 2013; Sharp et al., 2016), the excessive theory of mind, the tendency to make groundless inferences about the mental state that go so far beyond observable data that others may struggle to see how they are justified is a signal of the evolutionary mismatch that we have created for our young people and the source of the mental health risk which young people in the early 21st-century face.

That they deserve better support and social networking than they currently receive is hard to deny. Yet there must be reasons for this gap in appropriate support, and these may point up a second, perhaps even more pernicious, social process. There is a clash of generations between baby boomers (and the children of baby boomers) and the adolescents and young adults of today. The increased focus on the parent–child interaction in the second half of the 20th century, the dyadic concern of parents for infants, focused on enhancing self-agency may have had many desirable social outcomes in the form of reducing the cognitive and psychological disadvantages of neglect but perhaps also had some undesirable social consequences when it comes to the capacity of the child of the baby-boomer parent to engage in their own parenting.

Transgenerational transmission of this enhanced dyadic focus, which seems well established by now, and has undoubtedly improved the early years of infants and toddlers across society. But has the same pattern improved these parents' capacity to empower the next generation to achieve independence and overtake them as well as taking over from them as is nature's template for all living beings? I believe that here we encounter a problem. The same developmental pressures that have placed the infant at the centre of the socialisation process taking energy and attention away from the we-mode of the community and the social network, that same psychological pressure for self-importance may make that individual when older be less willing to step aside and give over power and authority to the emerging young. A simpler account for or a separate contributor to the evolutionary mismatch is, of course, increased longevity. As we live healthy lives for decades longer than has been the case in the environment of biological adaptation, evolution may not have prepared us to willingly relinquish our authority when perfectly fit and move over to our biologically prepared grandparenting mode. The narcissism of Western culture, probably rooted in the nuclear family and the valorisation of mother–infant interaction has perhaps served to undermine fresh opportunities for adolescents and young adults because of parents' attitudes to the challenge of the next generation of adults. It is generally recognised that the current generation of noughties is likely to be the first that is worse off than the generation that has preceded it, at least since we have focused on this particular indicator of transgenerational progression.

Our response to Covid-19 is perhaps an example of the way, for the most justifiable and humanitarian motives, the interests of the older generation have been prioritised across the globe over the interests of the young. Young people are less affected by the coronavirus than those in middle-age and above. In fact, under 45 excess deaths have decreased since Covid-19 in contrast to older adults whose lives are seriously at risk of being shortened by the virus. The public health initiative, at least in all Western cultures, appears to have prioritised the older generation against the young. As an adult in my late 60s, I have little to complain about. However, it is striking that rather than making my generation and a few above and below responsible for looking after ourselves and keeping ourselves safe, we forced young people to adopt an unnatural set of strategies of social isolation with the primary function of protecting the older generation from disease and a painful and uncomfortable death.

So, I see the increased prevalence of adolescent mental health less as a manifestation of the neurobiological changes, characteristic of that age group, and more of a consequence of social change consequent on preceding social changes that have prioritised the individual above the social group. It is hardly surprising that the sense of self-focus and the assumption of being of deserving of our central place might have translated at least in part into a way we treat the generation below us and in turn that generation experiences a sense of gloom, anxiety and hopelessness, feeling unsupported to some measure and abandoned by us to manage on their own in a social environment where competition has just become much harsher: they have all the 60-year-olds to contend with along with their peer group and beyond.

References

Bowlby, J. (1969). *Attachment and Loss, Vol. 1: Attachment.* London, UK: Hogarth Press and Institute of Psycho-Analysis.

Bowlby, J. (1973). *Attachment and Loss, Vol. 2: Separation: Anxiety and Anger.* London, UK: Hogarth Press and Institute of Psycho-Analysis.

Dunbar, R.I.M., & Sosis, R. (2018). Optimising human community sizes. *Evolution and Human Behavior, 39*(1), 106–111. doi: 10.1016/j.evolhumbehav.2017.11.001.

Fancourt, D., Bu, F., Mak, H.W., & Steptoe, A. (2020). *UK covid-mind study: Results Release 3* (pp. 1–23). London: University College London.

Fonagy, P., Gergely, G., Jurist, E., & Target, M. (2002). *Affect Regulation, Mentalization, and the Development of the Self.* New York, NY: Other Press.

Fonagy, P., & Luyten, P. (2019). Fidelity vs. flexibility in the implementation of psychotherapies: Time to move on. *World Psychiatry, 18*(3), 270–271. doi: 10.1002/wps.20657.

Gilbert, P. (2019). Distinguishing shame, humiliation and guilt: An evolutionary functional analysis and compassion focused interventions. In C.-H. Mayer & E. Vanderheiden (Eds.), *The Bright Side of Shame* (pp. 413–431). Cham, Switzerland: Springer Nature Switzerland.

Hayes, S.C. (2015). *The Act in Context: The Canonical Papers of Steven C. Hayes.* New York, NY: Routledge.

Hrdy, S.B. (2013). The 'one animal in all creation about which man knows the least'. *Philosophical Transactions of the Royal Society of London, Series B: Biological Sciences, 368*(1631), 20130072. doi: 10.1098/rstb.2013.0072.

Keller, H. (2018). Universality claim of attachment theory: Children's socioemotional development across cultures. *Proceedings of the National Academy of Sciences of the United States of America, 115*(45), 11414–11419. doi: 10.1073/pnas.1720325115.

McManus, S., Bebbington, P., Jenkins, R., & Brugha, T. (Eds.). (2016). *Mental Health and Wellbeing in England: Adult Psychiatric Morbidity Survey 2014.* Leeds, UK: NHS Digital.

Murphy, M., & Fonagy, P. (2013). Chapter 10: Mental health problems in children and young people. *Our children deserve better: prevention pays: Annual report of the Chief Medical Officer 2012* (pp. 176–188). London, UK: Department of Health.

Rossouw, T.I., & Fonagy, P. (2012). Mentalization-based treatment for self-harm in adolescents: A randomized controlled trial. *Journal of the American Academy of Child and Adolescent Psychiatry, 51*(12), 1304–1313. doi: 10.1016/i.jaac.2012.09.018.

Sadler, K., Vizard, T., Ford, T., Goodman, A., Goodman, R., & McManus, S. (2018). *Mental Health of Children and Young People in England, 2017: Trends and characteristics.* Leeds, England: Health and Social Care Information Centre. (NHS Digital).

Sharp, C., Ha, C., Carbone, C., Kim, S., Perry, K., Williams, L., & Fonagy, P. (2013). Hypermentalizing in adolescent inpatients: Treatment effects and association with borderline traits. *Journal of Personality Disorders, 27*(1), 3–18. doi: 10.1521/pedi.2013.27.1.3.

Sharp, C., Venta, A., Vanwoerden, S., Schramm, A., Ha, C., Newlin, E., … Fonagy, P. (2016). First empirical evaluation of the link between attachment, social cognition and borderline features in adolescents. *Comprehensive Psychiatry, 64*, 4–11. doi: 10.1016/j.comppsych.2015.07.008.

Tomasello, M. (2019). *Becoming Human: A Theory of Ontogeny.* Cambridge, MA: The Belknap Press of Harvard University Press.

Tuomela, R. (2005). *We-intentions revisited. Philosophical Studies, 125*(3), 327–369. doi: 10.1007/s11098-005-7781-1.

Acknowledgements

We would like to take the opportunity to thank all the amazing and brave adolescents we have met during the years, as well as their families. We are deeply grateful for the trust they have shown us, and we hope they have learnt from us as much as we have learnt from them.

We are indebted to the many gifted clinicians and researchers who have offered insights about mentalization, especially Professor Peter Fonagy, who has been a supervisor, mentor and collaborator of many of the contributors in this book, and a source of reliable support, inspiration and humour.

We would also like to acknowledge the support of the Anna Freud National Centre for Children and Families, where most contributors in the book attended or presented at MBT training events and conferences. All our colleagues who have contributed to this volume have our gratitude and deep respect.

Thanks also go to the editorial team at Routledge, especially Joanne Forshaw, for her encouragement, responsiveness, and flexibility, as well as the two anonymous reviewers for their constructive suggestions at the initial stages of the book.

We are grateful to Dr Adam Duncan for designing the paperback cover and for his editorial input and linguistic suggestions.

Thanks also to the Copyrights teams at Elsevier Publishing for permission to use the figures in Chapters 2 and 5, and at Oxford University Press for permission to reproduce the AMBIT wheel in Chapter 12.

Finally, we are most grateful to our family, friends and colleagues, for their thoughtfulness, support and understanding.

Introduction

Trudie Rossouw, Maria Wiwe,
and Ioanna Vrouva

The following dialogue between teenager Agnes and her father Olof is an excerpt from the Swedish movie 'Show me love' (the original Swedish title being 'Fucking Amål'), written and directed by Lukas Moodysson (1998). Olof, a caring father, is trying to comfort his daughter Agnes, who is feeling lonely and isolated following friendship struggles.

Olof: 'When our class met, I think it was our 25-year reunion, then they all found out that I had done very well for myself. Bengt, who was then the class king, he hadn't amounted to anything at all, really. Also, the girls who were considered the prettiest, they were not special any longer. You see, I think you should be glad that you do not have it so easy. Because those who have it easy often become quite uninteresting people in the end'.

Agnes: 'But you're speaking about 25 years' time. I'm sorry Dad, but I'd rather be happy now than in 25 years'.

Well, who would want to wait 25 years for better days? Adolescents, with their intense and highly present way of viewing life, can be rightly sceptical of adult advice and "wisdom". They long for connections with peers that will help them develop their sense of self and identity, but as many of us can still quite vividly remember, this process is far from painless, fraught with experiences of confusion, rejection, and humiliation. Understandably, adapting to the changing and often contradictory needs of adolescents presents their parents (and teachers) with multiple challenges. And when it comes to being an adolescent's therapist, pressures such as establishing an alliance in the face of high ambivalence, negotiating ruptures, preventing treatment dropout and managing multiple risks can test the most experienced clinicians. At the same time, the opportunity to follow these fascinating young people in their endeavour to connect with the people around them and find themselves and their place in life can be among the most rewarding experiences of our professional life.

The adolescent phase is tremendously significant and presents every young person and family with unique vulnerability, as well as opportunity. With every aspect of the adolescent mind and being under construction, and simultaneous changes in their neurochemistry, bodies and psychosocial worlds, the adolescent years, now understood to continue into our 20 s, is an uncertain, unsteady and often unsettling period of life. Changes associated with brain development leave the young person more prone to strong affect storms, but with an underdeveloped capacity to regulate and navigate them. Adolescents are uniquely sensitive to the facial expressions of other young people (Moore et al., 2012) and perceived rejection, and present with higher risk-taking behaviour as they seek stimulation and peer approval (Steinberg, 2008).

It has long been established that adolescents often feel lost and torn between their dependence on, and their disdain for their parents and other adult authority figures coupled with their pull to their peer group, amidst significant anxiety about not fitting in, not knowing who they are and what they want. Changes in social understanding and increased self-conscious awareness can result in the insecurity and anxiety of childhood being replaced by feelings of shame and self-hatred in adolescence. It is no wonder that 50% of adult mental illness originates in adolescence (Kessler et al., 2005), and internalising and externalising mental health problems such as depression, eating disorders, substance abuse, conduct disorder and psychosis typically first present in this period of life.

However, adolescence is not just a period of increased vulnerability, but also a time of great opportunity. Many great minds emerged in their adolescent years, such as Michelangelo, Mary Shelley and Ada Lovelace, whereas more recently a once struggling teenager, Greta Thunberg, succeeded at inspiring and mobilising people in all age groups worldwide to take protective action for the future of our planet.

So, what are the factors that can turn vulnerability into opportunity and strength? What are the essential components of mental health and personal growth in adolescence? At the heart of this book is the tenet that strengthening mentalizing development in this neurobiologically and psychosocially critical period of life not only alleviates distress, but also increases resilience (Fonagy, Luyten, Allison, & Campbell, 2016). The term mentalizing, first used by Peter Fonagy in 1989, refers to our ability to understand behaviour in terms of mental states, namely attribute psychological meaning to actions, and also make sense of our own internal and interpersonal experiences. Conceptualised as a developmental construct (Fonagy, Gergely, Jurist, & Target, 2002), mentalizing was applied clinically by Peter Fonagy, Anthony Bateman and their colleagues in the development of mentalization-based treatment for adults with borderline personality disorder (Bateman & Fonagy, 2004). MBT was further developed by clinicians and researchers worldwide for several other mental health conditions in adults (Bateman & Fonagy, 2019), with mentalizing becoming a transdiagnostic concept (Luyten, Campbell, Allison, & Fonagy).

MBT was also developed for interventions with young people (Midgley & Vrouva, 2012), including children (MBT-C; Midgley, Ensink, Lindqvist,

Malberg, & Muller, 2017), parents (Cooper & Redfern, 2016) and families (MBT-F, Asen & Fonagy, 2012a, 2012b, initially known as SMART, Fearon et al., 2006). Strongly connected to the above and other pioneering work with adolescents (e.g., Bleiberg, 2013; Sharp et al., 2009), Trudie Rossouw and Peter Fonagy developed and empirically evaluated MBT for adolescents (MBT-A) as a response to a need for effective and time-limited treatments for young people who self-harm (Rossouw & Fonagy, 2012). The model was later expanded with several other clinical applications presented in this book.

In the above randomised controlled trial (RCT), young people treated with MBT-A showed improvement not only with regards to self-harm but also in BPD (borderline personality disorder) traits as well as depression. In this study, MBT-A was offered as a combination of individual weekly MBT-A and monthly MBT-Family (MBT-F) treatment. The treatment duration was one year, even though several of the adolescents were able to terminate the treatment earlier than that. In several other services, however different formats of MBT-A packages exist, such as combining MBT-A individual with MBT-Group and MBT-F. Treatment duration also varies across services and may be both longer (up to 18 months) and shorter (6 months, with a briefer form of 3 months being currently examined), depending on the clinical need. Most MBT-A treatments are offered in outpatient settings, although there are inpatient units also offering MBT-A.

Embedded in the aforementioned work of Trudie Rossouw and Peter Fonagy, this book is a practical treatment guide for MBT-A and was created as a response to the many requests from trainees and supervisees for a practical text to enhance their knowledge, skills and practice; therefore, most chapters have a distinct clinical focus. Most contributors to this book are practising clinicians as well as researchers and have international experience in training and supervising clinicians in MBT-A. Working with adolescents themselves, they are attentive to the live clinical context and the day-to-day lived experience of practitioners, whilst also being familiar enough with the relevant theory and the empirical evidence supporting it, and they aim to meaningfully integrate theory, research and practice.

Mentalizing has been embraced by clinicians primarily trained in other modalities, such as psychoanalytic/psychodynamic, family/systemic, cognitive-behavioural, and interpersonal therapy. The purpose of the book is, therefore, to draw on clinicians' existing skills and insights and offer them further guidance in helping young people and their families navigate the turbulence of adolescence through developing a richer awareness of their thoughts and feelings, and those of other people, namely strengthening their mentalizing. The purpose of the book is not to tell clinicians 'this is how one ought to do the work; this is the only way'. We know from our experience working with many talented colleagues that engaging, meaningful and effective therapy is not exclusive to one therapeutic modality. However, it is also our experience that young people are more likely to benefit from therapy and psychosocial interventions when they feel that what is on their mind matters, when their thoughts and feelings are closely and sensitively attended to, and when they experience their therapist (and significant others in their life) as somebody whose mind is available and makes sense, who is prepared to meet the young person where they are at, and who remains open and willing to learn from the young person in order to understand them. So, in a way, the clinical examples described throughout the book are examples of efforts to stimulate mentalizing and foster epistemic trust in young people and their families.

We are aware that most clinicians reading this book already work in ways aimed at strengthening young people's reflective capacities, even if the theoretical language used may not include mentalizing and may be informed by different, but very relevant clinical concepts. As previous MBT authors have emphasised (e.g., Bateman & Fonagy, 2004; Midgley et al., 2017), the essence of the MBT approach is not novel, and mentalizing has been described as a "new word for old concepts" (Bateman & Fonagy, 2004). At the same time, as MBT encourages not only patients but also clinicians to subject their feelings and ideas to constant scrutiny (Holmes, 2005), interventions have been further modified and this has led to new learning about strengthening our therapeutic practice.

Although for many readers the book will serve as confirmation that their work fits with the mentalizing principles, for others, some interventions and examples might seem new and challenging and different from what they have learnt and applied before. Irrespective of their familiarity with MBT, we hope that the book will give most readers some helpful ideas in their work with adolescents and their systems. We believe that mentalizing work is at its best when the clinician is in touch with their creativity, and there are as many ways to be creative as there are therapists. Creativity is a sign of a free mind, which in turn is a sign of mentalizing. Hence, we hope the clinical examples given will provide a helping hand for clinicians to free their minds and find their creativity in their work with adolescents and their families, drawing on their own unique personal and professional attributes and experiences.

The overall organisation of the book is relatively simple: Part I is primarily theoretical and aims to provide an overview of the concept of mentalization as well as the neurobiological developments pertinent to adolescence. In Part II, we turn to clinical applications in working with young people using different formats, including individual and family therapy, and how this work can be most helpfully supervised. The last part of the book, Part III, discusses more specific clinical applications presented below.

Part I of the book has two chapters. The first chapter presents an overview of the concept of mentalization and the basic theory underpinning it. The author, Haiko Jessurun elaborates on the definition of the concept 'mentalization' and how it is rooted in socio–evolutionary and neuropsychological science, with developmental psychology and attachment theory at its heart.

The chapter describes what mentalizing difficulties look like, and their implications for clinical practice. In this chapter, Patrick Luyten, Saskia Malcorps and Peter Fonagy describe the extensive neurobiological changes taking place in adolescence, and the three systems (stress, reward and mentalizing system) evolved to enable humans to adapt to our complex social environment. Moreover, this chapter elaborates on the concept of epistemic trust introduced in Chapter 1. Even if this knowledge base may be unfamiliar to many readers with primarily clinical background, this chapter usefully reminds us that if we try as clinicians to understand these brain developments and importantly their implications to the experiences of adolescents, we can understand the young people we work with more fully, and therefore become more effective at helping them.

Taken together, we hope that the first two chapters will give the reader a clear overview of the concept of mentalization as well as an improved understanding of the mentalizing vicissitudes in adolescence.

The second part of the book illustrates the clinical work aimed at strengthening adolescents' mentalizing. The author of the third and fourth chapters, Trudie Rossouw, has developed in the United Kingdom, together with Peter Fonagy the MBT model for adolescents, empirically based on the RCT mentioned above. Trudie Rossouw takes us through the mentalizing stance and the mentalizing techniques when working with adolescents, as well as the structure of therapy. These two chapters represent the core MBT-A work and are imperative for the clinician who wishes to understand the key elements of the method and the model.

Most adolescents live with their families, and readers with CAMHS experience know well that family work is highly significant when working with young people who struggle with mental health difficulties. Building on the work of other colleagues in this area (e.g., Asen & Fonagy, 2012a, 2012b; Fearon et al., 2006) Holly Dwyer Hall and Nicole Muller describe MBT-F as 'a way of being with the family'. They present other vital components in family work, for example, holding the balance, highlighting and reinforcing positive mentalization, noticing and naming, mentalizing the moment, and therapist use of self. Furthermore, they discuss the aim of these interventions, which is to help families shift from coercive, non-mentalizing cycles to mentalizing interactions that can promote trust, attachment security and effective communication and problem-solving.

In the last chapter of Part II, Holly Dwyer Hall and Maria Wiwe describe the structure and function of MBT-A supervision. This chapter aims to benefit supervisors in developing a mentalizing approach to their supervisory practice whilst also helping clinicians to understand what to expect from mentalization-based supervision in work with adolescents.

The third part of the book describes clinical applications of mentalization-based work with adolescents affected by specific difficulties. In the first chapter of this section, Maria Wiwe and Trudie Rossouw present their work with adolescents who self-harm. The authors aim to describe in detail how to help adolescents who self-harm in the context of a breakdown in mentalizing, restore their ability to feel understood, understand themselves and consequently tolerate distressing mental states. The chapter includes a description of the mentalizing concept of 'the alien self' (Fonagy et al., 2002), and the clinical examples remind the reader of how academic language never fully captures the tremendous emotional pain these youngsters experience in their everyday life.

Following this, Ioanna Vrouva, Jason Maldonado-Page and Nicole Muller present a mentalization-based framework for thinking about gender identity development with adolescents. The three authors draw on their work in specialist and non-specialist settings in the UK and the Netherlands, reflect openly on the challenges they have experienced, and describe how the mentalizing stance helped them navigate those in a way that privileges each young person's unique mind, body and relationships with others.

Externalising problems such as conduct disorder is another highly significant area in adolescent clinical work. In Chapter 9, Svenja Taubner and Sophie Hauschild explain how conduct problems can be viewed as resulting from ineffective mentalizing and consequent loss of inhibition, especially among adolescents who show chronic offending behaviour. The work they describe includes a mentalizing assessment phase, followed by parallel individual and family work. This model is being tested in a feasibility study in Germany.

In the following chapter, Mark Dangerfield describes his work with youth presenting with at-risk mental states, namely early, low-level signs of psychosis. The author presents his work in an outreach mental health service for adolescents in Barcelona, which demonstrates the effects of relational trauma on at-risk adolescents' openness to learning through interpersonal experiences. The chapter also describes how the MBT therapist can attempt to sensitively engage such young people in understanding their own and others' minds.

Chapter 11, written by Nicole Muller and Holly Dwyer Hall, describes mentalization-based group therapy (MBT-G) with adolescents with an emerging personality disorder in community and inpatient settings. The authors depict this work from the initial stages of establishing the group composition and strengthening the therapeutic alliance with individual participants, all the way to facilitating endings. The chapter also highlights how creative activities can be used to facilitate mentalizing, and how specific mentalizing techniques can be used to attend to and clarify the different mental states among group participants and facilitate effective group work.

In the final chapter, Haiko Jessurun and Dickon Bevington describe the Adaptive Mentalization-Based Integrative Treatment (AMBIT) approach, previously also described elsewhere (e.g., Bevington, Fuggle, Cracknell, & Fonagy, 2017). AMBIT, directed towards difficult-to-reach-youngsters with multiple problems in multiple areas of their lives, has been developed over the last two decades and has been endorsed by a wide range of youth mental health services and other agencies.

Most chapters in the book use clinical examples with dialogue to illustrate the approach in a clear and practical way. The reader will notice imperfections and improvisations necessitated by the uncertainty of working with adolescents, and the unique personalities, experiences, style and culture of each clinician. In order to preserve confidentiality, all names and other identifiable details of all the adolescents and their families have been altered, or in some descriptions, a number of cases have been amalgamated.

The reader will be aware that, irrespective of the characteristics of each adolescent's and family's struggles, a consistent thread throughout the book is the mentalizing stance. The mentalizing stance involves a focus on the therapeutic process, rather than content. It is an attitude of care and compassion. We aspire to convey a real interest in our young people, their lives and what they are feeling. We are rather active in our interactions and aim to be as responsive as possible to what they communicate, verbally and non-verbally, working hard to get a better understanding of their experiences. We seek to clarify our patient's feelings, to help them feel as understood and supported as possible. We operate from a not-knowing base, where we do not assume to have significant knowledge or insight about young people before meeting them. When we see things differently or are not sure we understand, we question in a non-judgemental, explicitly supportive and open way. We make our own mind available to the young person as possible, and we are transparent about our misunderstandings and other limitations. That is what we call mentalizing work, and we are hopeful that readers will connect to this way of working and feel inspired to use it flexibly and develop it further, as we all continue to learn how to better understand ourselves and the young people we work with.

References

Asen, E., & Fonagy, P. (2012a). Mentalization-based family therapy. In A. Bateman & P. Fonagy (Eds.), Handbook of Mentalizing in Mental Health Practice. American Psychiatric Association Publishing.

Asen, E., & Fonagy, P. (2012b). Mentalization-based therapeutic interventions for families. Journal of Family Therapy, 34(4), 347–370. https://doi.org/10.1111/j.1467-6427.2011.00552.x.

Bateman, A., & Fonagy, P. (2004) Mentalization-based treatment of BPD. Journal of Personality Disorder, 18, 36–51. https://doi.org/10.1521/pedi.18.1.36.32772.

Bateman, A., Fonagy, P. (2019). A randomized controlled trial of a mentalization-based intervention (MBT-FACTS) for families of people with borderline personality disorder. Personality Disorders: Theory, Research, and Treatment, 10(1), 70–79.

Bevington, D., Fuggle, P., Cracknell, L., & Fonagy, P. (2017). Adaptive Mentalization-Based Integrative Treatment: A Guide for Teams to Develop Systems of Care (1st ed.). New York, NY: OUP.

Bleiberg, E. (2013). Mentalizing-based treatment with adolescents and families. Child and Adolescent Psychiatric Clinics of North America, 22(2), 295–330.

Cooper, A., & Redfern, S. (2016). Reflective Parenting: A Guide to Understanding What's Going on in Your Child's Mind. Hove, East Sussex: Routledge.

Fearon, P., Target, M., Sargent, J., Williams, L.L., McGregor, J., Bleiberg, E., & Fonagy, P. (2006). Short-term mentalization and relational therapy (SMART): An integrative family therapy for children and adolescents. In J.G. Allen & P. Fonagy (Eds.), Handbook of Mentalization-Based Treatment (pp. 201–222). Chichester, England: John Wiley & Sons.

Fonagy, P., Gergely, G., Jurist, E.J., & Target, M. (2002). Affect Regulation, Mentalization, and the Development of the Self. London: Karnac Press.

Fonagy, P., Luyten, P., Allison, E., & Campbell, C. (2016). Reconciling psychoanalytic ideas with attachment theory. In J. Cassidy & P.R. Shaver (Eds.), Handbook of Attachment (3rd ed., pp. 780–804). New York, NY: Guilford Press.

Holmes, J. (2005). Notes on mentalization – old hat or new wine? British Journal of Psychotherapy, 19, 690–710. https://doi.org/10.1111/j.1752-0118.2005.tb00275.x.

Luyten, P., Campbell, C., Allison, E., & Fonagy, P. (2020). The mentalizing approach to psychopathology: State of the art and future directions. Annual Review of Clinical Psychology, 16, 297–325. doi: 10.1146/annurev-clinpsy-071919-015355.

Kessler, R.C., Berglund, P., Demler, O., Jin, R., Merikangas, K.R., & Walters, E.E. (2005). Lifetime prevalence and age-of-onset distributions of DSM-IV disorders in the National Comorbidity Survey Replication. Archives of General Psychiatry, 62(6), 593–602.

Midgley, N., Ensink, K., Lindqvist, K., Malberg, N.T., & Muller, N. (2017). Mentalization-Based Treatment for Children: A Time-Limited Approach (1st ed.). Washington, DC: American Psychological Association.

Midgley, N., & Vrouva, I. (Eds). (2012). Minding the Child: Mentalization-Based Interventions with Children, Young People, and Their Families. New York: Routledge.

Moore III, W.E., Pfeifer, J.H., Masten, C.L., Mazziotta, J.C., Iacoboni, M., & Dapretto, M. (2012). Facing puberty: associations between pubertal development and neural responses to affective facial displays. Social Cognitive and Affective Neuroscience, 7(1), 35–43.

Rossouw, T.I., & Fonagy, P. (2012). Mentalization-based treatment for self-harm in adolescents: A randomized controlled trial. Journal of the American Academy of Child and Adolescent Psychiatry, 51(12), 1304–1313.e3. https://doi.org/10.1016/j.jaac.2012.09.018.

Sharp, C., Williams, L.L., Ha, C., Baumgardner, J., Michonski, J., Seals, R., … Fonagy, P. (2009). The development of a mentalization-based outcomes and research protocol for an adolescent inpatient unit. Bulletin of the Menninger Clinic, 73(4), 311–338. https://doi.org/10.1521/bumc.2009.73.4.311.

Steinberg, L. (2008). A social neuroscience perspective on adolescent risk-taking. Developmental Review, 28(1), 78–106.

Tahmasebi, A.M., Artiges, E., Banaschewski, T., Barker, G.J., Bruehl, R., Büchel, C., … Heinz, A. (2012). Creating probabilistic maps of the face network in the adolescent brain: a multicentre functional MRI study. Human Brain Mapping, 33(4), 938–957.

Section I

The concept of 'mentalization' and relevant neurobiological changes in adolescence

Chapter I

An introduction to mentalizing theory

Haiko Jessurun

At a certain time, our ancestors began to tell each other stories. Their brains had developed in a certain way, enhancing their frontal lobes, that made it more possible to symbolise and escape from the here and now and imagine the past and future. Using these stories, they could tell where food was to be found and where the danger was. Consider for a moment what this meant. What if the person telling you where the food was, was someone from a competing group of hole dwellers? Could he be trusted? So, alongside with the capacity to tell stories the need to know whom to trust had to find a way into our functioning. We had to be able to think about what might be going on in another's mind. And hand in hand, systems developed which helped us to grow in this capacity. Attachment plays a role in this; we tend to assign epistemic trust to those people we are attached to.

This all happened a long time ago and probably in a much more differentiated and sophisticated way than described here. Modern human beings, however, are driven by 'stories', some more 'true' than others, to try and make sense of our world, our relationships and ourselves. That is what mentalizing is all about. Considering that this amazing capacity developed late in the evolution of the human species, and that our brain develops along roughly the same path (from older to the newer systems, from inner to outer, and from back to front), it is important to appreciate that the pre-frontal lobe – in which this mentalizing ability takes place – is under heavy construction during adolescence. And this makes working with adolescents such a challenging task.

Broadcasting intentions

This chapter intends to introduce the basic concepts of mentalization. It will provide a working definition and discuss the several dimensions involved. Next, the developmental line will be described. Then the chapter will introduce mentalization-based treatment – now used to treat a range of mental health problems. In later chapters, treatment issues – especially when relevant to adolescents – will be addressed in detail.

Mentalization

From the vignette above, it is obvious that mentalizing is a key concept for human functioning; it is something we do all the time. Mentalizing has been defined (Allen & Fonagy, 2006, p. 54) as:

> [...] a form of *imaginative mental activity*, namely, *perceiving and interpreting human behaviour* in terms of *intentional mental states* (e.g., needs, desires, feelings, beliefs, goals, purposes and reasons).

The first element that is accentuated needs careful consideration: it is an imaginative mental activity. It takes place in the mind. And it is about imagination. Imagination here refers to an awareness of mental states in ourselves and other people, particularly in explaining our and their actions. It is the ability to imagine the phenomenological experience of the other, their thoughts and their feelings. It also reflects our ability to imagine the impact we have on the other as well as our ability to represent our own mental states to ourselves to develop self-awareness. That means that it constructs images, based upon our experience, things we may know about the present, and also from what we may have derived from other people's ideas or stories we tell each other. We have to imagine what is going on in other people's minds, just because we cannot know for sure – not even with all the modern technology, such as fMRI, are we able to see directly what happens in our and others' minds.

Because humans have such a great capacity for imagination, they can project things into the future or consider the past and can base their decisions upon those imaginations, instead of relying on our basic instincts. We are, as the novelist Sir Terry Pratchett said, not as such homo erectus, but even more homo narrativus. This can be seen in how from ages ago we started using stories to tell things, such as the Zhuang Zi, the Pentateuch, the New Testament, and the Koran – to name but a few important texts. And lots of these stories are about what makes people act like the way they do, about their beliefs, needs, feelings, and so on. And stories are about words – at least about symbolising – which was already apparent to Sigmund Freud, when he quoted an English writer (loosely translated), that civilisation started when the first savage threw instead of a spear an (abusive) word at his enemy (Breuer & Freud, 1893). So, stories – whether in words, images, body language or otherwise – deliver us knowledge (ἐπιστήμη – epistēmē) about the world and helps us make sense of ourselves and others.

And are not all stories true ...? We know that is not so. Not even the inner stories we tell ourselves are true all the time; when we use them to explain behaviour without taking into account mental states, they certainly are not. And some people even think that stories in specific established newspapers are definitely not true and are just fake news to bring them down. The context of a person telling the story is important to the person having to learn from it. This is about trust. Whom to trust is essentially a difficult task and having an inkling about what another person's motivation might be, is very helpful. And when we have epistemic trust (Gergely, Egyed, & Királi, 2007), which means that we are sure that the person that we are relating to has important things to tell about how things work, then we are really learning.

What a wonderful world it would be ... when we would all mentalize at any given time. But this is not the case; it is not even possible. Mentalizing takes effort, it is a slow process, especially when things become heated up a bit when the more ancient survival systems of fight, freeze and flight become more active, and we need to think about our and another's mind more consciously. When (relational) tension rises, when trust becomes challenged, and the attachment style kicks in, mentalization may be hampered, or it can even break down. And as this book focuses on adolescents, whose brains have not yet matured to support mentalizing, and given that adolescence is a period of Sturm und Drang, we must be prepared for non-mentalizing in our work.

Multidimensional

In describing mentalizing above, we have already touched upon the multi-dimensionality of the concept. Mentalization can be described as taking place in four dimensions, which have to be balanced in order for us to function well enough in the social world.

1 The first dimension is about mentalizing the other versus oneself. We have to try and understand our own behaviour in terms of mental states to be able to understand another person's behaviour in the same way, and vice versa. Neuroscience backs us up here; the same neural systems are used when we try to understand ourselves or others, or when we observe behaviour in another person, our neurons mirror the same behaviour.

This means that often, people who are not so good at reflecting upon themselves, are hampered as well when it comes to reflecting upon the mental states of other people.

2 The second dimension that we named more explicitly was automatic versus controlled mentalizing. When we are feeling secure, in an environment that is familiar to us and holds little relational dangers, when experience has taught us about the expected behaviours of the group, then mentalization can be automatic. Somewhat similar to when we know a route so well, that sometimes we arrive at our destination, not even conscious of the different turns we made along the way. Of course, all sorts of signals may alter this state to one of higher awareness, and this is when mentalizing needs to be more controlled. The controlled form of mentalizing is a slow process, a linear working through of the imaginations made about all kinds of mental states in the situation, considering them, reflecting on them.

One can imagine the problems arising when controlled mentalization is used when more automatic mentalization would be expected. Or when automatic mentalization dominates, when clearly issues have arisen that demand more reflection.

3 Cognitive versus affective mentalizing is the difference between the ability to name, recognise and reason about mental states, and to understand feelings without so many words.

People who tend to be highly sensitive have a sort of imbalance towards affective mentalizing and can get easily overwhelmed. But only cognitive mentalizing, without any emotional understanding of what something feels like, like the adolescent ascetic, is not helpful either. We need a balance between feelings and cognitions to understand things more fully.

4   Last but not least, there is the dimension of internal versus external mentalizing. Our mentalizing function can use input from observable external features (e.g., body language) or use what we can imagine about hidden and internal mental states. We, more or less, know (in any case in our own cultural habitat) how anger or shame might look. In some circumstances, we must make sense of something with few external cues, and then we need to have enough inner working models and a sense of who we are to understand somebody's mind.

For people feeling insecure about their identity – by the way, the major developmental task of adolescence is resolving the crisis of identity versus role confusion (Erikson, 1950) – there is increased tendency to seek external reassurance.

Developmental line of the mentalizing function

Consider a baby … a human baby comes to the world, with little capacity to take care of itself; except that it is in a way 'hardwired' for making relationships and that – under normal circumstances – it is born within some sort of caring system around him, which takes effort to provide food, and warmth, and love, and whatever is necessary for the well-being of the infant. And it is not totally helpless; it can gurgle, make little noises, and has a variety of cries at its disposal pretty quickly. At a certain point it smiles, parents do love this, but alas for a while the baby smiles at everyone. And all this interaction, in which the parents and other important people around the infant try to understand what this all means and try to adjust their behaviour to the signals that baby sends, and give this back to the baby, leads to a sense of self (Cooper & Redfern, 2016; Fonagy, Gergely, Jurist, & Target, 2002). What is happening here is that the parents form an internal representation of the baby's mental states and then communicate that understanding back to the baby through their *marked mirroring*. The baby internalises the mirrored/ represented mental state and this starts to form the building blocks of the baby's internal sense of self. Over time, this helps the child to become able to make sense of its own mental states and through generalisation, to make sense of mental states in others. *Marked mirroring* refers to the parent's ability to treat the child as an independent mind, as an agent in the world, even though it has little awareness of his own thoughts yet. (Fonagy et al., 2002).

To understand mentalizing and especially the different types of non–mentalizing, knowing how the capacity developed is important. Anna Freud (1965) describes the concept of developmental lines and its significance. The development of the mentalizing capacity also follows a clear path, with identifiable 'fixation points' (Fonagy & Allison, 2012).

It is clear that very early on, about six months of age, babies start to recognise causal relations between actions and the environment (Ensink & Mayes, 2010). From about nine months they tend to see actions in terms of underlying intentions of the other and starting to see themselves as acting with reasonable goals, as teleological (from τέλος – purpose, goal, end) agents, and they can choose different courses of action to achieve these goals. In this phase, they do not need to have the capacity to see themselves as anything other than in physical actions and constraints, and they do not have an understanding of inner, mental states (Fonagy & Allison, 2012). Actions are understood in terms of concrete and physical results. This reflects the teleological mode of non-mentalizing, which can be seen in later life when mentalization fails.

In the second year, when babies start to walk and talk and to develop more and more autonomy, they begin to understand that they and others act intentionally based upon inner states. Furthermore, they start to realise that their actions can result in changes of inner states. From 40 months of age, internal mental states are seen by children as the primary cause for behaviour (Dunn, Bretherton, & Munn, 1987; Dunn & Brown, 1993; Dunn, Brown, Slomkowski, Tesla, & Youngblade, 1991). They also start to develop a language for these inner states and a capacity for non-egocentric reasoning (Fonagy & Allison, 2012). However, at this stage, they cannot yet represent these inner states as independent from the external reality. There is no complete acknowledgement that there is a difference between what the internal state signifies and outer reality. This reflects, on the one hand, the psychic equivalence mode of non-mentalizing – in which we behave as if the real world faithfully mirrors our thoughts – and on the other hand, the pretend mode of non-mentalizing – where there is no connection between how things seem in our minds and how they are in reality.

Around the age of three or four, the understanding arises that actions by people are caused by what they believe. They see themselves and others as 'representative actors'. They know that someone does not always feel what they appear to feel and that their reactions can be influenced by all sorts of things, moods, earlier experiences, and so on. From the fourth year until the sixth year, when a sense of autonomy has been gained, and now children are experimenting with initiative, this sense will grow, and they start playing and experimenting with peers and devote energy to people with the same interests and style, to learn about themselves and others. At this stage psychic equivalence and pretend mode are fused and welded together and integrated into what we call mentalizing. However, it has to be noted that at this stage, all this is new and vulnerable and the pre-mentalizing modes can easily crop up and dominate social cognition for years (Fonagy & Allison, 2012).

The experience of the child grows, and from about seven years on, the young person starts to have access to memories of inner states to try and understand self and others. This can be recognised in the appearance of the second-order theory of mind, acknowledging mixed feelings, how expectations can influence the outcome of events, and recognition of 'white lies' (Fonagy & Allison, 2012). At about eleven/twelve years old, children have developed a pretty nuanced understanding of behaviour and thoughts of others, based on stable personality characteristics, on knowledge and experience, and preferences. At the same time, they are becoming better in talking about their emotions, and to think in terms of inner mental states, instead of other external things (Ensink & Mayes, 2010).

At the age of twelve, we drift into adolescence, known to be a turbulent period for different reasons (Fonagy et al., 2014). In the theory of mind literature, there is not much discussion about how mentalization develops in adolescence and beyond (Ensink & Mayes, 2010). In the previous years, what has been developed in the brain is the 'detection node', which deciphers and reacts to all sorts of social clues (Nelson, Leibenluft, McClure, & Pine, 2005). The *cognitive-regulatory node*, responsible for mentalizing, impulse inhibition and goal-directed behaviour, which in other words tells us what to do with all those social circumstances and goings-on, is not as developed. This delay, coupled with the intensified emotional force of interpersonal interactions during this period seems to explain why adolescents have powerful emotional responses to social stimuli, but their ability to regulate, contextualise, plan, or inhibit their behaviour in a context-appropriate manner is immature (Nelson et al., 2005). Other research has also shown that the social brain continues to develop in the adolescent years. This involves developments such as synaptic pruning, namely getting rid of unused neural connections to make the processes more efficient (Choudhury, Charman, & Blakemore, 2008). In addition, adolescents use quite different brain areas when they try to understand the social world; namely the more anterior areas, as opposed to the posterior lateral areas used by adults (Burnett, Bird, Moll, Frith, & Blakemore, 2008; Burnett, Sebastian, Kadosh, & Blakemore, 2011). Finally, in late adolescence and early adulthood, the brain systems that can inhibit reactions and direct behaviour become mature (Nelson et al., 2005).

When things get difficult

What we can determine from this developmental line, is that it is a long process before everything has matured in such a way that all the dimensions of mentalizing functions will be fluently in balance. It would be more accurate to say that balancing it out will remain a difficult task at all ages. At times, a child or young person can surprise us with some very good mentalizing, at other times we are confronted with not so good mentalization by someone who is to all outward appearances an adult.

We described this developmental line, assuming a reasonably normal and undisturbed process, where the attachment figures do a good enough job, and no traumatic events have occurred. However, we know this is not always – and perhaps more often – not true. Some circumstances lead to less than 'normal' (for any given value of that) development. For instance, the primary caregivers had problems of their own and therefore were less capable of mentalizing their baby, but instead mirrored back their own fear or anger. That would not lead to a sense of recognising oneself but to internalising the fears and so on of the other; in what is called the alien self (Fonagy et al., 2002). What if the pedagogical situation was such, that it did not generate trust in that others would tell us worthwhile things, but that experience taught us that people we depend upon saying things that are hurtful, wrong. Instead of epistemic trust, in such a case the balance would swing to epistemic mistrust.

To learn how to mentalize, we need to be mentalized. When this process has been inhibited during our years of development and dependency, we develop difficulties with mentalizing – perhaps one will develop a preference for a specific balance of the four dimensions, and our mentalizing functions might be more easily overwhelmed, resulting in falling back on pre-mentalizing modes easier and earlier in a (perceived) conflict.

When in our interactions tensions get too high (the emotional temperature rises), the balance will eventually be disturbed, sooner or later according to our strengths and weaknesses, and we will react in non-mentalizing ways of thinking and behaving. These ways of behaving are very similar to the ways we all have shown earlier in our developmental path. Under duress, we tend to fall back on the pre-mentalizing modes, which we described above. This is what we see happening all the time in our clinical work – our patients have all, in one way or another, developed an imbalance in their mentalizing functions. And the mentalizing of the young people we are working with is inherently imbalanced, because of their developmental stage, and the specifics and implications of this will be explored extensively in the second chapter. So here, we will describe these non-mentalizing modes briefly.

Non-mentalizing thinking

1   Teleological mode. This is:

> one of the prementalizing modes; in this mode, mental states are expressed in goal-directed actions instead of explicit mental representations such as words – for example, when self-cutting is used as a way of communicating extreme emotional pain (Bateman & Fonagy, 2012, p. 517).

When someone is in this mode, then everything must be shown. Mental states must be proven by physical evidence. Remember that this was the state in which the baby started, and hunger was relieved by the physical act of getting milk. We see this mode being in action, in those situations where for instance the person needs a constant confirmation with hugs, little presents, or an abundance of kiss-emoticons on the phone, to believe that they are cared for. The necessity of immediate responses to emails, WhatsApp, and so on, leads to high tension when this does not happen.

2   Psychic equivalence. Defined as:

> one of the prementalizing modes of thinking in which reality is equated with mental states, and the sense of representingness of mental states is absent; examples are dreams, posttraumatic flashbacks and paranoid delusions (Bateman & Fonagy, 2012, p. 516).

This is the mode where a feeling or a thought is experienced as without a doubt the reality, regardless of any other perspective. There is no other perspective. When you are a toddler, and you complain about the monster in the closet, this is a way of thinking that can easily be forgiven as age-appropriate. But later in life, we see someone who looks like he is overreacting, who suddenly can become very distrustful, though we do not see the why of it. Thoughts are treated as facts, so if you think something, it is true, or if you remember something it is happening in reality again, hence the experience of flashbacks as an example of psychic equation. If you think someone is lazy, it means he is lazy, etc.

> one of the prementalizing modes of thinking; unlike in psychic equivalence, mental states are decoupled from reality yet, unlike in mentalizing, are not flexibly linked to reality (Bateman & Fonagy, 2012, p. 515).

3   Pretend mode is defined as:

> one of the prementalizing modes of thinking; unlike in psychic equivalence, mental states are decoupled from reality yet, unlike in mentalizing, are not flexibly linked to reality (Bateman & Fonagy, 2012, p. 515).

When we were children, one of the important steps in our development was to reach 'pretend play'. We could pretend that a spoon and a fork are two people having a conversation, or we could pretend that our bed was a pirate ship. But even when we were young, reality always pulled us back. When in pretend mode, the problem is that at that point, reality's feedback does not have much influence over thoughts.

This might show itself in the use of psychology-like explanations, which seem to consider mental states – but not checking them (pseudo-mentalizing), or extensive theories where Occam's Razor has no control (hyper-mentalizing). It may be all cognitive, with little real understanding. Pretend mode may be difficult to spot. It looks so much like mentalizing, and we can easily be fooled. Even for us as therapists, who are after all humans as well and also like to avoid tension, patients can tell us intriguing stories, drawing us into pseudo-mentalizing ourselves.

Recognising which non-mentalizing mode is dominant at a certain time may be quite a challenge, not least because it really takes effort to not slip into non-mentalizing oneself when the tension grows. But even if we have the time and distance to reflect upon what is happening, it is not easy. Consider the next story:

> Sam is seeing her psychologist together with her mum Laila. Laila is telling the psychologist that "since Sam became a teenager she has really matured, she has become such a wise girl. She knows all about my flaws, and she is really accepting me as I am. I'm so very proud of her, I mean there are people struggling their whole life to get more accepting and Sam is only 13! So proud … I mean, I'll give you an example from the other day: I am a person who tends to get really angry when I'm hungry and tired, and that is just how it is. That is just who I am. And that is not a problem for Sam any more. Before she turned 13, she yelled back at me, but not any more. I'm sure that is because she now has reached a point in her life where she accepts me as I am."
> Sam sits in her chair looking like she is thinking about something else, judging by her eye-gaze, it looks like her mind has drifted far far away. (Jessurun, Wiwe, & Bevington, 2018)

When we look at this story, the non-mentalizing mode may switch per sentence. And there are three persons here. Now in this story, the mentalizing by the therapist is mostly shown in the last sentence, in which she tries to think about (based upon external cues) what might be going on for Sam. There is some good mentalizing taking place there, because of the tentative way in which it is presented. Mum is not showing very good mentalization in this example. The level of sureness about how Sam feels, without checking back, suggests a lack of connecting her theories with reality, which is pseudo-mentalizing and at other moments she connects the why of emotions with more concrete things, like hungry and tired, which is teleological. There seems to be little room for other perspectives because "that's just who I am."

Several approaches to stop this sequence of non-mentalization are possible; we could try to shift mum's attention to how her daughter seems to withdraw from the conversation and try to ask mum what she thinks might be going on. And then check back with Sam, to see whether what mum says about that is anywhere near where she was in her mind. With this example, we have started to think about the consequences for clinical work; and the goal of this book is to describe the clinical practice with a specific group in mind: adolescents and their families and other systems.

Mentalizing and clinical work

The concepts described above have found their way into clinical work. The main 'working mechanism' in these approaches, is helping the patients to mentalize by applying a mentalizing stance within the therapy: being curious and non-judgmental, exploring with the patient what is going on in his mind, what might be going on in other people's minds, being transparent and authentic about what is going on in our own minds, constantly taking into account that behaviour is to be understood as the result of intentional mental states, from a not-knowing attitude – meaning that minds are opaque and that nor the therapist nor the patient is capable of mind reading.

What will be explained in more detail in later chapters are the different techniques that can be used, when a young person – or in the case of a family session, (part of) the system – is in a non-mentalizing mode. Obviously, when the emotional temperature is too high, it needs to be cooled down to make mentalizing possible again. And when it is too low, there is no reason to mentalize, because nothing is going on, so there are techniques to raise the temperature. Different non-mentalizing modes need different approaches; for instance, when someone is in psychic equivalence mode, what is called for is validating the emotions. When the person is in hyper-mentalizing mode, in some way, he has to be stopped and helped to connect to what it feels like to be in that situation in the here and now.

Treatment based upon these was developed and evaluated in work with patients with borderline personality disorder (Bateman & Fonagy, 2008, 2009; Fonagy & Luyten, 2009). Mentalization-Based Treatment is by now an evidence-based form of treatment, with a protocol and a set of qualitative standards. What the treatment intends to do is to enhance the mentalizing capacities of the clients, basically by mentalizing the clients and helping them to mentalize themselves and others. This requires a certain therapeutic attitude, indicated above, and which will be explored further in the subsequent chapters.

During the last decade, mentalization theory and therapeutic techniques have been tried out and found effective or at least promising for several different psychiatric and psychosocial problems, such as:

- antisocial personality disorder (Bateman, Bolton, & Fonagy, 2013)
- eating disorders (Skårderud, 2007a, 2007b, 2007c)
- depression (Luyten, Fonagy, Lemma, & Target, 2012)
- conduct disorder (Reiter, Bock, Althoff, Taubner, & Sevecke, 2017)
- family violence (Asen & Fonagy, 2017a, 2017b)

and adapted for specific settings:

- family therapy (Asen & Fonagy, 2012a, 2012b; Bleiberg, 2013); MBT-F
- group therapy (Karterud, 2015); MBT-G

- a time-limited approach for children (Midgley, Ensink, Lindqvist, Malberg, & Muller, 2017); MBT-C
- a framework to work with hard-to-reach families and young persons (Bevington, Fuggle, Cracknell, & Fonagy, 2017); AMBIT
- parent work (Cooper & Redfern, 2016); MBT-P
- and of course, the subject of this clinical manual, the treatment of adolescents and their families, which started with research on adolescents presenting with self-harm (Fonagy et al., 2014; Rossouw & Fonagy, 2012); MBT-A.

Conclusion

Mentalization is a core human function, which is used to understand the behaviour of ourselves and others. It is, therefore, a very common thing to do. We mentalize all the time, but often not perfectly, and lots of the time, we slip into non-mentalizing modes. Good mentalization needs holding a balance between internal/external, self/other, implicit/explicit, and cognitive/affective dimensions.

The development of mentalizing follows a path from a teleological mode (concrete – quick fix), through a psychic equivalence mode (inner-out thinking) and pretend mode (as-if), and finally integrates the last two into true mentalizing. We learn to mentalize by being mentalized. We learn from those to whom we are attached and whom we trust that they have things to tell us that are important (epistemic trust).

When the tension gets high, our mentalizing function tends to falter. The (four-dimensional) balance is lost, and we react with one or a combination of pre-mentalizing modes. The collapse of mentalization in one person easily leads to the breakdown of mentalizing within an interpersonal system.

Mentalization-Based Therapy, in all its different applications, aims at helping the patient enhance his mentalizing capabilities. This is particularly significant when working with adolescents, given the specific mentalizing challenges they face at this developmental stage (socially, psychologically, and neurologically).

Acknowledgements

For this chapter, inspiration and information were found in the work of other authors. Of course, the work of Fonagy et al. (2002) on *Affect regulation, mentalization, and development of the self*, has been a significant resource. The books Minding the Child (Midgley & Vrouva, 2012), Adaptive Mentalization-based Integrative Treatment (Bevington et al., 2017), the Handbook of Mentalizing in Mental Health Practice (Bateman & Fonagy, 2012), and Reflective Parenting (Cooper & Redfern, 2016) were also essential sources.

References

Allen, J.G., & Fonagy, P. (2006). *The Handbook of Mentalization-Based Treatment.* Chichester: John Wiley & Sons.

Asen, E., & Fonagy, P. (2012a). Mentalization-based family therapy. In A. Bateman & P. Fonagy (Eds.), *Handbook of Mentalizing in Mental Health Practice.* American Psychiatric Association Publishing.

Asen, E., & Fonagy, P. (2012b). Mentalization-based therapeutic interventions for families. *Journal of Family Therapy, 34*(4), 347–370. https://doi.org/10.1111/j.1467-6427.2011. 00552.x.

Asen, E., & Fonagy, P. (2017a). Mentalizing family violence part 1: Conceptual framework. *Family Process, 56*(1), 6–21. https://doi.org/10.1111/famp.12261.

Asen, E., & Fonagy, P. (2017b). Mentalizing family violence part 2: Techniques and interventions. *Family Process, 56*(1), 22–44. https://doi.org/10.1111/famp.12276.

Bateman, A., Bolton, R., & Fonagy, P. (2013). Antisocial personality disorder: A mentalizing framework. *Focus, 11*(2), 178–186. https://doi.org/10.1176/appi.focus.11.2.178.

Bateman, A., & Fonagy, P. (2008). 8-Year follow-up of patients treated for borderline personality disorder: mentalization-based treatment versus treatment as usual. *American Journal of Psychiatry, 165*, 631–638.

Bateman, A., & Fonagy, P. (2009). Randomized controlled trial of outpatient mentalization-based treatment versus structured clinical management for borderline personality disorder. *American Journal of Psychiatry, 166*, 1355–1364.

Bateman, A., & Fonagy, P. (2012). *Handbook of Mentalizing in Mental Health Practice.* American Psychiatric Publishing Inc.

Bevington, D., Fuggle, P., Cracknell, L., & Fonagy, P. (2017). *Adaptive Mentalization-Based Integrative Treatment: A Guide for Teams to Develop Systems of Care* (1st ed.). New York, NY: OUP.

Bleiberg, E. (2013). Mentalizing-based treatment with adolescents and families. *Child and Adolescent Psychiatric Clinics of North America, 22*(2), 295–330.

Breuer, J., & Freud, S. (1893). On the psychical mechanism of hysterical phenomena: Preliminary communication. In J. Strachey (Ed.) (1955). *The Standard Edition of the Complete Psychological Works of Sigmund Freud, Volume II (1893-1895): Studies on Hysteria,* Vintage: Hogarth Press, 1–18.

Burnett, S., Bird, G., Moll, J., Frith, C., & Blakemore, S.-J. (2008). Development during adolescence of the neural processing of social emotion. *Journal of Cognitive Neuroscience, 21*(9), 1736–1750.

Burnett, S., Sebastian, C., Kadosh, K.C., & Blakemore, S.-J. (2011). The social brain in adolescence: Evidence from functional magnetic resonance imaging and behavioural studies. *Neuroscience and Biobehavioral Reviews, 35*, 1654–1664. https://doi.org/10.1016/j. neubiorev.2010.10.011.

Choudhury, S., Charman, T., & Blakemore, S.-J. (2008). Development of the teenage brain. *Mind, Brain and Education, 2*, 142–147.

Cooper, A., & Redfern, S. (2016). *Reflective Parenting: A Guide to Understanding What's Going on in Your Child's Mind.* Hove, East Sussex; New York, NY: Routledge.

Dunn, J., Bretherton, I., & Munn, P. (1987). Conversations about feeling states between mothers and their young children. *Developmental Psychology, 23*(1), 132–139.

Dunn, J., & Brown, J.R. (1993). Early conversations about causality: Content, pragmatics and developmental change. *British Journal of Developmental Psychology, 11*(2), 107–123.

Dunn, J., Brown, J., Slomkowski, C., Tesla, C., & Youngblade, L. (1991). Young children's understanding of other people's feelings and beliefs: Individual differences and their antecedents. *Child Development, 62,* 1352–1366.

Ensink, K., & Mayes, L. (2010). The development of mentalisation in children from a theory of mind perspective. *Psychoanalytic Inquiry, 30,* 301–337.

Erikson, E.H. (1950). *Childhood and Society.* New York: Norton.

Fonagy, P., & Allison, E. (2012). What is mentalization? The concept and its foundations in developmental research. In N. Midgley & I. Vrouva (Eds.), *Minding the Child: Mentalization-Based Interventions with Children, Young People and Their Families* (pp. 11–34). New York: Routledge.

Fonagy, P., Gergely, G., Jurist, E.J., & Target, M. (2002). *Affect Regulation, Mentalization, and the Development of the Self.* London: Karnac Press.

Fonagy, P., & Luyten, P. (2009). A developmental, mentalization-based approach to the understanding and treatment of borderline personality disorder. *Development and Psychopathology, 21*(4), 1355–1381.

Fonagy, P., Rossouw, T., Sharp, C., Bateman, A., Allisson, L., & Farrar, C. (2014). Mentalization-based treatment for adolescents with borderline traits. In C. Sharp & J.L. Tackett (Eds.), *Handbook of Borderline Personality Disorder in Children and Adolescents.* New York: Springer.

Freud, A. (1965). *Normality and Pathology in Childhood Assessments of Development* (Institute of Psycho-analysis (Great Britain), Ed.). London: Karnac Books: Institute of Psycho-Analysis.

Gergely, G., Egyed, K., & Királi, I. (2007). On pedagogy. *Developmental Science, 10*(1), 139–146. https://doi.org/10.1111/j.1467-7687.2007.00576.x.

Jessurun, H., Wiwe, M., & Bevington, D. (2018). *A Box of Mentalizing Games; A Manual for Games to Practice Mentalizing Skills* (1st ed.). Eindhoven: TweeMC.

Karterud, S. (2015). *Mentalization-Based Group Therapy (MBT-G): A Theoretical, Clinical, and Research Manual.* Oxford, United Kingdom: Oxford University Press.

Luyten, P., Fonagy, P., Lemma, A., & Target, M. (2012). Depression. In A. Bateman & P. Fonagy (Eds.), *Handbook of Mentalizing in Mental Health Practice* (pp. 385–417). Arlington VA: American Psychiatric Association.

Midgley, N., Ensink, K., Lindqvist, K., Malberg, N. T., & Muller, N. (2017). *Mentalization-Based Treatment for Children: A Time-Limited Approach* (1st ed.). Washington, DC: American Psychological Association.

Midgley, N., & Vrouva, I. (Eds.). (2012). *Minding the Child: Mentalization-Based Interventions with Children, Young People, and Their Families.* New York: Routledge.

Nelson, E.E., Leibenluft, E., McClure, E.B., & Pine, D.S. (2005). The social re-orientation of adolescence: A neuroscience perspective on the process and its relation to psychopathology. *Psychological Medicine, 35*(2), 163–174.

Reiter, M., Bock, A., Althoff, M.-L., Taubner, S., & Sevecke, K. (2017). Mentalisierungsbasierte Therapie einer Jugendlichen mit Störung des Sozialverhaltens. *Praxis der Kinderpsychologie und Kinderpsychiatrie, 66*(5), 362–377. https://doi.org/10.13109/prkk.2017.66.5.362.

Rossouw, T.I., & Fonagy, P. (2012). Mentalization-based treatment for self-harm in adolescents: A randomized controlled trial. *Journal of the American Academy of Child and Adolescent Psychiatry, 51*(12), 1304–1313.e3. https://doi.org/10.1016/j.jaac.2012.09.018.

Skårderud, F. (2007a). Eating one's words, Part I: 'Concretised metaphors' and reflective function in anorexia nervosa—an interview study. *European Eating Disorders Review*, 15(3), 163–174. https://doi.org/10.1002/erv.777.

Skårderud, F. (2007b). Eating one's words, Part II: The embodied mind and reflective function in anorexia nervosa—theory. *European Eating Disorders Review*, 15(4), 243–252. https://doi.org/10.1002/erv.778.

Skårderud, F. (2007c). Eating one's words: Part III. Mentalisation-based psychotherapy for anorexia nervosa—an outline for a treatment and training manual. *European Eating Disorders Review*, 15(5), 323–339. https://doi.org/10.1002/erv.81.

Chapter 2

Adolescent brain development and the development of mentalizing

Patrick Luyten, Saskia Malcorps, and Peter Fonagy

Adolescence is a time marked by important biological and psychosocial changes. Whilst in the past, adolescence was typically seen as a time of increased risk for the development of psychopathology, there is now increasing consensus, particularly within the mentalizing approach to development, that adolescence also provides new opportunities for growth and resilience and is associated with marked plasticity (Luyten, Campbell, Allison, & Fonagy, 2020). This chapter is written with this double focus in mind in an attempt to redress the balance and consider adolescence as a pivotal stage in development in explaining both risk and resilience.

The focus in this chapter will be on neurobiological findings concerning the development of mentalizing, our capacity to understand oneself and others as motivated by intentional mental states. We discuss neuroimaging evidence suggesting that adolescence is associated with the functional and structural reorganisation of three distinct, although highly related, biobehavioural systems, i.e. the stress-regulation, attachment/reward and mentalizing systems, as well as other related neural systems such as systems for cognitive control. These reorganisations occur at a time when the establishment of new and more complex relationships and a sense of agency and autonomy are two central and major developmental tasks (see Figure 2.1).

From an evolutionary perspective, the following three basic biobehavioural systems have evolved to enable humans to adapt to our complex social environment: (a) a system that has developed to deal with distress following threat (the stress/threat system); (b) a system that is centrally involved in producing rewarding experiences associated with the formation of interpersonal relationships (i.e., infant-parent, parent-infant, romantic attachment, and other attachment relationships) on the one hand, and experiences of agency and autonomy on the other (the reward system); and (c) a mentalizing or social cognition system, which underpins the human species-specific capacity to understand oneself and others in terms of intentional mental states (e.g. feelings, desires, wishes, attitudes, and values), a quintessential capacity in our complex interpersonal world (Fonagy & Luyten, 2018; Luyten & Fonagy, 2018).

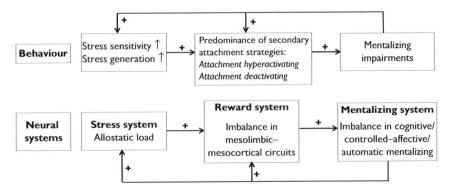

Figure 2.1 Chapter 2. Interaction of the Stress, Reward and Mentalizing Systems (adapted from Luyten, P., and Fonagy, P. (2018). The stress-reward-mentalizing model of depression: An integrative developmental cascade approach to child and adolescent depressive disorder based on the Research Domain Criteria (RDoC) approach. *Clinical Psychology Review, 64,* 87–98, doi:10.1016/ j.cpr.2017.09.008, © Elsevier).

The implications of the reorganisations in these three biobehavioural systems in adolescence, and their role in explaining both vulnerability and resilience, are vast and deserve our attention. They are essential to understand for every clinician working with adolescents. As we will show, research into the neurobiological changes that affect the neural circuits underpinning social cognition during adolescence has important implications for clinical work with adolescents, and particularly for those suffering from mental health issues. This chapter will guide us through this significant research.

We will discuss developmental cascades set in motion as a result of excessive and/or age-inappropriate stress, typically resulting in impairments in reward sensitivity and in the capacity for mentalizing (see Figure 1). Together, these impairments affect normative developmental tasks, typically leading to vicious cycles marked by a disturbed capacity for relatedness and agency/autonomy and associated mentalizing problems. Yet, throughout, we emphasise that even marked 'impairments' in mentalizing and attachment are in the eye of the beholder. From the perspective of the young person, they represent attempts at adaptation to a specific (interpersonal) environment. For instance, in an environment characterised by marked emotional neglect and violence, the use of instrumental aggression can be seen as an understandable strategy to ensure status and, in extreme circumstances, survival (Fonagy & Luyten, 2018). Similarly, for young people growing up in a context of abuse, the inhibition of mentalizing, typically combined with high levels of epistemic mistrust in others, are an understandable response to protect the self from further abuse and disappointment (Luyten *et al.* 2020). In this context, we also warn against overly simplistic interpretations of neurobiological findings implying a direct parallel between findings that suggest a reorganisation of neurobiological systems involved in emotion regulation in adolescence and typical impulsive and risk-taking behaviours in adolescence.

The stress system: dealing with adversity

We begin our journey through the rapidly accumulating literature on neurobiological changes in adolescence by a discussion of findings concerning the impact of stress and adversity on the developing adolescent brain. Most, if not all, psychological disorders are best conceptualised as developmental, stress-related disorders, with elevated and/or age-inappropriate stress playing a major role in their onset and perpetuation. In adolescence, as noted, major changes in sociocultural expectations occur leading to increased stress (Auerbach, Admon, & Pizzagalli, 2014; Davey, Yücel, & Allen, 2008; Forbes & Dahl, 2012; Spear, 2000) in the domains of both relatedness and agency/autonomy (see Figure 2). On the one hand, adolescence entails that peer and romantic relationships become increasingly important, which is expressed, for instance, in increased rejection sensitivity. On the other hand, demands for achievement, reflected in increased sensitivity to failure, intensify. The emergence of pubertal sexuality and (relational and instrumental) aggression, and associated bodily changes, provide further challenges in both domains. See Figure 2.2

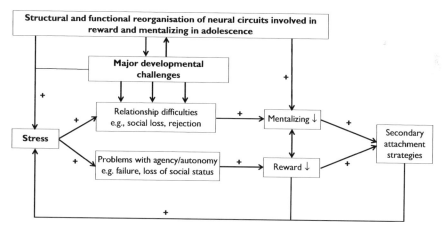

Figure 2.2   Chapter 2. Major developmental changes in adolescence and their relation to the structural and functional reorganisation of stress, reward and mentalizing systems (adapted from Luyten, P., and Fonagy, P. (2018). The stress-reward-mentalizing model of depression: An integrative developmental cascade approach to child and adolescent depressive disorder based on the Research Domain Criteria (RDoC) approach. *Clinical Psychology Review, 64,* 87–98, doi:10.1016/j.cpr.2017.09.008, © Elsevier).

The human biobehavioural stress system is a complex system of neural structures that are involved in detecting, integrating, and responding to threat. While the hypothalamic–pituitary–adrenal (HPA) axis system and the sympathetic nervous system make up the core structures of the stress system, the amygdala, hippocampus, and areas in the prefrontal cortex (PFC), including the anterior cingulate cortex, orbitofrontal cortex, and medial PFC (MPFC), also play import roles in this network (McEwen, 2007). Together, these structures serve *allostasis*, the capacity to continuously adapt to ever-changing circumstances (McEwen, 2007). When this fails, *allostatic load* ensues and the individual's self-regulatory capacities increasingly begin to fail (McEwen, 2000).

Research indicates that there is an even broader network of physiological systems responsible for establishing and maintaining allostasis, serving the fight/flight/freeze response in the face of acute stress (Gunnar & Quevedo, 2007; McEwen, 2007). This network includes the autonomic nervous system and the metabolic system, gut, kidneys, and immune system, each with their relatively distinct biomediators (e.g., cortisol, sympathetic and parasympathetic transmitters, metabolic hormones, and cytokines, respectively). These findings emphasise the embodied nature of adversity, and the intertwining of physical and mental health, particularly in those individuals with a history of early adversity.

Consistent with these views, there is now relatively good evidence to suggest that early adverse experiences may result in permanent alterations in the stress system associated with an earlier age of onset of psychopathology, greater symptom severity, higher levels of comorbidity, a greater risk for suicide and a poorer response to treatment across different psychiatric conditions (Teicher & Samson, 2013). High levels of stress, particularly during 'critical time windows' (Heim, Plotsky, & Nemeroff, 2004) in which the stress system is highly sensitive to environmental factors, typically result in HPA-axis overactivity (i.e. a constant state of fight/flight) and a consequently increased vulnerability to stressors throughout life (Kertes, Gunnar, Madsen, & Long, 2008). In humans, this critical time window in which the HPA axis is particularly sensitive to programming effects extends into early adulthood (Lupien, McEwen, Gunnar, & Heim, 2009). This leads to a cascade of physical and psychological consequences given the intricate relation between the stress system and other key biological and psychosocial systems, such as problems with sleep and attention, difficulties with motor control, coordination, learning difficulties and social and relational problems, as well as problems related to the immune system, pain-regulating systems, the metabolic system, and the reproductive system (Eiland & Romeo, 2013; Lupien et al., 2009). Specific genetic variation may make individuals more sensitive to environmental factors ('differential susceptibility hypothesis') (Ellis, Boyce, Belsky, Bakermans-Kranenburg, & van Ijzendoorn, 2011).

Core structures of the stress system, including the amygdala and hippocampus, undergo major structural and functional reorganisation in adolescence:

the amygdala and hippocampus increase in volume and reach their peak volume in adolescence, and their central functional role in adolescence is also demonstrated by studies suggesting that these areas show greater activation, compared to children or adults in various stress tasks. The PFC, in turn, is subject to cortical thinning during adolescence as a result of synaptic pruning and programmed cell death (Mutlu et al., 2013; Shaw et al., 2008).

Similarly, adolescence is associated with a considerable increase in HPA axis reactivity to stress, compared to children and adults (Casey, Getz, & Galvan, 2008). Adolescents have been shown to have both higher basal stress levels and heightened reaction to stress, and social rejection and academic stressors in particular (Masten et al., 2009; Sebastian, Viding, Williams, & Blakemore, 2010; Sebastian et al., 2011), consistent with the greater demands for autonomy, agency and achievement and the growing importance peer and romantic relationships (Auerbach et al., 2014) (see also Figure 2).

There is now also good evidence to suggest that young people who are at increased risk for the development of psychopathology also unwittingly generate in part their own stressful environment (i.e. active stress–generation or evocative person–environment effects) (Hammen, 2005). Several unhealthy and maladaptive behaviours such as smoking and unhealthy eating, risky sexual behaviours, including (sexual) re-victimisation, self-harm, and violence in (intimate) relationships (Afifi et al., 2009; Anda et al., 2006) further contribute to a vicious cycle leading to increased vulnerability to psychopathology.

The reward system: regulating attachment and agency/autonomy

Two areas of reward are central in adolescence: relationships, with a developmental shift towards growing importance of peer and romantic relationships (including sexuality), and agency/achievement (including instrumental aggression) (see Figure 2.2) (Blatt, 2008; Luyten, 2017). Both areas are often intertwined, as social status often increases relational attractiveness and vice versa. Yet, at least in Western cultures, boys place slightly more emphasis on agency/autonomy, while in girls there is a somewhat greater emphasis on attachment (Luyten & Blatt, 2013; Spear, 2000).

A mesocorticolimbic dopaminergic system underpins experiences of reward in the human brain. The mesolimbic pathways originate from the ventral tegmental area and project to ventral striatal regions and the hippocampus and amygdala. A mesocortical pathway consists of projections to the PFC and anterior cingulate cortex (Nestler & Carlezon, 2006; Pizzagalli, 2014; Russo & Nestler, 2013; Spear, 2000). Biomediators in these pathways involve dopamine, oxytocin, vasopressin, opioids and cannabinoids. They mediate feelings of acceptance, support, agency and validation on the one hand, and the emotional pain associated with social loss and rejection, which is increased in adolescence, particularly in women (Hsu et al., 2015; Spear, 2000).

The reward system plays a central role in the development and functioning of the stress system (Hostinar, Sullivan, & Gunnar, 2014; Strathearn, 2011; Swain et al., 2014). Developmentally, the attachment behavioural system is activated when faced with a threat, leading to proximity seeking an attachment figure. The capacity of attachment figures to offer marked, mirroring responses will help the child to develop the capacity to downregulate stress and to trust others as a source of comfort and support. The reward system underpins these affective responses as secure attachment experiences buffer the effects of stress in early development, resulting in 'adaptive hypoactivity' of the HPA axis (Gunnar & Quevedo, 2007). Hence, for children growing up in secure attachment contexts, others become rewarding and, at the same time, feelings of agency and autonomy develop and are equally experienced as rewarding. Hence, the capacity for self-regulation and co-regulation mutually reinforces each other. By contrast, in children growing up with unavailable, unresponsive or abusive attachment figures, capacities for co-regulation and self-regulation are typically impaired. These children either begin to excessively rely on attachment hyperactivating strategies in an attempt to find downregulation of distress, or attachment deactivating strategies, leading to so-called compulsive autonomy (i.e. the belief that one has to be able to deal with distress without the help of others). For insecurely attached individuals, relying on others is not rewarding, as there is always the underlying belief that others will not be available. On the biological level, insecure attachment is therefore associated with increased vulnerability for stress, as expressed in dysfunctions of the stress system (Auerbach et al., 2014; Pizzagalli, 2014; Strathearn, 2011).

The abovementioned biomediators are centrally involved in these processes. Oxytocin, for instance, has been shown to increase affiliative behaviour when faced with distress, and thus effective co-regulation of stress with others. Oxytocin furthermore reduces behavioural and neuroendocrinological responses to stress (Neumann, 2008) via downregulation of the HPA system (Feldman, 2017), and enhances mentalizing and trust in others (Domes, Heinrichs, Michel, Berger, & Herpertz, 2007; Heinrichs & Domes, 2008). Importantly, these positive effects of oxytocin seem limited to in-group members. In contrast, increased levels of oxytocin appear to lead to increased distrust, and less cooperative behaviour in relation to out-group members, even in securely attached individuals (Bartz, Zaki, Bolger, & Ochsner, 2011).

Individuals with an insecure attachment history show decreased basal oxytocin levels and, in these individuals, oxytocin administration leads to decreased trust and cooperative behaviour, and increased cortisol response to stress, even in relation to in-group members (Bartz et al., 2011; Feldman, 2017). Hence, attachment experiences are not perceived as rewarding, and by contrast, intensify distress. These findings are critically important for clinicians' understanding of their encounter with insecurely attached young people (and particularly those with a history of abuse). For these young people, relationships, including the therapeutic relationship, are not experienced as rewarding, but as a source of distress. At best, relationships with others (including mental health professionals) are experienced as ambivalent, and there is often a thin line between their wish and need to be understood and cared for, and over-stimulation of the attachment system (and the ensuing loss of mentalizing associated with such overstimulation discussed below). Hence, clinicians may easily overwhelm the young person with warmth and support, which, however well-intentioned, is experienced as aversive and even dangerous. Mentalization-Based Treatment, therefore, typically titrates interventions to take into account the negative effects of attachment activation on mentalizing (Bateman & Fonagy, 2019).

The reorganisation of the reward system in adolescence might have direct behavioural effects in adolescence, but the precise mechanisms and their effects on adolescent behaviour are still relatively poorly understood. Research findings based on studies with both animals and humans, do suggest, however, that the lowest levels of dopamine characterise adolescence in striatal regions and the highest levels of dopamine in prefrontal regions, resulting in a so-called "mini-reward deficiency syndrome" in adolescence (Spear, 2007). Any clinician working with adolescents is familiar with this 'syndrome': adolescents may be easily bored and, at the same time, the frustration of their strong needs for belongingness and/or achievement and the status that is associated may give rise to intense feelings of rejection and failure, or a combination of both, and subsequent frustration and aggression. These experiences may lead to different compensatory behaviours such as risk-taking, substance abuse and/or oppositional behaviour, which explains the high comorbidity observed between internalising and externalising problems in adolescence (Davey et al., 2008; Spear, 2000).

As noted, the precise mechanisms involved remain elusive. It has been suggested that the hypo-responsivity to reward in adolescence may be evolutionarily adaptive: the low incentive value of reward supports adolescents' explorative tendencies, autonomy strivings and relational and sexual desires. In combination with high levels of phasic dopamine in response to reward, this might indeed explain the normative 'Sturm und Drang' typically associated with adolescence (Davey et al., 2008). Yet, the observed impairments in reward sensitivity in adolescence might also be the consequence of down-regulation through high levels of dopamine in the PFC (which inhibit mentalizing, see also below), resulting from increased stress in adolescence (Pizzagalli, 2014; Spear, 2000). Furthermore, increased representational capacities in adolescence may lead rewards such as love and status to be increasingly experienced as temporally distant as adolescence is typically associated with a psychosocial moratorium, limiting the adolescent's feelings of agency and autonomy.

Particularly in vulnerable young people, a greater need for reward, together with the perception that reward experiences are temporally distant, may further increase distress. In combination with ensuing mentalizing impairments, discussed below, this may lead to compensatory behaviours (e.g., substance abuse, violence, or social withdrawal). Because this further decreases the incentive value of relationships with others who may provide corrective experiences, a vicious cycle ensues, characterised by social isolation or excessive reliance on peers that struggle with similar issues. In these circumstances, it often becomes extremely difficult to be able to re-calibrate one's mind in interaction with others.

As noted, this may be particularly difficult in those young people with a history of adversity. Hence, the absence of resilience, associated with social learning driven by epistemic trust, may be key, particularly if increased social pressures for agency and relatedness are not balanced by an environment that supports these two fundamental developmental tasks, creating a toxic mixture for many young people (Debbané, 2015; Escofet, 2012). Yet, from an evolutionary perspective, the insecure attachment strategies that young people develop under such circumstances are better seen as attempts at coping with the (perceived) unavailability, unresponsiveness, or intrusiveness of attachment figures and the broader socio-cultural context more generally (Belsky & Fearon, 2008; Ein-Dor, Mikulincer, Doron, & Shaver, 2010; Simpson & Belsky, 2008). Hence, to put it somewhat provokingly, the brain adapts itself to a specific environment in order to optimise survival and social functioning. Although this attempt at adaptation may be far from optimal from a normative perspective, once a certain minimally satisfying state of allostasis has been reached, the brain stops any further iterations in attempting to find a better solution. It is here that psychosocial interventions may be useful. This brings us to the importance of mentalizing in adolescence and in any intervention that aims at a behavioural change in young people.

The mentalizing system: understanding oneself and others

Although it is largely unknown why humans developed the capacity for mentalizing, it represented a major leap forward as this capacity enables complex communication and collaboration typical of human social systems. Furthermore, the development of advanced capacities for mentalizing, which are largely or completely absent in most other animal species, also enabled the capacity for self-consciousness and even further, the capacity for imagination and, as a consequence, for transcending physical reality (see Davey et al., 2008). Each of these capacities, however, also paradoxically increases vulnerability for psychopathology. Self-consciousness also led to the emergence of so-called self-conscious emotions (e.g., embarrassment, regret, shame, and guilt) which, although in essence adaptive, may become maladaptive when chronic and/or excessive. Moreover, the capacity for imagination not only allows humans to envision an ideal state of the self but also to become painfully aware of the discrepancy between the actual and ideal self-states.

More generally, the quintessential role of social embeddedness in the fabric of human social organisation may lead to feelings of utter isolation and loneliness in those who lack skills required for human collaboration and communication (Luyten *et al.* 2020).

These issues are central during adolescence (Crone & Dahl, 2012), which might explain, at least in part, the increase in the prevalence of psychopathology in this developmental stage. Hence, while changes in the brain, and the emergence of full mentalizing throughout adolescence, allow for increasingly complex communication, collaboration and imagination, they also increase vulnerability in biologically and/or environmentally less fortunate young people (Sharp, Vanwoerden, & Wall, 2018).

As is well-known, mentalizing is multi-dimensional (see Table 2.1). From a neural perspective, the different dimensions of mentalizing are subserved by a complex set of neural systems (Luyten & Fonagy, 2015).

As with the stress and reward system, neural systems involved in mentalizing undergo significant reorganisation in adolescence. Synaptogenesis (the formation of new synapses between neurons), synaptic pruning (the eradication of unused synapses) and myelination (the myelin-coating of neurons which enhances the transmission speed of electrical impulses) (Blakemore, 2008, 2018) lead to significant structural and functional changes in mentalizing regions. For instance, both the synaptic reorganisation, in which excess synapses are being eliminated and the increase in myelination of remaining synapses, most likely explain the decrease in the grey cortical matter and increase in white cortical matter observed in fMRI studies in adolescents.

It is assumed that these processes increase the efficiency of brain networks implicated in mentalizing, and particularly the involved cortical regions (Blakemore, 2008, 2018), which in turn are thought to foster the development of social cognition in adolescence, enabling the development of a more differentiated and integrated sense of self and identity on the one hand, and relatedness on the other (Fonagy & Luyten, 2016; Sharp et al., 2018).

However, it is hypothesised that during these cortical changes, mentalizing skills of adolescents may be temporarily disrupted, also referred to as the mentalizing or pubertal 'dip' in social cognition (Blakemore, 2008). These findings have led to an ongoing discussion whether the development of social cognition in adolescence follows a linear (with levels of social cognition simply increasing with age) or a non-linear trajectory (with levels of mentalizing actually decreasing in mid-adolescence because of the reorganisation of mentalizing networks). Some studies that focused on externally based mentalizing indeed found such a "dip" in the accuracy in mentalizing (Carey, Diamond, & Woods, 1980; Diamond, Carey, & Back, 1983; Tonks, Williams, Frampton, Yates, & Slater, 2007) or reaction time in mentalizing tasks (McGivern, Andersen, Byrd, Mutter, & Reilly, 2002) in mid-pubertal adolescents (12 to 13 years old). This pubertal dip in mentalizing has been related to hormonal changes.

Table 2.1 Chapter 2. Four dimensions of mentalizing: Core functions and underlying neural circuits

Dimension	Features	Neural circuits
Automatic	Unconscious, parallel, fast processing of social information that is reflexive and requires little effort, focused attention, or intention; therefore, prone to bias and distortions, particularly in complex interpersonal interactions (i.e. when arousal is high)	amygdalabasal gangliaventromedial prefrontal cortex (VMPFC)lateral temporal cortex (LTC)dorsal anterior cingulate cortex (dACC)
Controlled	Conscious, verbal, and reflective processing of social information that requires the capacity to reflect consciously and deliberately on and make accurate attributions about the emotions, thoughts, and intentions of self and others. Relies heavily on effortful control and language	lateral prefrontal cortex (LPFC) medial prefrontal cortex (MPFC) lateral parietal cortex (LPAC) medial parietal cortex (MPAC) medial temporal lobe (MTL) rostral anterior cingulate cortex (rACC)
Internal	Understanding one's own mind and that of others through a direct focus on the mental interiors of both the self and others	Medial frontoparietal network (more controlled)
External	Understanding one's own mind and that of others based on external features (such as facial expressions, posture, and prosody)	Lateral frontotemporoparietal (more automatic)
Self-Other	Shared networks underpin the capacity to mentalize about the self and others	Shared Representation system (more automatic) versus Mental State Attribution system (more controlled)
Cognitive-Affective	Mentalizing may focus on more cognitive features (more controlled), such as belief-desire reasoning and perspective-taking versus more affective features (more automatic), including affective empathy and mentalized affectivity (the feeling and thinking-about-the-feeling)	Cognitive mentalizing involves several areas in the prefrontal cortex, affectively-oriented mentalizing seems particularly related to the VMPFC

Studies suggesting a pubertal dip in mentalizing because of the neural re-organisation of brain areas involved in mentalizing are appealing because they may provide a straightforward explanation for the observed increase in both internalising and externalising problems in adolescence, and particularly the increase in acting out behaviour, such as self-harm, risk-taking behaviours, substance abuse, and violence in general (Sharp et al., 2018).

However, research in this area is far from conclusive as many other studies on externally based mentalizing found a systematic linear increase in menta-lizing skills across adolescence in the similar face and emotion recognition tasks as used in research suggesting a pubertal dip (van Rooijen, Junge, & Kemner, 2018; Vetter, Drauschke, Thieme, & Altgassen, 2018; Vetter, Leipold, Kliegel, Phillips, & Altgassen, 2013) with no indication of age, pubertal or peer-bias effects (i.e. that adolescents may simply be better in recognising faces of peers simply because they interact more with peers). Additionally, there is no strong evidence for a pubertal dip in research on other mentalizing dimensions, such as in the development of Theory-of-Mind (Keulers, Evers, Stiers, & Jolles, 2010; Vetter et al., 2013), perspective taking (Choudhury, Blakemore, & Charman, 2006) and empathy (van Rooijen et al., 2018), with studies con-sistently suggesting a gradual linear increase in mentalizing skills. However, more longitudinal studies are needed before firmer conclusions can be drawn, particularly as changes in mentalizing in adolescence might be heavily influ-enced by changes in cognitive functioning (including executive functioning and effortful control). Indeed, studies in this area suggest increasing cognitive and impulse control with age during adolescence.

Hence, although the jury is still out on the course of the development of mentalizing in adolescence, the rapid changes that are characteristic of ado-lescence both in the domains of relatedness and autonomy/achievement present considerable challenges to mentalizing in young people, even in normative development. Hence, with increasing arousal, it should not be surprising that adolescents may often lose the ability for controlled menta-lizing, and often switch to more rapid, automatic mentalizing, and eventually non-mentalizing modes of thinking about the self and others.

This seems particularly true for those young people with a history of early adversity, as adversity undermines not only mentalizing capacities but also the capacity for epistemic trust and thus the capacity to re-calibrate one's mind when faced with new challenges (Luyten, Campbell, Allison, et al., 2020; Luyten & Fonagy, 2019). As a result, these young people are increasingly cut off from corrective experiences and might end up in complete social isolation and loneliness and/or seek social recalibration of the mind with peers that suffer from similar problems. With the current availability of social media, the latter strategy, in particular, may rapidly spiral out of control. The inability to make sense of changes that come with the advent of adolescence may lead to excessive mentalizing (hypermentalizing) and/or the avoidance of mentalizing (hypomentalizing). Both can be seen as a defensive strategy to avoid thinking about the painful nature of these experiences and both may explain in part the mini reward deficiency syndrome characteristic of adolescence. Hence, yet again, from the perspective of the adolescent, these represent adaptation strategies, whilst the outside world typically tends to consider these strategies as pathological and abnormal.

Conclusion

Although there is no one-to-one relation between brain functioning and behaviour, knowledge of the adolescent brain is essential in our understanding of their subjective experience. Indeed, it is the essence of the mentalizing approach that mentalizing allows us to understand the experience of the other, and thus see the world from their perspective. Yet research on mentalizing has also taught us that this capacity is limited and that misunderstanding of others is commonplace. This is probably especially true for any adult trying to understand the adolescent and his or her brain. While adolescents often have major impairments in understanding how brain and environment, and their interactions, determine their sense of self and others, it behoves us to show modesty when it comes down to our own capacity to understand these influences in a human being that sees the world often very differently from how we do.

References

Afifi, T.O., MacMillan, H., Cox, B.J., Asmundson, G.J.G., Stein, M.B., & Sareen, J. (2009). Mental health correlates of intimate partner violence in marital relationships in a nationally representative sample of males and females. *Journal of Interpersonal Violence*, 24(8), 1398–1417. doi:10.1177/0886260508322192.

Anda, R., Felitti, V., Bremner, J., Walker, J., Whitfield, C., Perry, B., ... Giles, W. (2006). The enduring effects of abuse and related adverse experiences in childhood. *European Archives of Psychiatry and Clinical Neuroscience*, 256(3), 174–186.

Auerbach, R.P., Admon, R., & Pizzagalli, D.A. (2014). Adolescent depression: Stress and reward dysfunction. *Harvard Review of Psychiatry*, 22(3), 139–148. doi:10.1097/hrp.0000000000000034.

Bartz, J.A., Zaki, J., Bolger, N., & Ochsner, K.N. (2011). Social effects of oxytocin in humans: Context and person matter. *Trends in Cognitive Sciences*, 15(7), 301–309. doi:10.1016/j.tics.2011.05.002.

Bateman, A., & Fonagy, P. (2019). *Handbook of Mentalizing in Mental Health Practice* (2nd ed.). Washington, DC: American Psychiatric Press.

Belsky, J., & Fearon, P.R.M. (2008). Precursors of attachment security. In J. Cassidy & P.R. Shaver (Eds.), *Handbook of Attachment Theory and Research* (2nd ed., pp. 295–316). New York, NY: Guilford Press.

Blakemore, S.-J. (2008). The social brain in adolescence. *Nature Reviews Neuroscience*, 9(4), 267–277. doi: 10.1038/nrn2353.

Blakemore, S.-J. (2018). *Inventing Ourselves: The Secret Life of the Teenage Brain*. London, UK: Doubleday/Penguin.

Blatt, S.J. (2008). *Polarities of Experience: Relatedness and Self Definition in Personality Development, Psychopathology, and the Therapeutic Process*. Washington, DC: American Psychological Association.

Carey, S., Diamond, R., & Woods, B. (1980). Development of face recognition: A maturational component? *Developmental Psychology, 16*(4), 257–269. doi: 10.1037/0012-1649.16.4.257.

Casey, B.J., Getz, S., & Galvan, A. (2008). The adolescent brain. *Developmental Review, 28*(1), 62–77. doi:10.1016/j.dr.2007.08.003.

Choudhury, S., Blakemore, S.J., & Charman, T. (2006). Social cognitive development during adolescence. *Social Cognitive and Affective Neuroscience, 1*(3), 165–174. doi: 10.1093/scan/nsl024.

Crone, E.A., & Dahl, R.E. (2012). Understanding adolescence as a period of social-affective engagement and goal flexibility. *Nature Reviews Neuroscience, 13*(9), 636–650. doi:10.1038/nrn3313.

Davey, C.G., Yücel, M., & Allen, N.B. (2008). The emergence of depression in adolescence: Development of the prefrontal cortex and the representation of reward. *Neuroscience and Biobehavioral Reviews, 32*(1), 1–19. doi:10.1016/j.neubiorev.2007.04.016.

Debbané, M. (2015). Adolescent Attachment: From Brain to Culture. Paper presented at the European Society of Child and Adolescent Psychiatry, Madrid, Spain.

Diamond, R., Carey, S., & Back, K.J. (1983). Genetic influences on the development of spatial skills during early adolescence. *Cognition, 13*(2), 167–185. doi:10.1016/0010-0277(83)90021-5.

Domes, G., Heinrichs, M., Michel, A., Berger, C., & Herpertz, S.C. (2007). Oxytocin improves "mind-reading" in humans. *Biological Psychiatry, 61*(6), 731–733. doi:10.1016/j.biopsych.2006.07.015.

Eiland, L., & Romeo, R.D. (2013). Stress and the developing adolescent brain. *Neuroscience, 249*(0), 162–171. doi:10.1016/j.neuroscience.2012.10.048.

Ein-Dor, T., Mikulincer, M., Doron, G., & Shaver, P.R. (2010). The attachment paradox: How can so many of us (the insecure ones) have no adaptive advantages? *Perspectives on Psychological Science, 5*(2), 123–141. doi:10.1177/1745691610362349.

Ellis, B.J., Boyce, W.T., Belsky, J., Bakermans-Kranenburg, M.J., & van Ijzendoorn, M.H. (2011). Differential susceptibility to the environment: An evolutionary–neurodevelopmental theory. *Development and Psychopathology, 23*(1), 7–28. doi:doi:10.1017/S0954579410000611

Escofet, P. (2012). *Le microcosme juvénile: Sociabilité adolescente, école et violences*. Gollion, Switzerland: Infolio.

Feldman, R. (2017). The neurobiology of human attachments. *Trends in Cognitive Sciences, 21*(2), 80–99. doi:10.1016/j.tics.2016.11.007.

Fonagy, P., & Luyten, P. (2016). A multilevel perspective on the development of borderline personality disorder. In D. Cicchetti (Ed.), *Developmental Psychopathology. Vol. 3: Maladaptation and Psychopathology* (3rd ed., pp. 726–792). New York, NY: John Wiley & Sons.

Fonagy, P., & Luyten, P. (2018). Conduct problems in youth and the RDoC approach: A developmental, evolutionary-based view. *Clinical Psychology Review, 64*, 57–76. doi:10.1016/j.cpr.2017.08.010.

Forbes, E.E., & Dahl, R.E. (2012). Research Review: Altered reward function in adolescent depression: What, when and how? *Journal of Child Psychology and Psychiatry, 53*(1), 3–15. doi:10.1111/j.1469-7610.2011.02477.x.

Gunnar, M., & Quevedo, K. (2007). The neurobiology of stress and development. *Annual Review of Psychology*, *58*(1), 145–173. doi:10.1146/annurev.psych.58. 110405.085605.

Hammen, C. (2005). Stress and depression. *Annual Review of Clinical Psychology*, *1*(1), 293–319. doi:10.1146/annurev.clinpsy.1.102803.143938.

Heim, C., Plotsky, P.M., & Nemeroff, C.B. (2004). Importance of studying the contributions of early adverse experience to neurobiological findings in depression. *Neuropsychopharmacology*, *29*(4), 641–648. doi: 10.1038/sj.npp.1300397.

Heinrichs, M., & Domes, G. (2008). Neuropeptides and social behaviour: Effects of oxytocin and vasopressin in humans. *Progress in Brain Research*, *170*, 337–350. doi:10. 1016/S0079-6123(08)00428-7.

Hostinar, C.E., Sullivan, R.M., & Gunnar, M.R. (2014). Psychobiological mechanisms underlying the social buffering of the hypothalamic-pituitary-adrenocortical axis: A review of animal models and human studies across development. *Psychological Bulletin*, *140*(1), 256–282. doi:10.1037/a0032671.

Hsu, D.T., Sanford, B.J., Meyers, K.K., Love, T.M., Hazlett, K.E., Walker, S.J., ... Zubieta, J.K. (2015). It still hurts: Altered endogenous opioid activity in the brain during social rejection and acceptance in major depressive disorder. *Molecular Psychiatry*, *20*(2), 193–200. doi:10.1038/mp.2014.185.

Kertes, D.A., Gunnar, M.R., Madsen, N.J., & Long, J.D. (2008). Early deprivation and home basal cortisol levels: a study of internationally adopted children. *Development and Psychopathology*, *20*(2), 473–491. doi: 10.1017/S0954579408000230.

Keulers, E.H.H., Evers, E.A.T., Stiers, P., & Jolles, J. (2010). Age, sex, and pubertal phase influence mentalizing about emotions and actions in adolescents. *Developmental Neuropsychology*, *35*(5), 555–569. doi: 10.1080/87565641.2010.494920.

Lupien, S.J., McEwen, B.S., Gunnar, M.R., & Heim, C. (2009). Effects of stress throughout the lifespan on the brain, behaviour and cognition. *Nature Reviews Neuroscience*, *10*(6), 434–445. doi:10.1038/nrn2639.

Luyten, P. (2017). Personality, psychopathology, and health through the lens of interpersonal relatedness and self-definition. *Journal of the American Psychoanalytic Association*, *65*(3), 473–489. doi:10.1177/0003065117712518.

Luyten, P., & Blatt, S.J. (2013). Interpersonal relatedness and self-definition in normal and disrupted personality development: Retrospect and prospect. *American Psychologist*, *68*(3), 172–183. doi:10.1037/a0032243.

Luyten, P., Campbell, C., Allison, E., & Fonagy, P. (2020). The mentalizing approach to psychopathology: State of the art and future directions. *Annual Review of Clinical Psychology*, *16*(1), 297–325. doi: 10.1146/annurev-clinpsy-071919-015355.

Luyten, P., Campbell, C., & Fonagy, P. (2020). Borderline personality disorder, complex trauma, and problems with self and identity: A social-communicative approach. *Journal of Personality*, *88*(1), 88–105. doi:10.1111/jopy.12483.

Luyten, P., & Fonagy, P. (2015). The neurobiology of mentalizing. *Personality Disorders: Theory, Research and Treatment*, *6*(4), 366–379.

Luyten, P., & Fonagy, P. (2018). The stress-reward-mentalizing model of depression: An integrative developmental cascade approach to child and adolescent depressive disorder based on the Research Domain Criteria (RDoC) approach. *Clinical Psychology Review*, *64*, 87–98. doi:10.1016/j.cpr.2017.09.008.

Luyten, P., & Fonagy, P. (2019). Mentalizing and trauma. In A. Bateman & P. Fonagy (Eds.), *Handbook of Mentalizing in Clinical Practice* (2nd ed., pp. 79–99). Washington, DC: American Psychiatric Press.

Masten, C.L., Eisenberger, N.I., Borofsky, L.A., Pfeifer, J.H., McNealy, K., Mazziotta, J.C., & Dapretto, M. (2009). Neural correlates of social exclusion during adolescence: Understanding the distress of peer rejection. *Social Cognitive and Affective Neuroscience, 4*(2), 143–157. doi:10.1093/scan/nsp007.

McEwen, B.S. (2000). The neurobiology of stress: From serendipity to clinical relevance. *Brain Research, 886,* 172–189.

McEwen, B.S. (2007). Physiology and neurobiology of stress and adaptation: Central role of the brain. *Physiological Reviews, 87*(3), 873–904. doi:10.1152/physrev.00041.2006.

McGivern, R.F., Andersen, J., Byrd, D., Mutter, K.L., & Reilly, J. (2002). Cognitive efficiency on a match to sample task decreases at the onset of puberty in children. *Brain and Cognition, 50*(1), 73–89. doi: 10.1016/s0278-2626(02)00012-x.

Mutlu, A.K., Schneider, M., Debbane, M., Badoud, D., Eliez, S., & Schaer, M. (2013). Sex differences in thickness, and folding developments throughout the cortex. *NeuroImage, 82,* 200–207. doi:10.1016/j.neuroimage.2013.05.076.

Nestler, E.J., & Carlezon, W.A., Jr. (2006). The mesolimbic dopamine reward circuit in depression. *Biological Psychiatry, 59*(12), 1151–1159. doi:10.1016/j.biopsych.2005. 09.018.

Neumann, I.D. (2008). Brain oxytocin: A key regulator of emotional and social behaviours in both females and males. *Journal of Neuroendocrinology, 20*(6), 858–865. doi:10.1111/j. 1365-2826.2008.01726.x.

Pizzagalli, D.A. (2014). Depression, stress, and anhedonia: Toward a synthesis and integrated model. *Annual Review of Clinical Psychology, 10,* 393–423. doi:10.1146/annurev-clinpsy-050212-185606.

Russo, S.J., & Nestler, E.J. (2013). The brain reward circuitry in mood disorders. *Nature Reviews Neuroscience, 14*(9), 609–625. doi:10.1038/nrn3381.

Sebastian, C., Viding, E., Williams, K.D., & Blakemore, S.-J. (2010). Social brain development and the affective consequences of ostracism in adolescence. *Brain and Cognition, 72*(1), 134–145. doi:10.1016/j.bandc.2009.06.008.

Sebastian, C.L., Tan, G.C., Roiser, J.P., Viding, E., Dumontheil, I., & Blakemore, S.-J. (2011). Developmental influences on the neural bases of responses to social rejection: Implications of social neuroscience for education. *NeuroImage, 57*(3), 686–694. doi:10. 1016/j.neuroimage.2010.09.063.

Sharp, C., Vanwoerden, S., & Wall, K. (2018). Adolescence as a sensitive period for the development of personality disorder. *Psychiatric Clinics of North America, 41*(4), 669–683. doi:https://doi.org/10.1016/j.psc.2018.07.004.

Shaw, P., Kabani, N.J., Lerch, J.P., Eckstrand, K., Lenroot, R., Gogtay, N., ... Wise, S.P. (2008). Neurodevelopmental trajectories of the human cerebral cortex. *Journal of Neuroscience, 28*(14), 3586–3594. doi:10.1523/jneurosci.5309-07.2008.

Simpson, J.A., & Belsky, J. (2008). Attachment theory within a modern evolutionary framework. In J. Cassidy & P.R. Shaver (Eds.), *Handbook of Attachment: Theory, Research, and Clinical Applications* (2nd ed., pp. 131–157). New York, NY: Guilford Press.

Spear, L. (2007). The developing brain and adolescent-typical behavior patterns: An evolutionary approach. In D. Romer & E.F. Walker (Eds.), *Adolescent Psychopathology and the Adolescent Brain* (pp. 9–30). New York, NY: Oxford University Press.

Spear, L.P. (2000). The adolescent brain and age-related behavioral manifestations. *Neuroscience and Biobehavioral Reviews*, *24*(4), 417–463. doi:10.1016/S0149-7634(00)00014-2.

Strathearn, L. (2011). Maternal neglect: Oxytocin, dopamine and the neurobiology of attachment. *Journal of Neuroendocrinology*, *23*(11), 1054–1065. doi:10.1111/j.1365-2826.2011.02228.x.

Swain, J.E., Kim, P., Spicer, J., Ho, S.S., Dayton, C.J., Elmadih, A., & Abel, K.M. (2014). Approaching the biology of human parental attachment: Brain imaging, oxytocin and coordinated assessments of mothers and fathers. *Brain Research*, *1580*, 78–101. doi:10.1016/j.brainres.2014.03.007.

Teicher, M.H., & Samson, J.A. (2013). Childhood maltreatment and psychopathology: A case for ecophenotypic variants as clinically and neurobiologically distinct subtypes. *American Journal of Psychiatry*, *170*(10), 1114–1133. doi: 10.1176/appi.ajp.2013.12070957.

Tonks, J., Williams, W.H., Frampton, I., Yates, P., & Slater, A. (2007). Assessing emotion recognition in 9–15-years olds: Preliminary analysis of abilities in reading emotion from faces, voices and eyes. *Brain Injury*, *21*(6), 623–629. doi: 10.1080/02699050701426865.

van Rooijen, R., Junge, C.M.M., & Kemner, C. (2018). The interplay between gaze following, emotion recognition, and empathy across adolescence; a pubertal dip in performance? *Frontiers in Psychology*, *9*, 127. doi: 10.3389/fpsyg.2018.00127.

Vetter, N.C., Drauschke, M., Thieme, J., & Altgassen, M. (2018). Adolescent basic facial emotion recognition is not influenced by puberty or own-age bias. *Frontiers in Psychology*, *9*, 956. doi: 10.3389/fpsyg.2018.00956.

Vetter, N.C., Leipold, K., Kliegel, M., Phillips, L.H., & Altgassen, M. (2013). Ongoing development of social cognition in adolescence. *Child Neuropsychology*, *19*(6), 615–629. doi: 10.1080/09297049.2012.718324.

Section II

Clinical practice

Chapter 3

MBT technique when working with young people

Trudie Rossouw

Introduction

Young people are faced with the developmental task of establishing autonomy and self-directed identity. Still, they often feel overwhelmed by failures in self-experience, finding themselves in a sea of bewilderment when dealing with others or with relationships. This often leads to a sense of helplessness or feelings of self-hatred and a desire to give up. Frequently when we see these young people, they have dropped out of their social network and/or school and have given up any hope that they could achieve anything in their lives. Their interpersonal relationships fill them with anxiety and fear that they will be rejected or that they are not liked, and they spend a great deal of time "overthinking" the intentions of others. This frequently results in an increasing state of mental anguish, which fuels their sense of self-hatred. Very soon, the internal suffering can no longer be endured, and they respond with impulsive, acting out behaviour, such as self-harm in order to "get rid of" this unbearable internal state. They often develop avoidant behaviour and end up missing school or having rollercoaster interpersonal relationships of over-involvement, followed by avoidance of any closeness.

The therapeutic task with such young people is to help them get back on an adaptive developmental trajectory and achieve a sense of autonomy, identity, mastery and accomplishment. Our view is that by restoring their ability to represent the mind of the others as well as themselves more accurately, they will have a more realistic experience of themselves and others. Hence, they will be protected from the rollercoaster emotions which are caused by the relapses in their ability to mentalize. This, in our experience, reduces the interpersonal bewilderment and makes them more robust and resilient.

The underlying principle of this model is that difficulties in mentalization underpin all the struggles young people experience with affect regulation, impulsive behaviour as well as conflict in families and other interpersonal relationships. Being able to portray the mind of others more accurately reduces arousal, and hence protects against mentalizing failure. In their prospective study of 150 young people who were admitted to a mental health unit,

Hauser, Allen, and Golden (2006) found at ten-year follow-up that a surprising number of these young people performed in the top half of all adults in terms of social and emotional functioning. Hauser et al. (2006) identified three main protective factors in the high performing group, which were as follows:

They all showed a) a capacity for reflection about their thoughts, feelings and motivations, b) a sense of agency, namely a sense of oneself as effective and responsible for one's actions, and c) relatedness, namely the ability to reflect on the minds of others

In other words, the protective factors which helped these young people to do well could be summarised as their capacity to mentalize – i.e., their capacity to reflect upon their own internal state and on the mind of the other and also a sense of responsibility about themselves and the impact that they have on the minds of those around them.

In MBT-A therapy, the aim is to achieve precisely that – an increased ability in the adolescent to be mindful of themselves and those around them in a more accurate way, as well as being mindful of the impact they have on others. In achieving greater and more accurate awareness of the minds of others, impulsive behaviour will reduce, and hence risk will reduce too. This will also reduce the storminess of relationships which are so typical in the absence of mentalization, which I turn leads to more stability in interpersonal life. Such stability leads to a sense of hope as well as mastery over the tasks adolescents have to do every day.

Often coercive, non-mentalizing cycles in families maintain, reinforce and exacerbate non-mentalizing in young people and their caregivers, leading to parental rejection, criticism and punishment, or disengagement, withdrawal and acting out behaviour in young people. Thus, MBT-A aims to help families shift from coercive, non-mentalizing cycles to mentalizing interactions that can promote trust, security, closeness, effective communication and problem-solving. Such an aim requires minimising the parent's experience of incompetence or of being blamed or shamed for their children's problems. Similarly, such an aim can only be achieved if young people feel more understood by others and themselves, particularly in a kind and humane, non-judgmental manner, in order to combat the inner judgement these young people have about themselves. In MBT-A, parents and young people are invited to work as partners in a treatment designed to shift from focusing on behaviours to a mentalizing conversation that enables family members to grasp each other's point of view and share their own in a palatable way. Shifting away from trying to force change helps rekindle curiosity, respect, empathy, mutuality and agency in a family.

The therapeutic technique on how to achieve this aim will be discussed below and can be divided into the following stages:

The mentalizing stance
Technique Grid:

Support and empathy
Clarification, elaboration and challenge
Basic mentalizing
Mentalizing the patient–therapist relationship

The MBT technique was first developed by Bateman and Fonagy (1999, 2004) for use with adults with borderline personality disorder. It has since been adapted for use with children, adolescents and families (Midgley & Vrouva, 2012), adults affected by eating disorders, drug and alcohol addiction, trauma and several other mental health problems (Bateman & Fonagy, 2019). When applied to adolescents (MBT- A), the therapy showed increased effectiveness over treatment as usual in terms of reduction in self-harm ($p < 0.013$) as demonstrated by Rossouw and Fonagy (2012) in a randomised controlled trial. A reduction in emerging borderline personality traits ($p < 0.034$) was also found. These gains were maintained six months after treatment ended.

Mentalizing stance

The mentalizing stance describes the therapist's main attitude in their interaction with young people, their families and staff members in the wider team. The mentalizing stance is essentially an attitude of care and compassion. An MBT-A therapist shows warmth and respect to the patients and conveys a real interest in them. The MBT-A therapist is curious about them, their lives, and what they are feeling.

So often young people are caught in a frightening inner world of self-hatred which renders them vulnerable to expect similar feelings of disdain from the world around them. They often shut themselves off from the world around them as they already "know" what people are feeling and thinking about them. In the author's experience, these youngsters often relate to themselves in a dehumanising way. We need to embody humanity in our interactions with young people in therapy. We show authentic interest and curiosity about the young person's life and mind, and we explore the richness of all possibilities in a non-judgemental way. Active questioning expresses curiosity but should not be expected to yield an unequivocal answer, rather progress towards a conceptualisation of alternatives (Skårderud & Fonagy, 2012).

In the situations where young people harm themselves, it is at times hard for family members and staff to remain empathic and warm. Family and staff can often feel that self-inflicting injuries are deliberately destructive of their treatment, or that it is attention-seeking. Parents and staff can feel undermined, angry, powerless or very anxious. Not uncommonly, parents and staff can at times think "you are doing this deliberately to make me feel powerless or anxious".

Parents and staff can be helped to develop a greater understanding and reduce feelings of hostility or frustration by getting to know that self-harm in young people is hardly ever done for the purpose of "seeking attention", it is rather a desperate way to try and cope with unbearable feelings inside them. Until those feelings have been understood and until adolescents have developed greater abilities to mentalize, those states of dysregulation are likely to re-occur, and this should not be seen as anyone's fault or failure.

Adopting a not-knowing stance allows us to ask open questions, such as "what happened before you felt like hurting yourself?" In MBT-A, the therapist is quite active. The therapist does not adopt a neutral stance and avoids long silences. The active stance is particularly helpful when young people find it hard to relate to their inner world. An example would be a young person who said: "I just felt like cutting myself, it was just an over-whelming urge that came into my mind, it has no other "meaning" or "Nothing happened before I felt like that". The not-knowing stance means that as clinicians do not know what that feels like, we are left with a desire and a curiosity to get to know more. Hence the therapist would ask questions in order to try and learn more about the young person's experience, for example: "Just tell me a little bit more about what you were doing before you felt like that…where were you …or what were you thinking……or, if I was a fly on the wall, what would I have seen?" The message is: "I really want to know what you experienced, take me there so that we can look at it together". This stance is about getting to know the patient's experience and in doing so, the feelings will unfold themselves, and it will make it easier to explore or make emotional contact with the young person's affect.

In summary, the therapist stance requires the following competencies from an MBT therapist (Bateman, Bales, & Hutsebaut, 2012):

- An ability to communicate with the patient in a direct, authentic, transparent manner, using simple and unambiguous statements to minimise the risk of over-arousing the client.
- An ability to adopt a stance of 'not knowing' which communicates to the patient a genuine attempt to find out about their mental experience.
- An ability to sustain an active, non-judgmental mentalizing stance that prioritises the joint exploration of the patient's mental states.
- An ability to communicate genuine curiosity about the patient's mental states through actively enquiring about interpersonal processes and their connection with the patient's mental states.
- An ability to follow shifts and changes in the patient's understanding of their own and others' thoughts and feelings.
- An ability to become aware of and respond sensitively to sudden and dramatic failures of mentalization in the patient.

Support and empathy

The most frequently used technique in MBT-A is support and empathy. When our patients are dysregulated, they are emotionally overwhelmed, and hence would be inclined to lose their ability to mentalize. By being supportive and empathic, we also try not to overstimulate them in order not to increase their arousal levels, which would reduce their thinking capacities.

Our attitude is warm, interested and non-judgemental, and we are supportive and validating of their mental states. We work hard to foster a positive alliance, and we try and create a collaborative working relationship with our patients. Offering support and empathy includes the validation of feelings; reflecting what we have understood or using ourselves at times to try and get more in touch with feelings. An example would be: "I hear what you are saying – gosh I think if that happened to me, I would have felt......".

Our focus in therapy is the patient's mind and not their behaviour, and we are mostly interested in the here and now, and not the past. For example, if a patient talks about upset feelings and fears about her boyfriend leaving her, we do not think it is helpful to make interpretations of her distant past as it would distance us from her current feelings and the patient is likely to experience this as invalidating. Even though in theory those interpretations may be correct, they are likely to "go over the patient's head", they may end up feeling misunderstood and it may lead to a therapeutic rupture. Our view is that it is best to maintain the focus of our interventions on the level where the patient is most likely to connect with their emotions.

The following is an example of an adolescent patient presenting in a non-mentalizing state of mind:

Sally arrived at her session, saying that she cut herself at school.

Therapist:	*What happened?*
Sally:	*Nothing, I was changing between classes, and I just had an overwhelming desire to cut myself, so I went to the toilet to cut myself.*
Therapist:	*What happened before you felt like that?*
Sally:	*Nothing. I just wanted to cut myself. It just happens.*

So here we can see Sally in a non-mentalizing state of mind, unable to make sense or even connect with the feelings which underpin her actions – in other words, she is in a state of pretend mode or pseudo-mentalizing where we see a disconnect between actions and affect. Clearly, a patient in such a state of mind is a challenge to a therapist who is hoping to be supportive and empathic, as it is not easy to make an emotional connection with the patient in this state of mind. It is, however, crucial to do so to help the patient out of the pseudo-mentalizing state. Let us look at how the session progressed:

Therapist:	*I hear that you felt like that, but I am really curious to know a little more about your day before you felt like that. Can you remember what you were doing before? Where were you or what were you busy with?*
Sally:	*I was in my lesson and the bell went off and we started changing classes and then it happened. I felt I hated myself and I wanted to cut myself.*

Therapist:	*Slow down... Imagine I am a fly on your shoulder, what would I see, take me there.*
Sally:	*I was walking in the corridor, and I saw Mrs A, and you know I like her very much, well, I greeted her, but she walked past and did not greet me back. That is when I hated myself and wanted to cut myself.*
Therapist:	*Just help me understand – She did not greet you and she is your favourite teacher – how did that make you feel?*
Sally:	*As I said, it made me hate myself.*
Therapist:	*Wait a minute, I don't see how you got from her not greeting you to you hating yourself. If we were to draw a thought bubble above her head, what do you think would be in it?*
Sally:	*When she did not greet me, I knew she hated me. I thought that the French teacher was cross with me yesterday because I didn't hand in my homework and the French teacher is Mrs A's best friend and I thought that the French teacher told her that I was bad and now she was also angry with me and she hated me.*

So, by carefully exploring the detail of the event, the affect unfolded and became clear. It also became clear how this increased the arousal in Sally and triggered her into a state of hypermentalization, which finally led to her seeking an impulsive (teleological) solution to the unbearable internal state. Her felt experience bypassed this process of understanding as she went very fast from hypermentalization and hyperarousal to feeling overwhelmed and needing to act out; hence she was only aware of the desire to cut herself, disconnected from the mental states which underpinned it. Careful exploration helped to bring us back into contact with this state of mind. Once the state is clearer, it is possible to understand her feelings and help her to make sense of her feelings.

Therapist:	*I see, so when she did not greet you, you felt she hated you?*
Sally:	*Yes, I felt she was disappointed, and now she does not like me anymore. It made me so angry with myself.*
Therapist:	*It sounds as if you felt you lost her, and it was all your fault, is that right?*
Sally:	*Yes.*
Therapist:	*I can see how you can feel like that, but from my perspective it feels a bit as if when she didn't greet you, your mind went into overdrive a bit to try and make sense of why she didn't greet you, and you arrived at an understanding that really hurt your feelings – as if your mind arrived at the worst possible scenario in seconds, isn't it?*
Sally:	*Yes, it is the worst possible scenario.*
Therapist:	*If a friend of you saw her not greeting you, what would your friend have thought?*
Sally:	*She may have thought something else. She may have thought nothing of it, or she may have thought the teacher did not see me, or that she had something else on her mind.*

In this example, we see how the therapist maintained a supportive and curious stance and tried to make emotional contact with Sally. Once it was clearer what Sally felt before she acted out, the therapist validated her feelings, which helped her to feel understood. Then it was possible to explore a different perspective as a gentle challenge of her non-mentalizing perspective. If the therapist had presented a different perspective before validating her feelings, she might have felt misunderstood, and this might have increased her arousal, and she may have reverted to a non-mentalizing state.

In our work with young people, we often end up working with the wider system around the young person too, such as communicating with their school to help the school understand what they are going through, to be more supportive, or meeting with the parents to help them with their understanding of the young person. When young people present with a higher risk of harm to themselves or risk of suicidal behaviour, it is, of course, important to work with the system around them to help keep them safe. It is also important to have a clear and concrete crisis plan which can help both young people and their parents and others around them to maintain their safety. A detailed example of a crisis plan will be discussed later, but at this stage, it is important to mention that the supportive technique at times requires us to take concrete action. The concrete action fulfils two functions; on the one hand, it helps with the management of risk that these young people present with, and on the other hand, it supports them in their quest to manage in their lives by creating supportive and mentalizing scaffolding around them. This scaffolding protects and supports them against becoming over-aroused and hence helps to support their growing ability to mentalize.

In summary, the technique of support and empathy requires the following competencies from an MBT therapist (Bateman et al., 2012):

- An ability to establish and maintain a supportive, reassuring and empathic relationship with the patient.
- An ability to sustain a positive, supportive stance without undermining the patient's autonomy.
- An ability to critically consider the appropriateness of supportive interventions that may involve taking concrete action within therapeutic boundaries.
- An ability to judiciously praise the patient when the patient uses mentalizing with a positive outcome to encourage and support change.

Clarification, elaboration and challenge

We often move from support and empathy into clarification and then back into support and empathy and then back again into clarification, elaboration or challenge. Clarification is about using active questioning to try and clarify events or behaviour. In the example of Sally above, the therapist used clarification by asking questions about the preceding events before she wanted to cut herself. Clarification of events can frequently bring to the fore the mental states which underpinned the event. If we merely asked about the mental state without the detailed exploration of the event, it may not have led us any closer to the mental state – as it was the case with Sally. Just asking her what she felt before she cut only led to her stating that she hated herself.

Perhaps it may be useful for us to pause at this point. Sally's statement that she hated herself might be incorrectly perceived as the feeling state, which created her dysregulation. However, such a state of self-hatred is evidence of concrete mentalizing, and it is evidence of the alien self, described in Chapter 7. The aim is trying to make a connection with the mental state that fuelled the loss of mentalization. In this way, it is trying to link actions with feelings, and it helps to make sense of what we did and what we felt when difficult things happened. It can also help us to see our role in how someone else may have felt or our role in the behaviour of someone else.

It is crucial to validate our patients' feelings authentically. Our patients frequently encounter an invalidating environment; hence in the treatment of such young people, we must adopt a validating stance. Now, the tricky question is, how can we be genuinely validating if an emotion is the consequence of hypermentalization? If we refer to the example of the young person who wanted to cut herself because she believed the teacher hated her, then we could say that her perception that the teacher hated her was distorted, so how can we validate her intense feelings? From a technical point of view, it is essential to make contact with her feelings and see the experience from her perspective. From her perspective, she lost the only person she felt she could trust or be close to at school, so from that perspective, we can see that it was a devastating experience. The technique in MBT-A is to make contact with the patient's feelings first – such as saying:

> "I can see from your perspective that if you felt she hated you, that would be a pretty devastating feeling…. But can we just slow things down, I'm not sure I understand how you got there from her not greeting you…."

In this way, we validate her feelings and still gently challenge the non-mentalization.

Elaboration refers to the elaboration of feelings. It is not an uncommon phenomenon that patients may present in one state of mind, but that there is a different state of mind underneath. For example, someone who comes in angry and swearing can easily be perceived as angry and perhaps even dangerous. However, careful elaboration of the patient's feelings may expose a deep sense of shame underneath the rage. This technique also includes the exploration of feelings or actions in order to try and link the two or being curious about the link between feelings and actions in others. An example is as follows:

*A patient moved home and moved to a new school and then reported the
following:*

P: *I just want to die. I want to cut myself into pieces. I cannot stand this pain any more.
I am in such pain.*

T: *Is that the pain of losing people when you moved school?*

P: *No, it is the pain of being alive. I cannot do this anymore. Everyone around me is
happy and has purpose in their lives and I am just in such pain, no-one will ever
love me.*

T: *You know when I started a new job, I felt as if I did not fit in and as if everyone else
had a good connection, but I was an outsider, I am not sure if you are talking about
that sort of pain?*

P: *I just don't have purpose and I don't have friends. I just cannot take it anymore. I so
want to die, I think of it all the time and have visions in my head of what it may feel
like to die.*

T: *It sounds almost as if your mind is a bit attracted to that vision, is that right?*

P: *Yes.*

T: *I may be wrong, but to me, it sounds like a vision of getting away, like getting away
from something horrible or scary, which makes me think you are having feelings
inside you that are really hard — so hard that you want to get away, am I getting it
right?*

P: *It is hard. It is so hard. I feel so alone and I don't know how to make friends....*

In this way, the therapist helped the patient to make emotional contact
with her feelings underneath the suicidal fantasies, which would then
enable them to work with these feelings. Clearly, feeling alone and
overwhelmed by the change is quite normal and understandable, but
further exploration in the session helped to clarify that instead of her
feeling compassion for herself at the change, something else was taking
place in her mind. Under the force of her alien self, the understandable
feelings were attributed to her being unlovable, weird and unwanted,
and consequently, she withdrew from interactions. She also started to
hypermentalize about others and was reading all sorts of hostile intent in
their interactions with her. Having been helped to mentalize more
accurately about her own mind and the minds of those around her, she
was able to settle in the school and her suicidal feelings decreased.

Challenge refers to stopping non-mentalizing interactions and trying to
bring mentalization back. A challenge does not refer to a confrontational
interaction with the patient. If the patient feels that they "have done something wrong" and that they are "in trouble", the intervention will not succeed.
It is best done with warmth and if possible, with a sense of humour. A patient
is also more likely to take a challenge on board if their feelings are validated;
otherwise, there is a risk of them feeling stupid.

An example is as follows:

> *A patient comes to her session one day with a newspaper report about a young adult in the Netherlands who was given permission to have euthanasia. She came to the session in good spirits, saying, "Look what I found, this is possible, isn't this amazing?"*
>
> *The therapist read the report briefly and then leaned forward and looked the patient in the eyes and said with a smile "Are you serious?"*
>
> *The patient smiled back and said, "Yes, it is great, isn't it?"*

T: *(Still with a smile). You seriously thought I would think it is a great idea, too?*

P: *Yeah.*

T: *I don't think I read that bit of my job description, you know, the bit where it said I am supposed to kill you.(Both smile).*

T: *Are you romanticising about death again?*

P: *Yes, it is the only solution.*

T: *Tell me, what's been happening in your life for you to feel that way?*

Basic mentalizing

The crux of the work is helping young people and their parents to become better able to mentalize those around them, as well as be more aware of their own feelings and other mental states. By getting better at mentalizing, they can see how mental states are linked to their behaviour, which in turn has an impact on those around them. It can be described metaphorically speaking as opening the shutters in front of windows to help us notice the world around us more accurately. With the shutters closed, we are left with our mental images of what goes on around us, but there is no reality check; hence there is the risk that the mental images may soon be treated as facts (mode of psychic equivalence). In this state of mind, it is easy to fall prey to hypermentalization, or what our patients so beautifully describe as "over-thinking", which increases their arousal levels, consequently keeping the shutters more firmly shut.

Basic mentalizing is about helping someone to open the shutters in front of their eyes so that they have a more accurate understanding of the mental states of those around them. The MBT-A therapist uses the techniques described above, such as asking questions, seeking clarification, using elaboration and challenge where needed to generate curiosity and a not-knowing stance about the minds of others.

Let us illustrate this with the example below:

> *This is an example of a boy who was attacked in the playground by a group of other boys and beaten up. He then ran home, but on the way to his flat, he ran past the flat of one of the leaders of the bullies who beat him up, and he stopped and kicked the flower pots in front of the door to pieces.*

Later, the leader's mother spoke to the boy's dad angrily about the boy's destructive behaviour in breaking her flower pots. She made the boy's dad feel humiliated as if he was a bad father and not able to teach his child how to behave appropriately. When he saw his son, he was furious and shouted at him and slapped him in the face. He was unable to see that his son was injured from having been beaten up by the other boys. When his wife became supportive of his son, the dad shouted at her and left the room.

In this example, the dad was overwhelmed with his feelings of embarrassment and possibly a sense of powerlessness. He could neither see the boy's injuries nor could he allow his wife to have a different perspective. He had no curiosity about the boy's mind and made no attempt to try and understand what the boy was feeling when he kicked the pots or what was going on for him. He felt ashamed, and therefore everything else was filtered through that lens – the boy did it to him.

The consequence of this derailment of mentalizing could have the following ripple effects: The boy would feel his dad is angry, but he might also feel his dad does not love him, which might make him feel he is unlovable or that he is a bad boy.

If the dad could be helped to notice his own feelings, rather than just act on them, and then be more curious about the boy, he may have found out what happened. That would help him to understand the boy's intense feelings of rejection, humiliation and pain when he was attacked. It would rekindle his desire to protect his son. He would also be helped by having a more accurate portrayal of himself, and by not seeing himself as a bad dad, he would not feel humiliated.

This is what basic mentalizing in MBT is trying to establish: stopping and pausing a moment of mind blindness, trying to imagine what was going on for those involved and also trying to use imagination to envision the feelings someone else may have had when they did what they did. We try and ignite curiosity about mental states in order to see if we can arrive at a different perspective. This stage is imaginative, and it is exploring other possibilities. Although this might sound like a cognitive exercise, the emphasis is on the connection with the feelings rather than cognition. We can use ourselves if it seems that it may be helpful therapeutically. As an example, if the dad in this example spoke to us about what happened, we may say things like:

I think if one of my neighbours shouted at me like that, I may have felt very embarrassed, but that is me, I don't know if that is what you felt….

and

Sometimes when I am embarrassed, it is such a painful feeling, it becomes all I feel and then I feel like such a bad person and I cannot see anything else, was it like that for you?

With this technique, we try and validate the dad's feeling first; otherwise, he will feel more humiliated and not be able to mentalize. Once validated, he could then see his feelings more reflectively, and hence not be so overwhelmed by them – watching it like a cloud in the sky – able to see it but not being inside it.

Then it would be possible to try and help him to mentalize what was going on for the boy when he kicked the pots. If they are both in the session, we could ask the dad to ask the boy questions about that day to elicit curiosity in the dad's mind about the boy. Sometimes it helps to be playful and ask the dad to be an interviewer for a newspaper and to ask the boy about events of the day prior to him kicking the pots.

If the boy is not in the room, one could still get the dad to imagine life from the boy's perspective to try and understand what he feels and what was going through his mind at the time. If it is hard for the dad to do this, one could use playful techniques to help, such as saying:

> If I draw a picture of your son on this paper, and this is him kicking the pots, let's draw a thought bubble above his head, what do you think is going on in his mind?

If we imagine that the dad was not aware of the attack on the boy and he had no idea of what happened, he may say something like:

> I don't know – he was just naughty.
> We could say: You know I wonder, sometimes people do things because they have very strong feelings inside themselves – if it was that he had a strong feeling inside himself at the time, I wonder what it could have been?
> The dad may then say: Perhaps he was angry.
> That could then lead to us asking about the anger: Would he be angry with the mother who lived there or with her son?

The dad may then at some point start to remember that this boy is often horrible to his son and it may just open up a different insight in him, which may help him to have more curiosity about his son's mind and experiences.

Mentalizing the relationship between the therapist and the patient

Mentalizing the therapeutic relationship refers to reflecting on the interactions between the therapist and the patient. We take responsibility for the fact that we have an emotional impact on the patient and that we, at times, get things wrong or misunderstand them. When we misunderstand them or get something wrong, we own up to it and try and restore the connection between us. In MBT-A, we do not aim to make interpretations about the patient's unconscious or make reference to us being the receptors of unconscious projections. The emphasis is on relationships in the here and now, not unconscious projections from the patient's past. We take full responsibility for the fact that we have an impact upon our patients, and this can sometimes lead to an increase in arousal, and hence compromise the young person's ability to mentalize. It is important for us to own this and try and re-establish contact with the patient in order to re-instate mentalization.

It is impossible in our work not to misunderstand our patients from time to time or make errors in what we say. These experiences are painful for patients and likely to have a strong emotional impact, and it can lead to an immediate change in demeanour in a session. We must pick up when we have made an error and then take responsibility for it to try and repair the connection with the patient. If a patient says: *"You have not understood me"*. We would say: *"I am so sorry, I really want to understand you, please help me see where I got it wrong"*.

It is sometimes helpful for our patients if we are explicit with what we feel or what our intentions are, mainly when our patients are a bit blinded by their own mental states or, as described earlier, where the shutters are down. For example, if a patient is very angry, either with the therapist or with themselves, they are often likely to think the therapist is angry too. It is very helpful for patients if we explicitly state during these times *"I am not angry with you"*. Alternatively, when they feel overwhelmed with humiliation or shame, it can be helpful for us to state our feelings explicitly, to avoid them feeling we judge them too, by saying: *"I am not angry or judging you, I am on your side. All I want to do, is try and understand"*.

A simple example that epitomises the MBT technique was offered by Peter Fonagy, one of the founders of the mentalizing model. When once asked at a conference how to speak to an angry young person who is screaming at the therapist, he suggested the therapist could say: *"I really want to hear and understand what you say, but if you scream like that, I cannot think"*.

By communicating that, he stated explicitly his intention of wanting to hear and understand and by saying, *"when you scream like that, I cannot think"* he presented himself as another human being with his own limitations, therefore reducing the threat and the young person's arousal levels, and forcing the young person to mentalize him, which kick-started mentalization in the young person.

References

Bateman, A., Bales, D., & Hutsebaut, J. (2012). A Quality Manual for MBT. London: Anna Freud National Centre for Children and Families. http://www.annafreud.org/media/1217/a-quality-manual-for-mbt-edited-april23rd–2014-2.pdf.

Bateman, A., & Fonagy, P. (1999). Effectiveness of partial hospitalisation in the treatment of borderline personality disorder: A randomised controlled trial. American Journal of Psychiatry, 156, 1563–1569.

Bateman, A.W., & Fonagy, P. (2004). Psychotherapy for Borderline Personality Disorder: Mentalization-Based Treatment. Oxford, UK: Oxford University Press.

Bateman, A.W., & Fonagy, P. (2019). Handbook of Mentalizing in Mental Health Practice (2nd ed.). Washington, DC: American Psychiatric Press.

Hauser, S.T., Allen, J.P., & Golden, E. (2006). Out of the Woods: Tales of Teen Resilience. Cambridge, MA: Harvard University Press.

Midgley, N., & Vrouva, I. (Eds.) (2012). Minding the Child: Mentalization-Based Interventions with Children, Young People and Their Families. London: Routledge.

Rossouw, T.I., & Fonagy, P. (2012). Mentalization-based treatment for self-harm in adolescents: A randomized controlled trial. Journal of American Academy of Child an Adolescent Psychiatry, 51(12), 1304–1313.

Skårderud, F., & Fonagy, P. (2012). Eating disorders. In A.W. Bateman & P. Fonagy (Eds.), Handbook of Mentalizing in Mental Health Practice (pp. 347–383). Arlington, VA: American Psychiatric Publishing.

Chapter 4

The structure of therapy

Trudie Rossouw

1 Introduction

The MBT model developed for the treatment of adults combines MBT individual therapy with MBT group therapy. In our work with young people, we involve families in the treatment plan. In bringing families into the treatment plan, we believe we enable family members to support and scaffold the development of a home environment in which everyone becomes more curious about the feelings of others and more aware of their impact on others, as well as being more humanising in their own feelings about themselves. When young people find themselves adrift in a sea of self-criticism and fears of rejection from peers or feelings of isolation, they often turn to their bedroom as the only safe space they have, and in their attempt to have some control over a world that feels hostile, they close their curtains and their door to the outside world and isolate themselves. The consequence is that they are then trapped in their room with their mind as their worst enemy. Parents of young people in this situation often find themselves feeling very anxious and worried, but also very helpless. In the end, the situation results in the young person feeling stuck in their room with negative feelings about themselves, and the parents also feeling stuck in the painful feelings of helplessness – all of which leads to a growing sense of inadequacy in all involved. Working with the family, therefore, is a crucial component of the therapeutic process and our view is that as the family becomes more able to mentalize, family members become in a way therapists themselves who can support and scaffold mentalization at home at times when it breaks down.

MBT-A is a model in which individual therapy is usually combined with MBT-Family and or MBT-Group. In more intensive programmes, MBT-A individual therapy will be combined with both MBT family and MBT group and in less intensive programmes it will be combined with MBT family. The individual sessions are usually at least once a week, but the family sessions do not need to take place weekly. There is emerging clinical evidence to suggest that six sessions of family work can be sufficient, and stretching it out to twice a month, gives families more time to apply what they have learned. In those programmes where MBT group is used, group therapy usually takes place once a week, but in some more intensive models such as inpatient units or day-patient programmes, it is sometimes offered twice a week.

The structure of MBT-A follows the same structure as the adult model in that it has the following stages of therapy:

Initial phase - Assessment and Psychoeducation
- Assessment
- Contract
- Formulation
- Crisis plan

Psychoeducation

Middle phase - Bulk of the work
- Improving mentalizing and impulse control
- Enhancing awareness of mental states of others
- Helping with adolescent tasks

Final phase - Concluding the work
- Increasing independence and responsibility
- Consolidating stability
- Developing follow-up plans
- Understanding and processing the meaning of the ending and focussing on affective states associated with loss
- Discharge planning and liaison with partner organisations

2.1 Initial phase – assessment

Whenever we meet a new family or young person, we do so with a mentalizing mind, which means we are curious, open-minded and we maintain a not-knowing stance with an attitude of warmth, empathy and authenticity. In other words, the mentalizing stance that we maintain throughout the work is the same stance we maintain during the assessment process. The assessment process can take place during the first session, or if required, it can take place over a few initial sessions. Our view is that it should not be longer than three sessions and our view is also that after the first session, families and young people usually want some form of feedback or clear idea about the treatment plan. If there are concerns about risk, this needs to be addressed in the first session too and a crisis plan needs to be developed with the young person and the family. So, the first session will include the assessment, but it also needs to include some concrete planning at the end, even if the assessment is to continue over more than one session. The assessment phase is usually concluded with the discussion of the formulation, which will be discussed in greater detail later.

The aim of assessment, as can be expected, is to get an idea of the following:

- The usual information a clinician would want to gain from any assessment, such as the reason for referral, history of difficulties, other relevant background information and developmental history.
- The clinician will also often need to assess the young person's mental state, do a risk assessment and get to know precipitating and perpetuating factors, which is covered in most first assessment sessions with young people.
- However, in the MBT-A assessment, the clinician is also hoping to get an understanding of the mentalizing difficulties experienced by the young person and the family, so the clinician would pay attention to evidence of good mentalizing or examples of non-mentalizing functioning and hence may ask a few mentalizing tracer questions, such as "when he did that, what do you think he was feeling…"
- At the end of the assessment, the MBT-A clinician would want to be in a position to do the following:

  - Have an idea of the presenting problems and the diagnosis when this is useful
  - Draw up a draft formulation of the young person's difficulties
  - Describe the treatment plan
  - Develop a clear safety or crisis plan, when indicated

The main difference between doing an assessment with an MBT-A hat on and any other assessment is that in this assessment, we mentalize with the young person and/or family together in the session. It is important that all leave the assessment feeling recruited to work alongside the clinician as partners in the treatment, rather than the clinician being the expert that will solve the problem or find out who is at fault.

2.2 Contract

The term contract always sounds like a legal document, which is not the aim here! It is more a description of the treatment plan in a concrete way which makes explicit for the young person and family what the treatment will entail, how often the sessions will be, what is being offered and how long it will last. It makes the practical arrangements clear from the start so that the young person and the family know what they can expect, have a clear understanding of what is offered and can sign up for it willingly, or in other words, consent to participate in it. A written information sheet about MBT-A is given to the young person and can be found at the end of this chapter.

We do not bring in concrete expectations that the young person would stop self-harming or anything along such lines. However, if there are behaviours associated with risks such as self-harm, suicidal behaviour, violence, drug-taking or other risk-taking behaviour, these will have to be addressed either in the contract and in the crisis plan or in the crisis plan alone. We do not support contracts that state, 'if you harm yourself your treatment will be terminated'. Young people turn to impulsive or self-destructive behaviours as a way of coping and if we do not understand that and pull treatment away when they will most likely turn to their old coping styles. It is like leaving someone when they have fallen and not helping them get back on their feet. These issues need to be addressed in a mentalizing framework where we have mentalized the possible feelings underneath the behaviours. We can communicate concern that the risky behaviours can have dangerous consequences or can be undermining of treatment, but that we understand it may have been the only way for some young people to manage difficult feelings until now. We can convey the hope that together, we may be able to find other ways of helping with those feeling states so that they become more understandable and manageable over time. In the meanwhile, particularly in cases of high risk, we can look at some alternative strategies that they can use, which will provide safer ways of coping. As we see the risky behaviour through a mentalizing lens, it may therefore make more sense to include these discussions in the crisis plan and formulation, rather than in the contract. This will be illustrated with examples below.

2.3 Formulation

As clinicians complete an assessment, they would be in a position to formulate an understanding of the young person and their family, as well as the issues that brought them to seek professional help. In other words, the clinician would be in a position to mentalize them and see them and the struggle they present with through a mentalizing lens. This is what a draft formulation is. When we discuss this with the young person (and the family), we develop the formulation together. The clinician brings to the family the draft version for discussion and together they elaborate on the formulation. Some practitioners do the discussion of the formulation verbally and some practitioners present a written draft formulation to young people for discussion. The benefit of the latter is that although it could be described as teleologic in that the discussion is captured in a concrete written format, it can be very helpful for young people to hold onto it and refer back to it at a later stage, especially at times when they may feel overwhelmed and hence unable to remember the session's discussion without a concrete reminder to scaffold them.

As different therapists frequently offer the individual MBT-A work and the MBT family work, the formulation of the young person is often discussed in the young person's individual therapy and not shared with the rest of the family. In the family sessions, formulations are developed, but those tend to focus more on family interactions and less on one particular individual. The formulations which develop in family work are usually discussed during the sessions and not pre-sented in written format. It is useful for professionals involved in the young person's care (such as the MBT individual, group and family therapists) to discuss their formulations to ensure as coherent a treatment plan as possible.

Below is an example of a formulation shared with a young person in therapy:

Background Information

When you were referred to this service you reported a two-year history of feeling de-pressed and harming yourself. At times you have felt so depressed that life did not feel worth living.

You thought your parent's divorce three years ago, your mother's subsequent de-pression, your father's drinking and his recent violent relationship with his girlfriend all played a role in you becoming depressed. You spoke about feeling guilty as if it was your fault. Before you came for help you entered into a relationship in which you allowed someone to treat you in a disrespectful manner, almost as if you were being punished. All of this made you feel terribly bad about yourself.

Personality style

You are a very brave young person who has had to cope with a lot in your life. You were also very brave to speak to me about your feelings and difficult things that happened in your life. You are kind and caring to others and you have been a very reliable friend to your peers. It is sad to notice how you cannot see your own beautiful qualities and how you constantly expect people to dislike you. This can make you feel so anxious in social situations that you tend to withdraw yourself, but the problem with this way of coping is that it does not allow others to be close to you and in that way it reinforces your view that they do not like you. You also told me that in your relationships things can be up and down at times. You explained that you have a desire to be close to people but as soon as you are close to them, you feel overwhelmed by anxieties that they will let you down or reject you. This, you said, can make you feel so anxious that you can feel as if you are on a rollercoaster emotionally with extreme mood swings. From our discussions I had the impression that sometimes when you have strong feelings inside you, you cope with them by either cutting yourself or by switching your emotions off until you feel empty. Is that what happens to you?

When we spoke about you switching off your emotions, I thought about it afterwards and although I can see that it feels as if this coping style helps you at the time, I did wonder whether it also makes you feel disconnected from what you or other people feel and whether it is then difficult to understand what is going on. I wondered if it may be at times like this that you feel action is the only option available to you – and whether it may be at these times that you have a tendency to harm yourself. What do you think about that?

In listening to the way you spoke about yourself, I found myself feeling very sad about the constant negative ways in which you see yourself. I was also struck by how you seem to relate to other people in a self-sacrificing manner and how at times you allow them to take advantage of you. Perhaps in therapy we can work on all these aspects and help you to develop a desire to look after yourself and to allow others to look after you, rather than hurt you.

You are a courageous and thoughtful person and you deserve more than what you currently allow yourself to have. Hopefully in the therapy we can work together to help you feel better about yourself.

Looking at the above formulation, it reminds the reader of something like a personal letter. It is presented to the young person as a draft and then discussed together to see if the young person agrees with it. Otherwise, the risk is that it may be experienced as intrusive mentalization, i.e. the therapist telling the young person what they are feeling. Hence, we use phrases in the formulation such as: "is that correct?" Such phrases invite comment from the young person at each stage and read as a tentative statement rather than a fact. The reader will also notice comments such as "it makes me feel sad to see how negative you feel about yourself". In this way, we explicitly present ourselves as humans with feelings. So often these youngsters relate to themselves in a dehumanising manner and when they do, they anticipate that we view them in the same light. By explicitly stating our intentions, we help them to mentalize us more accurately. We also embody humanity, which they so often have lost in their relationships with themselves.

2.4 Crisis planning

Although crisis planning is discussed at this stage, it often happens before the formulation in the sequence of therapy, depending on the level of risk at the outset. If a young person presents with self-harm or suicidal feelings, or indeed any other form of risk such as violence, the safety plan will need to be discussed at the first session. The safety plan aims to think about the risk in mentalizing terms and to address the underlying feelings as well as have some understanding of the trigger factors and then to think about safer alternatives that can be used. The safety plan is drawn up with the family and the young person and our view is that it is best if it can be discussed in the session, but also that it can be provided to the young person and their parents in written format so that they can take it home with them and refer to it at a later stage.

In the author's experience, she initially used to give written crisis plans to young people, but soon realised that this had little value. Young people live in a cyber world and not a paper world anymore. She, therefore, developed a mobile app that she uses as part of the crisis planning discussion with young people. Given that the app is very general, it will not be helpful if crisis planning is exclusively just the app. It needs to be personalised and mentalized in the way that is mentioned above. This can be discussed in the session, followed by the discussion and illustration of the app. The combination of having something readily accessible on the young person's mobile phone with the personalised understanding of the crisis and this risk provides a more useful crisis planning. The author also provides a separate crisis plan for parents to guide them and help them in their role as parents. Below there is an example of a discussion of a crisis plan with a young person, as well as a discussion about the app and the crisis plan with parents.

2.4.1 Crisis plan for a young person

The following is an example of a crisis plan for a young person:

CRISIS PLAN

Trigger factors that you and I identified are times when you feel rejected, humiliated or bad about yourself. As we have discussed, these feelings do not just arrive out of the blue, they are likely to have been triggered in a close relationship. When you have those feelings, you tend to rush into an action to take the feelings away.

When you feel like that again, I would like you to try and stop the action by trying to delay it for 10 minutes. Then use the 10 minutes to try and reflect on what was happening a few moments before you had the bad feeling. That might help you to understand more clearly what it is that you feel as well as what might have happened in a close relationship which may have contributed to the feeling.

Once you have this understanding more clearly it may be easier to think about a solution or to see things from a different perspective. Once that has happened you may not feel as if you need to rush into action anymore.

If that fails and you still feel at risk of harming yourself, use the tools on the COPING SKILLS app to help you. It will help you with tools such as trying out alternatives to self-harm or tools to help you use your senses to try and calm you down.

Sometimes you harm yourself in order to numb yourself emotionally. When you get into such a state of mind, try to remember that it is not a useful state of mind to be in and it is harmful to you.

Try and bring yourself back to reality – do something to occupy yourself, like talking to someone, playing a game, writing a poem, painting or watching something that can hold your attention on TV. Don't just sit and stare into space with your mind full of negative thoughts about yourself.

If all else fails, call the clinic and ask to speak to me and I will call you back when I can.

The COPING SKILLS app is a combination of distress tolerance skills, borrowed from DBT, mindfulness exercises, a mentalization exercise and guided meditation as well as progressive muscle relaxation tapes. It also has a functionality where young people can link it to calming music of their own, and also images and photos which hold good memories for them. The app is only £1.00 to download. It is helpful to go through the app with young people in the session so that they can understand how to use it. Below (Figure 4.1) is an image of the app.

Figure 4.1 Coping skills App.

2.4.2 Crisis planning for parents

The crisis plan with the parents includes some basic understanding of self-harm and risk in young people and practical advice on how to behave and what to say/do when young people self-harm. It also includes advice on basic safety measures at home to reduce the risk. See below:

Parents endeavour to protect their children from suffering and pain. Therefore, when one's child presents with self-harm behaviour, it stirs up incredibly strong emotions. You may experience helplessness, anxiety and various other strong emotions. Hopefully this crisis plan will give some guidance at the start of the therapeutic journey.

*Firstly, let's address some **basic safety measures** around the home:*

- *Keep medication locked away*
- *If your child harms themselves by cutting themselves, it may be helpful if you keep the knives out of reach and restrict access to razors*
- *It may also be helpful if you remove sharps from your child's bedroom*

*Next, encourage **communication** about self-harm and allow your child to tell you when they feel at risk. Young people will find this very hard to do and for some young people it is easier to agree on an emoji that they can send their parents on their phone as a code that they are at risk of harming themselves.*

If your child is at higher risk, be with them and ensure that they are not on their own. Sometimes when parents are concerned about their children's safety, they either sleep with them on a mattress on the floor or they let the young person sleep with them.

Now, let us turn to speaking a little bit more about self-harm in young people. Young people mostly harm themselves when they have very strong feelings inside them that they find hard to manage. Here are 3 Dos and 3 Don'ts which may help you at times of risk:

Dos:

- *Listen*
- *Understand*
- *Let them know you are there for them*

Don'ts:

- *Panic*
- *Blame*
- *Punish*

Don't blame your child and don't blame yourself. Just try and understand what your child felt before they wanted to harm themselves and help them to speak about the feelings and the events leading up to the feelings. If the events involved you, listen and try to understand their perspective without becoming defensive. You don't have to hold the same perspective, but it is important that you validate their feelings. If there was a misunderstanding between you which you contributed to, own up to it. You are not here to win battles but to restore the connection between you.

If your child is very aroused, speaking too much is not helpful. Just be kind and supportive and say things like: "I am not angry with you, I am here to help you and keep you safe. Something has made you so upset. I don't know what it is and if it is something I have done, I am sorry. I really want to understand. Talk when you are ready, but until then, I will just be with you to keep you safe."

If your child wants to hurt themselves, you could say: "I really don't want you to hurt yourself. You deserve so much more. Let's try one of the alternatives. I will help you, shall we get a bowl of ice?"

If your child is suicidal, you could say: "Killing yourself is not an option. I love you and do not want you to kill yourself. You are not alone. We will get through this together. I am going to stay here with you to keep you safe. Let's try and think of something that will help right now. Will distraction help such as going for a walk or watching TV?"

If all else fails, call the clinic or if it is after hours, you may have to take your child to the emergency department.

3 Psychoeducation

Psychoeducation aims to help young people and families develop curiosity about mental states in themselves and others, as well as to learn that there is a link between behaviour and feelings. During the course of treatment, we are hoping to address states of non-mentalizing, such as psychic equivalence, to restore mentalization. It is helpful at the outset if young people and families have some understanding of some of the basic principles of mentalization. The process in which the psychoeducation is delivered varies from service to service. There are some services where the first few sessions of the therapeutic process are dedicated to psychoeducation (MBT - Information). This is usually done in a group format. Another model is to invite families for a day workshop. In services where this is not possible or available, psychoeducation can be done by explicitly making statements which stimulate curiosity and give the message that mental states are opaque.

3.1 Informal psychoeducation in sessions

Where workshops or psychoeducation groups are not available or possible, psychoeducation can be done more informally, particularly during the initial sessions, by weaving it into the treatment where relevant. Here are a few examples of psychoeducational statements which could be used in response to material from the session:

> "You know, many times when people do what they do, it is because they have feelings inside them and if we are curious about that, it can help us to try and make more sense of other people".

We could also address non-mentalizing when it occurs, by saying something like:

> "It sounds as if you have made an assumption about what X was feeling. You know when we make assumptions about what people feel, we can easily get it wrong - ...."

Or

> "Can we pause for a minute, I was wondering if you are beginning to overthink a bit, and you know when we overthink, we start making massive assumptions about other people's minds and then we start to treat these assumptions as if they are facts, when they aren't– we cannot really see into other people's minds."

Or

> "When we are anxious our minds can sometimes run away with us and make assumptions of what other people are thinking or feeling, but the best thing to do when we catch ourselves making assumptions or overthinking, is to stop, pause and perhaps ask the other person what they are thinking or feeling."

3.2 Psychoeducational workshops

Psychoeducational workshops can be conducted over the course of a whole day or over a couple of sessions. They are usually offered in a group format and best delivered by two clinicians. The format is as follows:

- Icebreaker exercise and introductions
- Short didactic input on the adolescent brain
- Clip from a film which gets paused from time to time and the participants are invited to discuss – why did the character say or do that – what was the character feeling?
- The section about *Making sense of relationships* in which we explain the link between behaviour and mental states underneath it. We also emphasise that mental states are opaque, and it is usually possible to refer to sections of the film to demonstrate this. We also refer to the film to demonstrate how blinkered our own feelings can make us and how this can stop us from being curious about the mental states in others. We also talk about the trap we can all fall into when we assume others share the same mental state as the one we are experiencing or imagining.
- This can be followed by further video clips or discussions from people's personal lives.
- Techniques such as *stop and pause* are discussed in order to stop rushing into non-mentalizing states and to help people think about exploring what others are thinking and feeling. This could be practised using videos which can be paused at times to practise the technique.

The latter part of the workshop is dedicated to two sessions, one on *Understanding self-harm* and one on *Understanding and managing violence*.

- *Understanding self-harm*: In our service, instead of giving didactic input on self-harm, we wrote several statements on cards which were handed out to everyone. Participants took turns to read the statements on the card and then they had to say whether they thought the statement was true or false. The group discussed each statement thereafter. We used statements such as, "*Self-harm is done for attention*", or "*My child is suicidal when they harm themselves*", or "*Self-harm often happens when someone is overwhelmed with intense feelings, etc.*"

We then spend some time discussing how to help someone who is harming themselves and we draw from the examples given in the crisis plan discussed above.

- *Understanding and managing violence*: Again, we use the group to discuss this together rather than offer didactic input. We gave an example of an outburst of violence of a child towards his parent and then the group is handed a group of cards with actions written on it and they are tasked to arrange the cards in the most helpful order of what needs to happen next. Each card contains an action in a mentalizing sequence, going from "*giving space*" to "*calm down*" to finally discussing the event and owning up to their own contributions to the event. The last card is for *reparation*.

4 Bulk of the work – main phase

This phase will cover most of the therapeutic work done. MBT group and MBT families will be described in other sections of this book, but the therapeutic tasks described in this section also describe the bulk of the work in MBT-group and MBT-family. For the duration of the work, we follow the techniques discussed earlier. We doggedly hang onto the aim of the work, which is to enhance mentalization when it is absent. The aim is not to gain insight for insight's sake or make the unconscious conscious. As we discussed in the previous chapter, we are active in work and convey a stance of curiosity, warmth and not-knowing. Support and empathy are the techniques used most of the time and we move between support and empathy and affect elaboration or challenging most of the time in our attempt to foster basic mentalizing. Work with young people is creative and can involve writing things down, drawing thought bubbles above someone's head in pictures to try and imagine what they are thinking and feeling or doing role plays. We try and put the brakes on the action, particularly impulsive action, and kick start mentalizing.

STOP and PAUSE, is a very common mentalizing intervention and in the *pausing* we use empathy to make emotional contact and then, once the young person feels understood and is not hyper-aroused, we use exploration or elaboration to think together about the underlying feelings, thoughts or assumptions the person is making. We use STOP and PAUSE each time a non-mentalizing interaction is happening and we use it to calm the emotions down and then to create space for mentalizing.

Whenever we notice a non-mentalizing interaction, we can assume that there has been a strong emotion which triggered a loss of mentalizing abilities. We then use the STOP and PAUSE technique to end the interaction and then try and rewind to where the person last had the ability to mentalize – next we try and understand the event that happened that derailed the young person's ability to mentalize. We then try and mentalize the feelings which could not be mentalized at the time. The technique in doing this is as follows:

Non-mentalizing action – STOP and PAUSE – expressing empathy and trying to validate what the young person felt at the time, even if this is based on them not mentalizing – then trying to rewind to the moment where the young person lost the ability to mentalize – then asking for detail and using validation, empathy as well as elaboration and exploration to open things up and in the process trying to kick start mentalizing by gently addressing the non-mentalizing errors which may have escalated the emotions or driven the person into impulsive action.

Unlike structured therapies, MBT-A does not have prescribed structures for each session. The content of the sessions is mostly based on what the person brings to therapy. We do not try to make unnecessary links to the past or past events as this often invalidates the feelings the person has about the here and now. The bulk of the work involves a continuous focus on the young person's mind and improving mentalization, which inevitably improves impulse control and enhances the awareness of mental states in others.

In our RCT study of MBT-A for young people who self-harm (Rossouw & Fonagy, 2012) we found that if we controlled for improvement in attachment security as well as in mentalization, the superiority of the MBT-A group over the treatment as a usual group in terms of reduction in self-harm, disappeared. This means that the improvement in self-harm was mainly due to the improvement in mentalizing and in attachment. One could argue that the improvement in attachment could also be attributed to the improvement in mentalizing.

A further task in the middle phase is helping the adolescent with relevant developmental tasks. As illustrated in the first two chapters of this book, mentalization is commonly affected by the changes of adolescence. However, the period of adolescence has a few well-known tasks associated with it, such as:

- Moving from strong parental attachments to attachments in the peer group
- Starting to form a clear and coherent identity
- Becoming independent
- Managing and negotiating a much more complex social and romantic world as well as a much more demanding and challenging educational world, and more recently, an additional important task is also learning to manage the complexities of social media

In their striving for independence and effectiveness in their social world, young people often find themselves overwhelmed emotionally and in a sea of bewilderment in trying to deal with relationships, which often leaves them unable to succeed in their developmental tasks. Often, when they come for treatment, they have given up trying and feel like a failure both in the interpersonal world as well as in their educational worlds. They often return to a state of self-hatred and hopelessness, both of which can drive impulsive, self-destructive actions. Our role is to help them back onto more adaptive developmental trajectories so that they can achieve a sense of mastery, autonomy and independence.

When young people's lives are filled with anxiety and fear about the minds of others, fuelled by hypermentalizing the actions of others, they often end up in mental anguish, which fuels self-hatred. This suffering soon leads to impulsive behaviour or avoidance, or both. Young people start to avoid school and social situations and withdraw to their rooms, often with the curtains drawn and their only interactions being online. In those situations, we often need to offer developmental scaffolding or help them out of their avoidant patterns. The avoidant pattern may be understood as a non-mentalizing pattern which can be addressed using the *STOP and PAUSE – validate the feeling –*

rewind and explore, as has been mentioned. Additionally, we often have to provide some concrete support, such as a clear structure to help them back to school. This will involve working with the school and parents to get a clear plan agreed. At times the young person may need more actual support such as someone to accompany them to school the first time. In our service, we used occupational therapists with great effect to help young people become more able to do tasks such as go to school, use public transport, help themselves in shops and general self-help tasks, which are part of the adolescent world, but which are at first too anxiety-provoking for some young people.

Young people with a deep sense of themselves as not having anything good inside them, easily feel overwhelmed with anxiety when faced with school tasks. Our task again is to STOP and PAUSE and help them not to rush into avoidance, but actually, help them to attempt the work and not run away. Sometimes this feels a bit like constantly reminding them – *just do a little, like just putting one foot in front of the other – look in front of you and just do what is in front of you - like climbing a mountain – don't look up and don't look down, just do what is in front of you and don't blame or criticise yourself, or compare yourself with others.*

It sounds simple, but under the force of avoidance, these youngsters often rush into a state of panic and fear, resulting in them being unable to do anything, which drives a further sense of failure. We sometimes need to help stop this concretely by kindly using words such as in the above sentence. The author sometimes asks young people to put the sentence on their phones in the note section so that they can draw from that when they find themselves panicking.

5 Final phase – concluding the work

In the final phase, we are hoping to achieve the following:

- Increase independence and responsibility
- Consolidate stability
- Develop follow-up plans
- Understand and process the meaning of the ending and focus on affective states associated with loss
- Discharge and liaise with partner organisations

In our study (Rossouw & Fonagy, 2012), we noticed a dip in mood as therapy approached the end. Although this dip is not maintained after the end of therapy, it is important to bear in mind the emotional impact of the end of therapy. It will be best managed if the ending is planned long in advance. The end ought to go hand in hand with the young person becoming more in-dependent in their own lives and being more able to stay on task with their developmental trajectory. We would anticipate a greater period of stability, both in terms of emotional regulation as well as greater stability in their sense of identity and less presence of the "alien self" or intense self-hatred. We are hoping to see a greater sense of stability in their view of themselves as well as their view of others. This will dovetail with greater accuracy in their ability to portray the minds of others.

In our experience, it has been helpful to have clear follow-up plans as well as adjusted crisis plans. Some services allow a slow ending of sessions, with sessions reducing to fortnightly from weekly for a couple of months and then sessions once a month for a few months. Other services have an ending date but keep a few sessions "in reserve" in case the young person needs to come back for a "top up". These arrangements are usually quite useful as it allows for a re-fuelling, as the tasks of adolescence progress. The change from adolescence to young adulthood brings another challenge and young people can benefit significantly from being able to "drop in" for a few sessions to support their development.

There are services in which this is not possible and, in those cases, it will be essential to make arrangements with partner services or organisations to provide support in this vulnerable transitional phase for young people, or to help young people identify other social supports in their lives.

Information about mentalization-based therapy for adolescents (MBT-A)

What is mentalization?

Mentalization is the ability to think about our thoughts and feelings. Mentalization also helps us understand other people's thoughts and feelings. When we mentalize, we try to see ourselves from the outside and others from the inside. Mentalization is a capacity we all use in everyday life. However, people can find it more difficult to mentalize in certain situations than others.

What happens when we mentalize well?

When we mentalize well, we take a step back to think about our own and others' thoughts and feelings. We are curious and try to understand ourselves and other people's actions, based on different emotions, beliefs, wishes, intentions, thoughts, etc. For example, we mentalize well when we notice that we may have been a bit clingy towards a friend because we were feeling anxious about meeting a new group of people at a party. Or we may wonder whether a sibling has been behaving unkindly towards us because of the negative feedback they received at the parents' evening. When we mentalize well, we notice that we cannot be 100% sure about others' emotions, but we remain curious and willing to understand ourselves and other people. And when others mentalize us well, this gives us the experience that our feelings make sense, and this helps us feel understood and relate better to others.

What happens when we struggle to mentalize?

We all struggle to mentalize sometimes, especially when we are affected by strong, challenging feelings, such as anger, fear, despair, shame and rejection. Adolescence is an important period of life for mentalizing, as relationships with peers and parents get more complex and it becomes more challenging to understand ourselves and others. Our feelings can be very powerful and take over the rational brain quite quickly, which means our feelings are often more in charge of our thoughts.

Consider the following scenario. *Imagine a boy during a lesson getting increasingly agitated as some other students sitting nearby are teasing him about his new haircut. He gets increasingly embarrassed and angry and tells them to "shut up". The teacher (who had not noticed what was going on) hears this and warns him that he'll have to go to the headteacher's office. A sudden rush of fury, driven by adrenaline, overwhelms the boy and he kicks his chair, shouting abusive words at the teacher. The teacher, being new and feeling anxious about appearing "weak" in front of the class, takes the boy to the head-teacher's office and suggests that he is excluded.*

In this example, the boy, the other students and the teacher all struggled to be curious and notice their own and other people's feelings, and it appears that their feelings took precedence over any rational thoughts about what to do in the situation or consider what might have been the other person's actual intentions or thoughts. The reaction of the boy when the teacher warned him also shows how painful it can be when we feel misunderstood by others.

How can MBT-A help?

MBT-A was developed to help young people like you build a better understanding of what's going on in your mind, especially when you are upset or have other strong feelings. MBT-A can help to make sense of your thoughts and feelings and to link these to your actions and behaviours.

In your sessions, you and your therapist will be exploring what happened in your week and how you felt at different times, and also what goes through your mind in your meetings with your therapist. You will also be talking about what you think and how you feel towards other important people in your life, and how you try to understand why they behave in the way they do, especially when things get difficult. Your therapist will encourage you to slow situations down in your mind, in order to get more of a sense of what happened in yourself and other people.

Think back to the boy in the scenario. If he had been more aware of how he was feeling and thinking and how these thoughts and feelings were causing him to become increasingly agitated, he might not have reacted so impulsively or aggressively towards the teacher. Likewise, the classmates and the teacher might have acted differently, if had they better understood their own and the boy's feelings in the situation.

The more you can explore and name how you feel, the more you can bring the feeling into your awareness and regulate it if necessary. Sometimes, just talking and understanding something better can make the feeling less intense and more manageable. Hopefully, talking in the MBT-A sessions about your and other people's thoughts and feelings will help you understand yourself and others better. This should also help with managing life's ups and downs more robustly and effectively and improve the quality of your relationships with important people in your life.

Reference

Rossouw, T.I., & Fonagy, P. (2012). Mentalization-based treatment for self-harm in adolescents: A randomized controlled trial. Journal of American Academy of Child an Adolescent Psychiatry, 51(12), 1304–1313.

Chapter 5

Working with parents and families of adolescents

Nicole Muller and Holly Dwyer Hall

'I don't know what to do. It was easy when he was little, but now he cuts himself! I'm scared, I don't know what to do...'
Mother of 16-year-old Tom

Introduction

'Love gives structure and is an anchor in understanding the world around you' (Schomakers, 2018, p. 128). But love has many different faces and the bonds of love within a family change over time and perhaps most strikingly, throughout adolescence. In a society with changing family structures and many varied cultural differences and personal choices, relations between parents and adolescent children can be tested as adolescents assert their individuality and autonomy. This moving away from family and the familiar whilst simultaneously managing ongoing feelings of dependency along with rapid hormonal and neurological changes can leave both adolescents and parents feeling lost and scared. Parents can struggle to see beyond their adolescent's overt behaviours to consider the underlying mental states informing the adolescent's apparently illogical and extreme actions. Often, parents and family members react with their own strong feelings, thereby perpetuating familiar but unhelpful patterns.

Rossouw (2017, p. 469) eloquently notes 'we have little awareness of these patterns, their scope, architecture, and intricacy or, how they shape us as we co-create and co-perpetuate them. This mutual shaping is the "familiarness" of intimacy. Even when the familiar is filled with pain, we cannot get outside the familiar and change the repetition of the dance.' Encouraging adolescents and parents to be curious about these patterns can present a variety of clinical dilemmas specific to this transitional stage. Adolescents frequently do not want parents involved in their treatment and may not be in agreement with the presenting concerns and referral for help. Parents who might once have felt competent in their parenting role fear being criticised by clinicians or their children whilst putting family communication under the microscope. It takes tremendous courage, trust and at times, desperation on the part of families to ask for help and engage in a process requiring vulnerability in examining family patterns of communication.

Mentalization-based Treatment for Families (MBT-F) aims to engage families in just such a process, supporting them to enhance mentalization within their family relationships thereby reducing non-mentalizing interactions which can lead to increased affective storms, impulsive enactments and coercive control. Beginning with a brief outline of the rationale for family work and the basic structure and processes employed in MBT-F, clinical vignettes will then illustrate MBT-F mentalizing techniques in addressing specific mentalizing difficulties encountered when working with families and adolescents. Particular attention will be given to the therapist's stance in engaging family members in working collaboratively and motivating their curiosity in seeing their familiar dance and where possible eliciting desired changes.

Why increase mentalizing within families?

Improving family functioning is a critical treatment target for suicidal youth (Brent et al., 2013), with family conflict having been identified as a key risk factor for adolescent suicide and suicidal behaviour. Both direct conflicts and the absence of communication (Bilsen, 2018) along with extremes of high or low parental expectations and control (Beautrais, 2000) are associated with increased risk of suicide and suicide attempts among young people. Likewise, family cohesion and alliance has been identified as a protective factor (Breton et al., 2015; Bridge, Goldstein, & Brent, 2006). Clearly, parents play a critical role in maintaining youth safety, and strengthening the relationship between parents and teens is essential in increasing the likelihood that the adolescent will go to the parent for help.

Caregiver mentalization has been identified as a key factor by which attachment security is inter-generationally transmitted (Fonagy & Allison, 2014; Sharp & Fonagy, 2008). Secure attachment experiences underpin the establishment of epistemic trust, enabling adolescents to believe in the authenticity of interpersonally transmitted knowledge and learn from their social environments (Fonagy & Allison, 2014). Beyond attachment security, good parental mentalizing is associated with greater social cognitive development (Meins et al., 2002) and the higher performance of children in social cognition tasks (Laranjo, Bernier, Meins, & Carlson, 2010).

It is within the family context that relationships tend to be at their most fraught, their most loving and their most intense emotionally (Fonagy & Allison, 2014), with the potential for mentalizing being both facilitated and undermined. Problems with mentalizing create stressful family interactions that further undermine an individual's capacity to make sense of themselves and others, creating cycles of inhibition of mentalizing in a family (Figure 1). The feeling of being misunderstood generates powerful emotions that can result in coercion, withdrawal, hostility, overprotectiveness, rejection and extreme acts of violence. These kinds of interactions give rise to relational problems that undermine family coping, creativity and resilience. See Figure 5.1

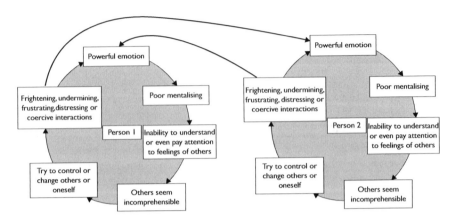

Figure 5.1 Vicious Cycles of Mentalizing Problems - Within the Family (published in Bleiberg, E. 2013. Mentalizing-based treatment with adolescents and families. *Child and Adolescent Psychiatric Clinics of North America, 22*(2), 295–330. doi.org/ 10.1016/j.chc.2013.01.001, © Elsevier).

MBT-F aims, structure and processes

MBT-F aims to help parents keep mentalizing about themselves, their adolescent and additional family members and looks to break through impasses in communication and coercive cycles of non-mentalizing resulting in controlling behaviours. The focus of treatment is on helping family members maintain their capacity to mentalize even in stressful situations, thereby promoting trust and security. MBT-F focuses on emotions as cues to what goes on within individual family members and pays specific attention to emotional regulation. A primary aim of the approach is to increase the empathic understanding that parents and caregivers have for their adolescent and if developmentally appropriate, vice versa (Asen & Fonagy, 2012). It is an empowering approach, based on the assumption that when mentalizing is improved, families will find their own solutions to the problems they are struggling with.

Within MBT-A programmes, family sessions take place once or twice monthly alongside the adolescent's weekly individual sessions. Ideally, sessions include all family members to observe the natural flow of interactions and understand how these impact on the family's mentalizing and presenting concerns. Sometimes it can also be helpful to see parents or different sibling groups independently to offer more specific support and stimulate mentalizing.

MBT-F is best characterised as 'a way of being' with the family. Having a genuine interest and curiosity about what each family member feels whilst maintaining a warm, respectful stance ensures everyone feels present and included. Four core principals held together by a fifth, **empathy**, underpin the operationalisation of the Mentalizing Stance in MBT–F (also see Keaveny et al., 2012).

An Inquisitive stance – A genuine and authentic curiosity to investigate others' perspectives benignly, playfully and explicitly, eschewing our need to know or 'get it right' in favour of active questioning and a willingness to accept our own mistakes and contributions to misunderstandings.

Holding the balance – A series of balancing acts are required to promote safety and mentalizing including balancing different family members' contributions, exploring in-session and out-of-session content, balancing cognition and affect and attending to explicit (conscious and reflective) and implicit (automatic, rapid, mainly not conscious) mentalizing processes.

Intervening to terminate non–mentalizing interactions – Once there is a clear idea of the nature of the core mentalizing problems, sensitively stopping non–mentalizing interactions which are unlikely to produce significant changes in family interactions and marking this as an area for further investigation and understanding.

Highlighting and reinforcing positive mentalizing – Actively searching for episodes of 'good mentalizing' or steps towards this, positively highlighting these and encouraging the family to notice the potential of mentalizing to deepen people's ability to connect feelings, thoughts and intentions and make sense of interactions.

The active pursuit of these four core principals whilst empathically validating family members' thinking and feeling, getting them to describe these thoughts and feelings **and** the effect they have on interactions will ensure a focus on mental states and not behaviours. This also enables clinicians to develop a tentative understanding of the mentalizing profile of the family and individual members. From here, it becomes possible to explore unhelpful repeating non–mentalizing patterns using the **MBT–F Loop**. Having identified a non–mentalizing pattern, the therapist, **Checks** with the family for consensus, invites them as collaborators to **Notice and Name** this pattern and then they agree together it is worthy of exploration and understanding. Next, the therapist supports the family to **Mentalize the Moment** by asking questions about how each of them feels in this pattern and the impact these feelings have on their understanding of one another and family interactions. Here, family members gain a deeper understanding of the mental states underlying family behaviours, helping them to identify what needs to be different for each person to ensure the pattern does not continue. The family can then **Generalise** from this explicit and detailed investigation of this non–mentalizing pattern to similar situations, further defining what each of them might do to make a difference to interrupt and reduce non–mentalizing interactions. See Figure 5.2.

The MBT–F model provides a framework within which the therapist can inhabit a mentalizing stance when being with a family, identifying mentalizing vulnerabilities and strengths and working together to gain a shared understanding

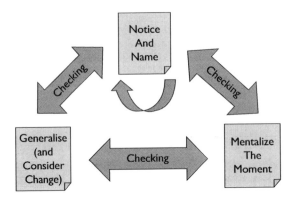

Figure 5.2 The MBT- F Loop (published in Bleiberg, E. 2013. Mentalizing-based treatment with adolescents and families. *Child and Adolescent Psychiatric Clinics of North America,* 22(2), 295–330. doi.org/10.1016/j.chc.2013.01.001, © Elsevier).

of the difficulties whilst creatively imagining new ways of being in relationship with one another. Within this structure, the therapist can employ the Mentalizing Loop and a range of heterogeneous techniques, activities and games to stimulate mentalizing and support families to identify familiar interactions, and where possible change unhelpful repeating patterns. See Figure 5.3

The following vignettes describe different mentalizing family profiles and illustrate the various ways in which MBT-F techniques can enhance mentalization and support families to initiate their desired changes.

Families where there are considerable mentalizing strengths and where failures in mentalizing are intermittent, with mentalizing being temporarily inhibited by intense emotional arousal or the intensification of attachment needs

Several constructs have been developed to refer to the capacity of the parent to treat the infant or child as a psychological agent, a separate person with a mind of their own (Bleiberg, 2002; Sharp & Fonagy, 2008). What these constructs have in common is the capacity of the parent to regulate and fully experience their own and their adolescent's emotions in a non-defensive way without becoming overwhelmed or shutting down (Slade, 2005). In these families, parents are resilient and can contain their own 'ghosts in the nursery', offering attuned and marked responses to family members. In these primarily secure attachment relationships, the adolescent is free to explore as there is an open atmosphere, with parents and adolescents trusting that differences, difficulties and mistakes will be tolerated and forgiven. Parents hold a developmental perspective when considering an adolescent's behaviour and family

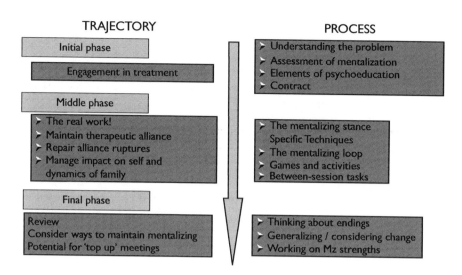

Figure 5.3 MBT-F Trajectory and Process (published in Bleiberg, E. 2013. Mentalizing-based treatment with adolescents and families. *Child and Adolescent Psychiatric Clinics of North America, 22*(2), 295–330. doi.org/10.1016/j.chc.2013.01.001, © Elsevier).

members have a sense of narrative continuity to family life whilst also appreciating the changeability of relationships. These parents show an interest in what their children are experiencing and are able to listen and use humour whilst exercising flexibility in dealing with stressors. Adolescents have a sense of their own agency in managing their emotions whilst also feeling able to allow their parents and increasingly their friends to offer guidance. These families possess some level of epistemic trust and are mostly open to the challenges of therapy with the family's mentalizing strengths, further supporting the clinician's mentalizing. In the work with these families, we aim to restore mentalization in them and help them overcome the hurdles that temporarily block their ability to be sensitive to one another.

Families where mentalizing frequently breaks down, resulting in high levels of coercive and controlling behaviours

Mentalizing abilities are inversely related to parental negative controlling behaviours (Perry, Dollar, Calkins, Keane, & Shanahan, 2018). Criticism, corporal punishments and intrusive control of a young person's thoughts and feelings (Hughes, Deater-Deckard, & Cutting, 1999) rarely promote a young person's capacity to make sense of themselves or others. Such high parental control has been found to accompany higher internalising symptoms in children and young people.

Often underlying such controlling parenting practices are elevated levels of fear and anticipation of judgement impacting on a parent's capacity to remain open and flexible in managing their child's behaviour.

These families can exhibit features of avoidant attachment relationships, fearing intimacy and emotional contact. Consequently, emotions in others can be experienced as 'needy' or 'attention-seeking' with parents often feeling frightened, confused and powerless in the face of their child's expressed emotions. Parents' mentalizing style is mostly unreflective with a rigid adherence to their own perspective and a focus on external behaviours with over-detailed descriptions lacking any contingent affect. Children can struggle to recognise their emotions or learn to act as if they do not have emotions, sometimes developing a pseudo-independence or resulting in concrete actions such as self-harm to manage intolerable and as yet unnamed feelings.

Such families need much support and genuine empathy to help them with their feelings of powerlessness and self-criticism. They can come to therapy fearful of the therapist's curiosity whilst equally seeking authoritative certainty and expertise in providing immediate solutions to the problems they are experiencing. Early sessions need to focus on normalising feelings and gently supporting family members to tolerate, notice and name feeling states, 'identifying, processing, and expressing affects' (Jurist, 2005) and staying with a process that can feel tremendously destabilising. Therapists can feel inadequate under the pressure of the family's need for solutions. It can be difficult to resist joining with a family's coercive controlling responses by providing teleological solutions through excessive risk management or following rigid treatment protocols.

Lisa and her family

Eighteen-year-old Lisa lives with both her parents, her two sisters and brother. Religion plays an important role in the family's approach and understanding of life. Lisa is struggling with her family's chosen faith and suffers from anorexia, social anxiety and is exhibiting behaviours consistent with an emerging avoidant personality disorder. With her capacity to mentalize significantly underdeveloped, she manages her intense feelings through cutting and frequently feels suicidal. Her parents are exhausted with worry and experience Lisa's behaviours as deeply controlling and intentionally hurtful.

Lisa and her family arrive suspicious of therapy yet desperate for help, wanting guidance and solutions. Anticipating criticism Lisa's parents work hard to present themselves as 'normal', detailing the effectiveness of family beliefs on their other children but not Lisa. Lisa's normal developmental needs, her wish to be with friends, the questioning of her faith and her confusion about her feelings are pathologized whilst her more worrying behaviours of cutting and suicide attempts are normalised as *'typical attention-seeking'* or something Lisa could *'snap out of'* if she only had *'more self-control'*. These comments seem to confirm Lisa's view of herself as worthless and of her feelings as not important, causing her to avoid contact with others, including the therapist.

The therapist found it difficult to maintain an **empathic, inquisitive not-knowing stance**, as Lisa's parents experienced her questions as criticisms, often ignoring them and redirecting conversations to *'solutions, strategies and reward systems.'* Feeling under attack, the therapist had to work hard not to respond similarly either unsympathetically, controlling the sessions, or like Lisa, avoiding meaningful contact by retreating into herself. In supervision, she reflected on how the opposite pole of coercion is not freedom but con-nectedness, and how finding a way to connect with this family and help them to feel understood and safe in her company was essential. She reflected on her own **mistakes**, fears and feelings of shame, using these as helpful resources to support her in being in contact with how frightening the family might be finding therapy. It was crucial to recognise the **positive steps towards mentalizing** and the family's will and courage, *'you're working so hard to get to these sessions, it is a tribute to how much you care about each other.'* Equally, playfully naming her understanding of how frustrating and confusing the therapy process might be for them, *'I wish there was an easy magic strategy I could offer but I think if there was, well you would have figured this out for yourselves. Instead you have to come here and put up with me encouraging you to be curious about your feelings, how frustrating!'*

Active **'therapist use of self'** interventions further enabled the therapist to be non-judgmental, human and authentic with the family as she made her own thoughts and feelings available for investigation and reflection. Lisa's dad is pushing the therapist for an answer, his wife talks of the negative impact of Lisa's behaviour on her siblings, Lisa is furious with her parents and shouts *'it's too much pressure.'* *'Yes, it really is… for me too!'* exclaims the therapist. Lisa and her parents stop their isolated talk and collectively look at the therapist who offers, *'when everyone is talking at once and each of you is feeling so very much and you ask me "what should we do?" I feel a real pressure to get things right and sometimes it stops me from thinking. Then I worry I might suggest something which isn't helpful as I haven't really slowed down enough to listen and get a better understanding of what is going on.'*

The family were responding to the therapist's empathic, supportive com-ments and attempts to slow down, elaborate and clarify thoughts and feelings. Now, the intense feelings emerging in sessions could be **'noticed and named'** and utilised to make sense of the unhelpful interactions. Discussing Lisa re-cently being found standing at a railway station, Lisa's mother raising her voice asks, *'why do you want to kill yourself? We're doing so much to help you. I cannot understand. I must be a bad mother, if my child wants to kill herself'*. Lisa's father stares out of the window and Lisa cries, looking as though she might run out of the room. The therapist **notices and names** what she thinks is happening, **checking** out as she describes, '*mum I can feel how worried you are right now, I understand, she's your daughter... you're really worried?* Mum agrees, '*and I think*' the therapist tentatively offers '*you feel this pressure we've talked about before, a kind of responsibility to find an answer or solution fast?*' Mum agrees and the therapist explains how it seems when a solution can't be found, "you cannot understand" it feels horrible, desperate?' Mum nods in agreement, 'then it seems you blame yourself "I'm a bad mother" or blame Lisa, she's not accepting the help everyone is offering?' Lisa's mum confirms this, and the therapist observes and checks for agreement that during this interaction both Lisa and her father seem to '*go away in their minds, shut down or may even want to physically get away, run?*'

Confirming with family members that this kind of interaction is a frequent occurrence, the therapist suggests '*it can help to give such a sequence a name so we all know what we are talking about.*' Lisa suggests they call it '*fix and hide*'. From here the therapist and the family **mentalize the moment** through describing and exploring their individual perspectives on what it feels likes to be in this '*fix and hide*' situation.

The therapist encourages family members to ask one another what it is like for them in a '*fix and hide*' moment. Lisa responds to her mother's question telling her she feels '*guilty, the worst daughter, lonely and ashamed.*' The therapist notices a change in Lisa's mother and asks, '*what do you think about what Lisa has said?*' Lisa's mum becomes a little tearful, '*I thought you just didn't care, maybe we can both blame ourselves.*' The therapist wonders if this is helpful for mum, this new way of understanding Lisa's hiding and her mother says it makes her '*feel less angry*' with Lisa so '*it probably is* (helpful) *but then I feel quite sad and that is hard.*' The therapist agrees and highlights how hard mum is working now, '*you're working so hard to manage this sadness and not "fix it" or "blame" and I think this is having a positive impact on others.*'

The therapist nods towards Lisa who is thoughtfully looking at her mother, encouraging the family to notice the positive impact of their current more mentalizing interactions. The therapist wonders '*what it is like for Dad in these moments?*' Lisa's dad describes how he withdraws, fearing he will be criticised by Lisa and her mum for not doing enough to help. Lisa's mum asks him if he thinks she is critical of him. He tells her that at times he feels she excludes him and doesn't talk things over with him. He also speaks about fearing how when they do work together, Lisa might feel worse like it is two against one, so he thinks it is better to stay out of it. Lisa jumps in and says sometimes she likes it when they talk together about her but not when they blame her or expect her to do something she is not capable of. The therapist keeps an eye on arousal levels, offering empathy and frequently checking for understanding and clarifying any misunderstandings as family members actively show curiosity and compassion for one another.

After **mentalizing the moment**, the therapist then helps the family generalise from this experience and look at other examples where something similar happened, and to consider how they might respond differently. Lisa and her parents agree that when a '*fix and hide*' moment next occurs, as a starting point, they will remind each other they do not need to 'fix it'. They agree that before anyone takes action, sets a new rule or blames the other, they will each take 10 minutes on their own before coming back together to try and talk. They agree when they do talk, they need to try and name what they are feeling without suggesting that the other person needs to fix this feeling, just listen.

Lisa and her parents were developing skills in basic mentalizing; pausing before acting and reacting, taking time to notice their feelings and becoming increasingly curious about one another without the need to control. These developing skills helped them to consider further ways of organising family life so Lisa could explore her independence and her parents might feel less responsible for her care, letting go of their need to control.

Families where mentalizing is severely compromised owing to parental psychopathology, trauma and addiction with episodic, arousal state-dependent breakdown of mentalization

Traumatised parents have often missed out on having someone in their own lives to offer comfort when they were in stressful situations. Lacking sufficient marked contingent mirroring of their own experiences, as parents their capacity for self-representation and sense of self-agency is compromised making it difficult for them to recognise emotions, pain and fear in their child without feeling or re-experiencing their own pain (Lyons-Ruth & Jacobvitz, 1999). Mental disorders such as depression, anxiety, personality disorders and problems with substance abuse further impact on the parents' capacity to accurately reflect on their own and their child's mental states, leading to confusion, misunderstanding and overwhelming affective states. Additional socio-economic stressors are associated with parental psychopathology, causing even further stress or exhaustion (Fonagy, Steele, Steele, Higgitt, & Target, 1994), further threatening a parent's and a family's sense of security and capacity to mentalize. In these families with multiple problems, interactions are often characterised by emotional unavailability, threatening or unpredictable behaviour, unclear boundaries, role confusion, difficulties in estimating the intentions of others and parental difficulties in appreciating the developmental stage of their child, along with incongruent communication (Benoit, Bouthillier, Moss, Rousseau, & Brunet, 2010; Madigan et al., 2006). The mentalizing profile of such families can include a hyper-alertness to one other's emotional dysregulation with frequently increased levels of arousal in the face of relatively small emotional upsets, real or imagined. Family members can struggle to move from the level of action to mental representation, risking episodes of intra-familial violence.

With the parent's mind closed to seeing their child's perspective, the adolescent feeling ignored, misunderstood and rejected is likely to intensify their behaviour to get through to and be seen by their parent, displaying behaviours in keeping with an anxious preoccupied attachment style. Here, parents can perceive the behaviour of their adolescent as specifically aimed at them, increasing their emotional arousal, and further debilitating the parent's mentalizing capacity. The adolescent's behaviour can also trigger memories of the parent's own traumatic experiences, rendering the parent temporarily incapable of tuning into their child, with the parent's trauma then becoming the child's. Here the adolescent can feel there is no room to separate from their parents.

These families often arrive at therapy enacting the difficulties in full view of the clinician whilst feeling equally terrified by the prospect of being in a relationship with an outsider. Parents can present as hostile towards their children and clinicians. Clinicians can easily be drawn into immediately working with the unfolding interactions without having first accurately assessed the family's capacity to mentalize and openness to change (Muller and Kate, 2008). Clinicians need to sensitively match the mentalizing capabilities of family members moving at a pace which helps to regulate arousal and clearly communicates the intentions of the therapist. Giving due attention to our ostensive cueing, the quality of our eye contact, the emotional tone of our voice and responding in ways which contingently mark individuals' feelings and behaviours help to communicate the compassion and trustworthiness of the therapist and supports the development of epistemic trust. Essential to this is supporting each family member to feel recognised as a person in their own right with their own self-agency and that the therapist believes their subjectivity to be important, helping to make the therapist and the therapy, a potentially reliable source of information which is personally relevant to family members.

Kevin and his family

Kevin is 19 years old and lives with his father. His parents divorced when he was ten years old having had a tempestuous relationship exposing Kevin to considerable interparental hostility, which culminated in an acrimonious divorce. His parents described dysfunctional childhoods with Kevin's father struggling with drug addiction throughout Kevin's early years and his mother having significant episodes of severe depression. Permanently excluded from school and possibly taking drugs, Kevin has little sense of himself at any given moment in time oscillating between aggressive outbursts and extreme passivity. He has experimented with sniffing his ADHD medication, fuelling his father's fears that Kevin will end up like him. With Kevin's mentalizing underdeveloped, he struggles to put his complex feelings into words, instead of letting his body do the talking, one moment going missing, the next trashing his room, provoking his father into closer contact with him.

Kevin and his parents arrive for their first session seemingly open to the therapist whilst appearing equally destabilised, looking anxious and fearful. Within minutes a full-blown argument has erupted between Kevin and his father, both seeking to secure the therapist's attention and agreement on their view of the problems. Kevin's mother sits quietly in the corner, looking uneasily at the therapist. The therapist quickly works to **manage arousal** and sensitively **terminates the non-mentalizing** whilst cueing to the family her wish to be helpful. Gently raising open hands above her head, she sighs and speaks with a gentle but firm *'woah, hey let's slow down'* slowly bringing her hands down *'wow, so much to say!'* She resists noticing and naming or ex-amining the problematic interaction as arousal levels are high, making it un-likely the family could take in her words and mentalize. Instead, she **empathically validates** what she imagines they are feeling, taking respon-sibility for the unsettling nature of the situation. *'It's not easy coming here, meeting me for the first time, I can see each of you really wants me to understand what it is like for you.'* Kevin and his dad settle, his mother nods yes as Kevin's dad explains, *'we want to get this all sorted, this kind of argument.'*. The therapist agrees *'yes, of course and I want to be of help. I have made a note of what you've just described and shown me now. I've put in on my notice board* (motioning to an imaginary notice board, pinning the note to it) *and we'll come back to it. But before we do, I'd like to spend some time getting to know each of you, here and now, and for you to get to know me. I think it will help us to later think more carefully about these difficulties.'*

Through managing arousal and slowing down the process, the therapist is avoiding becoming saturated with the problems and resists moving to an ur-gent teleological sorting out. Equally, she optimises the families' capacity to mentalize, giving them a lived experience of the principles of the therapy (Asen & Fonagy, 2017a; 2017b; 2019) and setting up how the work will continue to unfold. In a later session, she expands this to increase **perspective-taking** and kick start Kevin's father's mentalizing of the impact of his threatening behaviour, supporting him out of **psychic equivalence,** where his internal feelings are experienced as external facts.

Kevin's father is screaming and pointing aggressively at Kevin, *'Look at what he is doing to me! He's doing this deliberately, I'm so fed up. Why can't he just stop?'*. With concern and curiosity the therapist who is herself feeling unsettled, clarifies, *'you feel he is doing this to you?'* *'I know he is'* shouts Kevin's father, becoming in-creasingly louder while walking to the door, *'I've had enough — nothing is working, I don't want him home, you can keep him here till he stops lying!'* The therapist with much empathy offers, *'I genuinely want to understand what you're feeling right now, please stay, let's try and understand this a little more.'* Kevin's father sits down, and the therapist thanks him, then explains how, *'when you shout, well, I find it hard to think. I feel a little threatened, although I don't think you mean to threaten me.'* *'No, I don't, I'm just angry'* explains Kevin's father. By expressing the impact of dad's threatening stance on her thinking, the therapist sides with the other family members whilst also validating the emotions of Kevin's father, helping to clarify that he does not intend to threaten. *'Yes, I can understand feeling angry especially if you believe Kevin is doing things deliberately,'* Kevin's father agrees and the therapist tries to introduce a little **uncertainty** as well as moving the discussion away from possible triggering events or 'the facts'. *'Well, Kevin may or may not be lying or doing something deliberately to you, I don't know for certain, it's hard to know what is happening for Kevin.'* Kevin's father, looking confused and thoughtful, adds *'I don't know.'* The therapist, noticing dad's mentalizing coming online **positively highlights** how his *'not knowing'* is helpful, albeit an uncomfortable place to start, and suggests they might **pause and rewind** to the point before he became angry. In doing so, Kevin's dad voices how he thinks he feels overwhelmed and Kevin is able to tell his dad that sometimes he is frightened of talking to him.

With sessions quickly getting heated and the family struggling with turn-taking, shared joint attention and affect regulating, the **building blocks of mentalizing**, the therapist thought that developing these mentalizing skills in an **embodied way** might help new patterns of family interactions to emerge. She initiated a musical activity to stimulate mentalizing inviting them to join her in playing the drums, asking each of them to play a rhythm with the others following, next encouraging them to improvise with one another. During these musical activities, eye contact increased with family members gradually learning to follow, listen and then lead. After they had played the instruments, the family would reflect on their playing, what they liked, what was good, what didn't work, with temperatures rising marginally compared to other sessions. The family noticed how they can *'work well together'* and *'have fun'*. During one session, the mother, supported by the therapist, played a strong repeating rhythm around which her son and ex-husband improvised a lively tune, which brought a smile to her otherwise saddened face. She reflected on how she feels she is *'quiet'* but keeps *'a basic structure'*, smiling even more brightly as her family acknowledged how her steady beat enabled them to play more freely.

As family members developed a greater sense of themselves as individuals and the contributions they brought to family life, Kevin's father gained some understanding of how Kevin's sniffing his ADHD medication exposed him to feelings of guilt, as he couldn't protect his son from his own drug use. Kevin initiated this conversation when explaining how he thought his father got angry with him because, *'he feels guilty, he was a bad example for me'*. Kevin's father answered *'yes I do feel guilty. I think I have been a bad father'*. The therapist underlined how brave Kevin's father was being **here and now** with Kevin, and also acknowledged Kevin's effort to consider what his father might be feeling thoughtfully. She wondered how dad was feeling now listening to his son without being feeling preoccupied with his own feelings of guilt. Kevin's dad thought he was *'making up for the past'* and this felt *'good'*. The therapist explained to the family how she thought their current bravery in being able to consider Kevin's felt experiences years ago was a helpful step in understanding one another and taking some responsibility for times when things went wrong, thereby promoting their sense of agency here and now. If they could be curious and open to Kevin now as he expressed what life was like for him then and now, they would be helping him learn to express these feelings and repair something in himself and their relationship (Muller, 2011). With the help of the therapist, the family created a Life Story Book with Kevin's father tearfully asking Kevin about certain times throughout the family's life together and listening carefully as Kevin described how scared and angry he had been. The act of creating the Life Story Book further supported the development of self-agency along with helping the family to cultivate a more nuanced, coherent and emotionally rich family narrative.

Conclusion

Working with adolescents and caregivers in MBT-F involves supporting important relational figures in the task of making sense of and thoughtfully responding to the adolescent's struggles, avoiding reacting and perpetuating familiar but unhelpful patterns. Engaging both the adolescent and their family during this heightened period of development with its thrust towards autonomy requires great sensitivity on the part of clinicians. As we hope the above vignettes show, compassion, playfulness and curiosity are essential to the work, enabling clinicians to creatively adapt to the varying menta-lizing needs of family members and offer genuine human responses. In slowing down, attending to and expanding upon the here and now feelings within sessions, MBT-F supports families to have *ordinary conversations about the extraordinary* – the confusing, revealing, exciting and at times, scary thoughts and feelings underlying intricate yet often familiar interac-tions. These repeated experiences of being mentalized develop a family's confidence and skills in tuning into emotional cues and using this important information in considering *'what to do'* in times of crisis. With these, parents, carers and important familial relationships can provide an anchor for the adolescent as they navigate the wild seas of change inherent in this period of life.

References

Asen, E., & Fonagy, P. (2012). Mentalization-based therapeutic interventions for families. *Journal of Family Therapy, 34*(4), 347–370. https://doi.org/10.1111/j.1467-6427.2011.00552.x.

Asen, E., & Fonagy, P. (2017a). Mentalizing family violence part 1: Conceptual framework. *Family Process, 56*(1), 6–21.

Asen, E., & Fonagy, P. (2017b). Mentalizing family violence part 2: Techniques and in-terventions. *Family Process, 56*(1), 22–44.

Asen, E., & Fonagy, P. (2019). Mentalization-based family therapy. In A.W. Bateman & P. Fonagy (Eds.), *Handbook of Mentalizing in Mental Health Practice* (pp. 107–128). Arlington, VA: American Psychiatric Publishing.

Beautrais, A.L. (2000). Risk factors for suicide and attempted suicide among young people. *Australian and New Zealand Journal of Psychiatry, 23*(3), 420–436. https://doi.org/10.1080/j.1440-1614.2000.00691.x.

Benoit, M., Bouthillier, D., Moss, E., Rousseau, C., & Brunet, A. (2010). Emotion regulation strategies as mediators of the association between level of attachment security and PTSD symptoms following trauma in adulthood. *Journal of Anxiety, Stress and Coping, 23*(1), 101–118. https://doi.org/10.1080/10615800802638279.

Bilsen, J. (2018). Suicide and youth: Risk factors. *Frontiers in Psychiatry, 9*, 540. https://doi.org:10.3389/fpsyt.2018.00540.

Bleiberg, E. (2002). The future of Menninger research: The Child and Family Program and developmental psychopathology. *Bulletin of the Menninger Clinic, 66*(4), 385–389. https://doi.org/10.1521/bumc.66.4.385.23394.

Bleiberg, E. (2013). Mentalizing-based treatment with adolescents and families. *Child and Adolescent Psychiatric Clinics of North America, 22*(2), 295–330. https://doi.org/10.1016/j.chc.2013.01.001.

Brent, D.A., McMakin, D.L., Kennard, B.D., Goldstein, T.R., Mayes, T.L., & Douaihy, A.B. (2013). Protecting adolescents for selfharm: A critical review of intervention studies. *Journal of American Academic Child and Adolescent Psychiatry, 52*(12), 1260–1271.

Breton, J.J., Labelle, R., Berthiaume, C., Royer, C., St-Georges, M., Ricard, D., Abadie, P., Gérardin, P., Cohen, D., & Guilé, J.M. (2015). Protective factors against depression and suicidal behaviour in adolescence. *Canadian Journal of Psychiatry. Revue Canadienne de Psychiatrie, 60*(2 Suppl 1), S5–S15.

Bridge, J.A., Goldstein, T.R., & Brent, D.A. (2006). Adolescent suicide and suicidal behaviour. *Journal of Child Psychology and Psychiatry, 47*(3–4), 372–394.

Fonagy, P., & Allison, E. (2014). The role of mentalizing and epistemic trust in the therapeutic relationship. *Psychotherapy, 51*(3), 372–380.

Fonagy, P., Steele, M., Steele, H., Higgitt, A., & Target, M. (1994). The Emanuel Miller Memorial Lecture 1992. The theory and practice of resilience. *Journal of Child Psychology and Psychiatry, 35*, 231–257. doi:10.1111/j.1469-7610.1994.tb01160.x.

Hughes, C., Deater-Deckard, K., & Cutting, A.L. (1999). "Speak roughly to your little boy"? Sex differences in the relations between parenting and preschoolers' understanding of mind. *Social Development, 8*, 143–160.

Jurist, E. L. (2005). Mentalized affectivity. *Psychoanalytic Psychology, 22*(3), 426–444. https://doi.org/10.1037/0736-9735.22.3.426.

Keaveny, E., Midgley, N., Asen, E., Bevington, D., Fearon, P., Fonagy, P., Jennings-Hobbs, R., & Wood, S. (2012). Minding the family mind: The development and initial evaluation of mentalization-based treatment for families. In N. Midgley & I. Vrouva (Eds.), *Minding the Child: Mentalization-Based Interventions with Children, Young People and Their Families* (pp. 98–112). London: Routledge.

Laranjo, J., Bernier, A., Meins, E., & Carlson, S.M. (2010). Early manifestations of children's theory of mind: The roles of maternal mind–mindedness and infant security of attachment. *The official Journal of the International Congress of Infant Studies, 15*(3), 300–323. https://doi.org/10.1111/j.1532-7078.2009.00014.x.

Lyons-Ruth, K., & Jacobvitz, D. (1999). Attachment disorganization: Unresolved loss, relational violence, and lapses in behavioral and attentional strategies. In J. Cassidy & P.R. Shaver (Eds.), *Handbook of Attachment: Theory, Research, and Clinical Applications* (pp. 520–554). The Guilford Press.

Madigan, S., Bakermans-Kranenburg, M.J., Van Ijzendoorn, M., Moran, G., Pederson, D.R., & Benoit, D. (2006). Unresolved states of mind, anomalous parental behavior, and disorganized attachment: A review and meta-analysis of a transmission gap. *Journal of Attachment and Human Development*, *8*(2), 89–111. https://doi.org/10.1080/14616730600774458.

Meins, E., Fernyhough, C., Wainwright, R. DasGupta, M., Fradley, E., & Tuckey, M. (2002). Maternal mind–mindedness and attachment security as predictors of theory of mind understanding. *Child Development*, *73*(6), 1715–1726. https://doi.org/10.1111/1467-8624.00501.

Muller, N. (2011). Mentaliseren Bevorderende Therapie voor Families waarbij uithuisplaatsing dreigt of heeft plaats gevonden (MBT-F when a child is taken away from the family). *Tijdschrift voor Kinder en Jeugdpsychotherapie*, *38*(4), 47–57.

Muller, N., & Kate, C. ten. (2008). Mentaliseren Bevorderende Therapie in relaties en gezinnen (MBT-F in partner relations and families). *Tijdschrift voor Syteemtherapie*, *20*(3), 117–132.

Perry, N.B., Dollar, J.M., Calkins, S.D., Keane, S.P., & Shanahan, L. (2018). Childhood self-regulation as a mechanism through which early overcontrolling parenting is associated with adjustment in preadolescence. *Developmental Psychology*, *54*(8) 1542–1554. https://doi.org/10.1037/dev0000536.

Rossouw, T. (2017). Working with families. In P. Luyten, L. Mayes, P. Fonagy, M. Target, & S. J. Blatt (Eds.), *Handbook of Contemporary Psychodynamic Approaches to Psychopathology* (pp. 469–481). Guilford Press.

Schomakers, B. (2018). *Het begin van de melancholie. Over verdriet, verlangen en werkelijkheid.* The beginning of melancholy. About sadness, desire and reality. Uitgeverij Klement.

Sharp, C., & Fonagy, P. (2008). The parent's capacity to treat the child as a psychological agent: Constructs, measures and implications for developmental psychopathology. *Social Development*, *17*(3), 737–754.

Slade, A. (2005). Parental reflective functioning: An introduction. *Journal of Attachment and Human Development*, *7*(3), 269–281. https://doi.org/10.1080/14616730500245906.

Chapter 6

Varifocal vision in a world of storm and stress

Supervising MBT-A practice

Holly Dwyer Hall and Maria Wiwe

The urgency in Mary's voice message struck to the heart of the listener. 'I'm hoping we can move our supervision session to this week, I'm really stuck, one of my adolescents, Tom, he might drop out, and he's risky. I referred to social care, he's furious.' Mary, an experienced psychotherapist and MBT practitioner often worked with complex cases characterised by risk and nuanced decision making. Yet somehow this case had got under her skin, and recognising she was 'stuck' in her thinking, she was reaching out for another mind to think with.

Working as clinicians with adolescents struggling with mental health issues, inevitably, our own mentalizing capabilities will be affected. We can feel despair, fear, sorrow, anger and hopelessness as well as immense joy, pleasure and excitement as we support adolescents in their recovery and development into adulthood. Intense emotions, interpersonal difficulties and the increased experimentation and risk-taking associated with adolescence can present particular clinical challenges and breakdowns in mentalization in adolescent and clinician. Supervision of practice is essential in ensuring such non-mentalizing states do not result in increased efforts on the part of the clinician to control self and other, leading to inflexibility and negative therapist attributes associated with poor outcomes and treatment breakdown (Ackerman & Hilsenroth, 2001, 2003). But what might such a supervision look like?

This chapter gives an overview of an MBT-A model of supervision that strives towards freeing up the mind of clinicians and supporting them to regain and sustain their mentalizing when faced with the inevitable challenges encountered in working with adolescents. The model makes use of the Thinking Together (see Chapter 12) supervisory practice developed within the AMBIT programme (Bevington, Fuggle, Cracknell, & Fonagy, 2017; Bevington, Fuggle, & Fonagy, 2015) alongside the shared experiences of the authors and colleagues who participated in the first MBT-A supervisor's course with Trudie Rossouw and Peter Fonagy in 2015.

Drawing on supervision case material 'the mentalizing stance' which lies at the heart of Mentalization-based Therapies will be translated to the supervisory context. This will show how working in collaboration with the clinician, the mentalizing supervisor aims to foster not a super or superior vision but rather a varifocal or flexi-vision. This flexible vision further enables the clinician to support the adolescent's efforts in understanding and making sense of their own and others' minds. We will see how the supervisor's empathic, curious yet also challenging stance creates a secure base from which the supervisee can begin to define shared affective states with their patients which lead to breaks in mentalizing, mentalizing impasses and feelings of being 'stuck'.

This chapter aims to benefit supervisors in developing a mentalizing approach to their supervisory practice whilst also helping supervisees to gain some understanding of what an MBT-A Supervision might look and feel like in practice.

MBT-A supervision method and structure

Trajectory and process

MBT-A Supervision can take place in a variety of settings and formats: group, individual, face to face or through online platforms; and might occur in time from 5 minutes to 50 minutes or beyond, with a frequency dictated by the identified need of the supervisee in explicit agreement with the supervisor. It is a supervision approach marked not by the structure of time and place but rather by the process it aims to engender, that is mentalizing. In particular, it involves sufficiently mentalizing the supervisee so that they might, in turn, regain and maintain their mentalizing with their adolescent patients, families and networks. Bearing in mind this overarching aim, the MBT-A supervisor anticipates and encourages the supervisee to bring something to the supervision which gives her trouble mentalizing. The supervisor, together with the supervisee, aims to actively and quite specifically seek out the problems they are facing to avoid the supervision operating without direction. The supervisor asks the clinician to formulate in what way the supervisor can be most helpful, asking the supervisee to 'mark the task' thereby establishing a well- defined difficulty to focus their minds upon. In doing so, the supervisor is instituting the collaborative nature of the supervisory process whilst ensuring the supervisee gets what is needed from their process of joint thinking. Sometimes, this well-defined difficulty is easily established.

Supervisor: 'So, what do you need from today's supervision?'
Clinician: 'I find myself getting stuck as soon this patient talks about flashbacks, I become rigid and list skills for managing.'
Supervisor: 'And what happens with your patient?'
Clinician: She tunes out, we're both going through the motions, going over the skills she never puts into use and it feels unhelpful.'

At times, a lengthier supportive, yet challenging, exploration needs to take place.

Clinician:	(confidently) 'I want to spend the next hour getting an overview of the case, kind of gathering my thoughts, a meta-perspective would be helpful.'
Supervisor:	'Ok, yeah, taking a meta-perspective can indeed be helpful but I'm wondering why now, what is it about now that makes you feel a review or meta-perspective is needed? Might help us to get a bit more detail of what you feel is needed, mark our task.'
Clinician:	'Well... (thinking) I feel lost, not sure where to go.'
Supervisor:	'Not an easy feeling, lost! Helpful you've brought this, let's make sure I don't get lost with you. Can you recall when you started feeling lost, what was happening?'
Clinician:	(pausing) 'A few sessions ago, I got this strong feeling - this kid is ready to finish therapy. He said a few things about ending, but I never took it up with him. Hmm, (laughing) maybe I need reassurance it's ok to finish therapy with him.'
Supervisor:	'It sounds like this meta-perspective needs us to think together about endings and how you and your patient are thinking, feeling and talking about this. Also, maybe reviewing what the agreed treatment hopes and expectations were and what's been achieved?'

Having 'marked the task', the supervisor and supervisee establish what information is needed to enable them to turn their minds to resolving the presenting dilemmas, many of which are likely to involve some shared affect state between the clinician and adolescent impacting on their ability to keep mentalizing; feeling frightened, overwhelmed, pressured, hopeless. The supervisee is encouraged to share brief information about the case, what was described in Chapter 12 as 'state the case', then move towards a more detailed description of a particular moment, event or interaction in which it seemed mentalizing in therapist, patient or both derailed. Once these details have been established the supervisory pair work towards 'mentalizing the moment' being open and curious about the difficulties, actively tuning into the minds involved in the quandary and hopefully uncovering new perspectives. Essential to this is re-establishing the supervisee's capacity to mentalize, requiring the supervisor to resist the impulse to empathise with and mentalize the patient – 'Oh, this poor patient, they sound so lonely, don't you think?' But rather, initially, the task is to focus all efforts on mentalizing the supervisee – 'It feels hard to be with this patient when he is in this state, quite isolating, is that how it feels for you or something different?' By tuning into the supervisee's subjective experience, the supervisor is offering their empathic understanding, supporting the supervisee to feel understood, increasing the supervisee's capacity to mentalize so they might jointly think together about the patient and the presenting concerns. If the supervisor is successful enough in mentalizing the supervisee, the validation is likely to calm the supervisee, create conditions for their own mentalizing to come back online, and for epistemic trust to be established so that the supervisee is more able to take in and process the supervision. With the supervisee more mentalized and some joint mentalizing around the problem having taken place, multiple possibilities and perspectives for addressing the presenting issues can then be generated and considered by the supervisee. The supervisor guides the supervisee's discoveries by supporting them to reconnect to the original well-defined task, to 'return to purpose' and establish how they might approach their work with these new ideas in mind.

> *'You've explained well how you get stuck and lose your mentalizing when he raises his voice, I think we understand a lot more about this. I'm wondering what your thoughts are on how you could avoid getting stuck in that "spin" next time?'*

The emphasis here is on progress and actively supporting the supervisee to plan how to put their understanding into practice. This might involve role-playing or trialling some of the ideas within the safety of the supervisory setting before returning to the clinical situation.

The supervisory trajectory aims to support mentalizing processes. Although at times, it might feel formulaic, particularly the earlier stages of marking the task and stating the case, it aims to protect the supervisory dyad from entering into potentially aimless narratives lessening the effectiveness of supervision. It is easy early on to fall into Pretend Mode with supervisees, offering lengthy descriptions of cases, with supervisors responding with equally lengthy intellectual explanations often alluding or directly telling the supervisee what to do. Without the adequate exploration of the feeling states being evoked in the clinical encounter, these supervisory offers are unlikely to meet the needs of the patient and most certainly do not work towards developing the supervisee's skills in using a mentalizing approach. It is worth noting that the supervisory dyad can deviate from the identified task and be curious and responsive to arising thoughts and feelings, but to do so with half a mind as to what might be drawing their thoughts away and how these may or may not relate to the agreed focus. Ultimately, the Thinking Together model aims to decrease instances of the supervisor as the expert with superior-vision in favour of increased collaboration between two minds freely working together, sustaining mentalizing and generating multiple perspectives, a varifocal flexivision. Thus, the supervisor attempts to be 'on-model' by prioritising a mentalizing focus, supporting the supervisee to notice breaks in their mentalizing and to regain and maintain a mentalizing stance.

To be 'on-model' enough

The supervisor will be looking for the core principles of a mentalizing approach in the supervisees' work as well as in her supervision approach. However, being 'on-model' will look different for each adolescent and therapist dyad varying according to the needs of the adolescent and the personality and style of both patient and therapist. The MBT-A supervisor welcomes and values the expression of this individuality within the clinical encounter. Equally, the MBT-A supervisor also needs to ensure that the clinical skills of MBT-A are understood and competently applied to the clinical setting. The supervisor must confidently and lightly hold their expertise in mentalizing theory and thoughtfully find ways to share knowledge and experience. There is a subtle distinction between helping the supervisee to be 'on-model' whilst at the same time refraining from conveying criticism or fault-finding, with the former best supporting the supervisee's confidence in mentalizing. Through respect, transparency and warmth the supervisor can most helpfully convey when she believes the clinician to be 'off-model' or when breaks in clinician mentalizing are present, inviting the supervisee to consider what might be happening. In this sense, the supervisor also needs to normalise the going back and forth between effective and ineffective mentalizing. When the supervisor notices that the supervisee shifts into a more ineffective, or even non-mentalizing way of being, the supervisor tries to give a 'nudge' back to more effective mentalizing.

> 'This passage intrigues me as it seems you get caught up in explaining to her why she behaves in that way. This feels different from earlier when you were working together to understand how she got into the argument with her boyfriend. Can you see a difference? Could we pause and look at what passed through your mind at this moment?'
>
> 'Did you find yourself in psychic equivalence? Please let me know if I'm unclear, I'm thinking about the state of mind where our inner feelings take over everything - if we feel it's hopeless, it is hopeless. What we feel inside becomes an external reality. Do you recognise that?'
>
> 'From your descriptions it sounds as if an 'Alien Self' has got a grip on this patient. I notice you haven't used this MBT-A idea to describe this situation and I'm wondering if it's something you feel comfortable with? Shall we take a few minutes to review the concept and see if it makes sense in relation to this patient and self-harming? Then, if it does, we might think about how you can use it with your patient.'

In these instances, the supervisor, like the clinician in an MBT-A session, might engage in a form of psychoeducation with the supervisee, reviewing and reinforcing the supervisee's knowledge base of MBT-A through revisiting concepts and considering how they make sense in relation to the clinical material. Again, the supervisor invites collaboration and seeks agreement with the supervisee on what might be helpfully revisited. Throughout the process, the supervisor continually checks out and clarifies whether their pedagogical endeavour is making sense to the supervisee and is felt to be clinically relevant and helpful.

Going alongside – understanding the therapist's subjective sense of themselves as an MBT-A therapist

In order to ensure the supervisory endeavour is meaningful and supportive to the supervisee, the supervisor needs to have a comprehensive understanding of the therapist's subjective sense of themselves as an MBT-A therapist. Having a detailed profile of the clinician's level of MBT-A knowledge whilst being mindful of their stage of practice and professional needs concerning implementing a new model will strengthen the supervisory relationship and increase the supervisee's effectiveness in delivering MBT-A. Many supervisees are accomplished therapists with well-developed basic therapy skills and further competencies in particular techniques. Some of these skills will sit well within an MBT-A model, whilst others might not. The supervisor needs to draw the supervisee's attention to approaches which are contraindicated within MBT-A whilst emphasising existing techniques which might complement a mentalizing approach. It is not unusual for highly experienced clinicians to struggle in re-orientating themselves to the MBT-A model, evoking feelings of anxiety and low professional confidence, which undermines their capacity to maintain a mentalizing stance. A key element of the supervisory process is sensitively understanding and managing these processes in addressing the supervisee's developing mentalizing skills.

Supervisor: *'I'm getting a feeling that our conversation about use of therapist self is a little unsettling?'*

Clinician: *'Well, it feels, ahh, odd. I'm just not used to being that transparent with my own emotional reactions.'*

Supervisor: *'I see and I'm kind of talking about transparency as if it was the most natural thing in the world!'*

Clinician: *'Yeah, a little bit.'*

Supervisor: *'I'm sorry, I wasn't mindful of that, I just went off on my own little journey on the delights of transparency without checking out if you'd like to come with me!'*

Clinician: *'I think I get it, in theory, it makes sense - modelling feelings, being human and showing how my mind is different from hers, but doing it feels uncomfortable!'*

Supervisor: *'What about exploring that a bit, the uncomfortableness of trying to be more transparent?'*

Clinician: *'When I trained years ago one of my first supervisors told me to never talk about my own feelings, no self-disclosure, but I think this is different from what he was referring to at that time.'*

Part of 'going alongside' a supervisee will also involve getting an understanding of the supervisee's previous supervisory relationships. It can be useful when first meeting to both explain the aims of a mentalization-based supervision and what the supervisee can expect in working with you, as well as gaining some understanding of what they found helpful or unhelpful in previous professional help-seeking relationships. Equally, establishing the supervisee's more general aims for developing their MBT-A practice is useful in getting a sense of where they are at now and where they hope to go. Is the supervisee in the early stages of MBT-A practice and looking to integrate mentalizing approaches to current cases? Or, are they experienced in the model and working toward establishing themselves as an MBT-A practitioner, supervisor or trainer? Having a clear understanding of the supervisee's hopes and expectations of you as a supervisor, alongside their professional ambitions, will increase the likelihood of a strong collaborative working alliance benefitting the supervisee and their adolescents.

Also, it seems to be the case that as clinicians, we benefit the most from supervision if it is active in terms of using role-play or video-taped sessions (Hilsenroth & Diener, 2017). We would encourage working with these means, whenever possible. Otherwise, audio recordings, transcripts, notes and an active engagement in thinking together about the well-defined difficulties will support the effectiveness of the supervisory process. Yet another part of 'going alongside' a supervisee is to introduce these means in a mentalizing way. Showing video-clips of oneself working can create anxiety in most clinicians. The supervisor needs to show a non-judgemental and mentalizing stance in this respect.

The mentalizing supervisory stance

Embedded in the aforementioned supervisory processes and tasks is the mentalizing supervisory stance, the supervisor's way of being with her supervisee which embodies 'the mentalizing stance' and lies at the core of all MBT models and mentalizing endeavours. This is the supervisor's ability to communicate in a direct, authentic and transparent manner, showing warmth, respect and a genuine empathic curiosity towards her supervisee. By 'walking the talk' the mentalizing supervisor not only models a mentalizing stance but crucially provides the supervisee with a lived experience of being understood by another, thereby supporting their mentalizing abilities within their clinical work. MBT-A supervision is conducted through the supervisor actively embracing a mentalizing stance alongside further mentalizing interventions which are consistently deployed within the supervisory setting.

Not-knowing

There is a genuine acceptance that neither supervisor nor supervisee (or adolescent patient) experiences interactions other than impressionistically and this not-knowing is utilised as an invitation to be curious about what is happening in the reported clinical encounter and simultaneously in the supervisory process. The supervisor makes sure that the supervisory dyad works around maintaining curiosity, avoiding labelling, continuously keeping in mind that the less you label and categorise the adolescent, the more you recognise that you do not know everything about the adolescent, and the more open you are to the adolescent being different from what you think, therefore, the more effective the mentalizing.

This curiosity inspires an active questioning about the supervisee's experience whilst equally inviting reflection on the patient's experience as imagined by the supervisee. This active and open questioning serves to validate the supervisee's experience of themselves with their adolescent patient and the clinical dilemmas they face – it does not aim to illuminate or prove the supervisor's theory about what is happening. Indispensable to this attitude is the maintaining of a non-judgemental attitude to the supervisee's reported accounts of the clinical situation. The MBT-A supervisor needs to bear in mind the levels of pressure on the clinician, be that organisational, emotional, work-load, demands from the adolescent, their parents, et cetera, and how these will inevitably impact on the clinician's mentalizing capacity. Consequently, the MBT-A supervisor aims to not only adapt to the supervisee's knowledge and experience level but importantly adapt and scaffold mentalizing interventions to the supervisee's mentalizing capacity at any given moment. To do otherwise risks further impairing the clinician's capacity to mentalize, isolating them from learning opportunities and destabilising the collaborative supervisory alliance. Equally, the supervisor anticipates that their own mentalizing will be impacted upon and monitors for mistakes along the way. The supervisor further exhibits integrity and courage in acknowledging these misattunements and works alongside the supervisee to make the implicit explicit, helping to make sense of the misunderstanding.

Supervisor:	*'I need your help here, I perceive myself as pushing you towards becoming more active, it's not very helpful is it? I think I just told you what to do in a really unhelpful way!'*
Supervisee:	*'No, no, it's just well, I'm just fed up with this case, nothing is working, and I can't stand borderline behaviour. I probably shouldn't say that, not very therapeutic of me but …'*
Supervisor:	*'Not at all, you may well be feeling fed up and understandably so, it feels a real struggle being with this girl! I think I might have missed just how hard it is or maybe I wanted to make it better for you, leaping in with some advice as even I am finding something unbearable.'*
Supervisee:	*(laughing) 'It really is hard she sends me to a really frustrating place… (sighing). I think I find it all too much and just retreat, go inside myself so in some ways, I do need to become more active.'*
Supervisor:	*'Feels very powerful and impactful. I'm wondering, what is it about her? You know, what is this borderline behaviour you mentioned? What is she saying, doing that's leading you to feeling fed up? I'm trying to imagine myself there in the room.'*

Supervisee: 'Argh... she comes in a flurry of risk and emotional turmoil, in a way that feels authentic, 'I tried to kill myself last night, I took 20 Ibuprofen then I threw them up.' And I feel for her and acknowledge how tough it is...'

Supervisor: (with genuine interest) 'And then?'

Supervisee: 'I try to understand more about how she is feeling, what was happening before the overdose and she opens up, starts to really describe.... then she shuts me out. I feel played, we're working together then suddenly nothing is going to help!'

Supervisor: 'Ah, yeah (with much expression) so you're in, close, then you're out, far away, frustrating when you feel someone is opening up, letting you get close and then, as you say shuts you out, stops you from doing your job!'

Supervisee: 'Yes, then I feel rather useless and retreat.'

Supervisor: 'Well (with some sympathy) an understandable response, I might also feel 'played with' with all the pushing and pulling although I'm not sure that is her intention. I guess if we go back to your helpful description, she comes in and opens up, it feels genuine, and you feel you're working together. I'm wondering what it's like for her to 'open up' as you describe?'

Supervisee: 'Hmmm... thinking about it, I imagine she feels terrified, that fear of getting close, I'm recalling her assessment sessions and how worried she was about the team and me, what we would 'do' to her. Oooh, it's starting to make more sense this "I'm in then I'm out" feeling I'm getting.'

The example shows how empathy and support underpin the mentalizing stance and are essential in ensuring the 'not knowing stance' provokes curiosity as opposed to fear in the supervisee.

Empathy and support

The supervisee, like anyone, needs to feel safely understood before they can be curious about themselves or others. The supervisor explicitly and transparently conveys to the supervisee that she endeavours to see the presented dilemma from their perspective. This effort on the part of the supervisor should not be conflated with quickly telling the supervisee 'I totally get it'. Instead, this work entails a substantial undertaking on the part of the supervisor to try to make a mental map of the clinician's subjective position as to the presented impasse with the adolescent. This empathic validation seeks to support the supervisee to really describe what they are thinking and feeling, as well as considering how these thoughts and feelings might impact on their understanding of and interactions with their adolescent patient. This is supporting the movement from implicit to explicit mentalizing. In this way, the supervisor also continues to hold a relational focus emphasising the power of relationships to both enhance and derail mentalizing. Additionally, the supervisor seeks to normalise feelings and develop the supervisee's capacity to notice and name their own feelings. Thereby, the supervisee can gain confidence in speaking with their adolescent patients about feelings in a genuine way. Having safely found themselves in the mind of the supervisor, the supervisee can return to being actively curious about themselves and their patient in collaboration with the supervisor.

Exploration and co-creation

The mentalizing work is co-created through an emphasis of joint attention on the well-defined difficulties as the supervisory dyad explores a variety of perspectives. This sense of collaboration and joint attention does not equate to an unequivocal agreement; rather, there is an acceptance of different perspectives and a willingness to identify these and explore.

'So you have an idea that this adolescent is unhelpfully stuck in pretend mode, endless talking with no feelings, this may be so. Yet, I have a sense there is something hopeful or helpful about this, maybe developmentally appropriate, before she didn't speak at all, only cried, as if all her feelings were facts. Shall we pursue both of these possibilities and see how it might influence your responses?'

'I can see how you feel sad when my patient speaks of her mother's death, yet it feels different in the room, I experience her as angry, furious and there is a tension.'

Throughout their exploration and co-creation, the supervisory dyad also holds a number of balances:

- being attentive to the clinical material as reported by the supervisee
- being attentive to the processes occurring in the here and now supervisory encounter;
- focusing on cognitions (thoughts or beliefs about situations)
- focusing on affects (the feelings about it; both as they were experienced in the clinical encounter and in the here and now discussion)
- The supervisor is alert to their role in holding a balance between mentalizing the supervisee, supporting them to mentalize themselves as a worker, and mentalizing the adolescent patient
- Equally, the supervisor seeks a balance between a natural unfolding in the supervision process to allow enough implicit mentalizing to take place. The purpose of this is to gain some understanding of both the supervisee's and their client's more rapid and automatic responses whilst supporting a movement to a more controlled and reflective explicit mentalizing.

At times this requires the supervisor to gently challenge and nudge the supervisee from non-mentalizing towards mentalizing, being mindful of the emotional temperature best set to keep mentalizing online. Too hot and arousal increases and mentalizing goes offline, too cold and the supervisory dyad slips into Pretend Mode, cognitively alive and intellectually active whilst affectively deadened. Here, the supervisor might need to inject a little anxiety into the situation to break out of Pretend Mode and an overreliance on intellectualising. It is a frequent occurrence that well-educated and experienced psychotherapists do tend to get stuck in the cognitive pole of mentalizing at the expense of the affective, with this dominating supervisory discourse.

Affective focus, simple and short

To work around this dilemma, the MBT-A supervisor is assigned to keep a continuing emotional focus, monitoring any tendency to talk too much or avoid emotions. The task here is to stay with the affects to identify, explore and modulate them. Another way of helping oneself as a supervisor to keep out of the cognitive trap is to be short and straightforward in one's discourse.

> 'Gosh, I would have felt pressure at that moment. How did you feel?'
> 'Could we stay with that emotion for a bit?'
> 'Do you think there were other emotions you were experiencing at that moment?'

Accordingly, the MBT-A supervisor must strive towards using words that stimulate reflection around affects and mental states, subsequently being attentive to not getting stuck in behavioural language. Furthermore, we strongly recommend the use of humour (especially the self-mocking kind) and playfulness. Getting in touch with these sides and it is a sign mentalizing goes on-line again.

> Supervisor: 'Gee, you know, I am usually the one being called 'the Ice Queen', well especially by my husband, but today I think you beat me to it!

Besides the affect focus, self-disclosure and transparency in the service of modelling feelings and being explicit with what is happening in one's own mind, as separate and different from others, is an important mentalizing intervention in both the clinical and supervisory setting. It demonstrates an open-mindedness which supports the move from implicit to explicit mentalizing, particularly upon the levels of attention and affect regulation. Within the supervisory setting, the supervisor feels free to notice and name her feelings in response to the reported clinical material and, here and now moments within the supervision, allowing her mind to become a further resource for playful curiosity. This encourages a range of pro-mentalizing activities, normalising feelings, highlighting alternative perspectives and safely regulating arousal. Finally, it can be a particularly useful intervention when supervisees are finding it difficult to develop skills in noticing and naming their own feeling states or developing the confidence in speaking explicitly about their own internal processes.

Returning to purpose

Let us return to Mary and her supervisor. How do the above tenets of the mentalizing stance and further mentalizing techniques and interventions make themselves known in this brief extract from their supervisory session?

Listening to Mary's message, her supervisor found herself wondering; She's so experienced, what's this request for an early session about, what can't wait? Not sure I'll have much to offer. Hold on, her mentalizing has gone a bit offline, she's human, she's being proactive, call her back and offer an earlier time this week, think together.' Mary arrives at the rearranged session and quickly identifies that although her 15-year-old patient Tom arrived for their last session, she is nonetheless continuing to worry that he might drop out. Mary has a sense that she is missing something. She has an idea that she gets stuck when there might be a difference of opinion about the actions taken to keep Tom safe but feels she is missing something of the feelings involved and wants to focus on this. She has brought a section of video from the last session when it felt incredibly tense, and she felt overwhelmed with worry and could no longer think. Having defined the task, they watch this brief extract together.

Supervisor:	*(sighs) What a session!*
Mary:	*(laughs) Yeah! God, it's a relief to hear you say that, because it was so tense!*
Supervisor:	*Wow, what's it like watching it back now?*
Mary:	*I can feel my worry, I notice I worry a lot about this boy, and it affects me.*
Supervisor:	*Yes, it feels that way, tense with worry. Was there a particular moment you noticed this worry affecting you, maybe more than other times?*
Mary:	*In the beginning, I was so concerned he wouldn't show up, thinking I had crossed a line referring to social services, then it disappeared because I was so happy seeing him arrive. Then I worried he would leave, then happy he stayed, relief, then worry. I was walking on eggshells, worried about offending or upsetting him so didn't really say anything.*
Supervisor:	*(actively curious) Do you think he picked up on this eggshell walking?*
Mary:	*(thinking) Yeah... yeah I do.*
Supervisor:	*(genuinely) Yeah, I had a similar feeling. In that moment when you shared with him that you were happy to see him and was worried that he might not come back. That seemed like a helpful naming of your thoughts and feelings, being open and honest with him. He didn't seem offended to me. But what do you think he made of this?*
Mary:	*Err.... It is something about this boy that I... he is shutting everyone out. But, I feel that he wants to relate to me. Something about his face and his eyes. I think he picks up on me being worried but also that I'm actually interested in his wellbeing. I think that is important to him, maybe that's why he comes back.*

Supervisor: So in your mind you've got a sense, an idea, that he recognises that you worry about him but also that you have some feeling of interest or concern for him. What do you think that's like for him to notice that you have these feelings of worry or concern for him?

Mary: I believe this is where we get trapped. My experience is that when I show or name my feelings he goes into his machine mode and talks about having no feelings, like a robot.

Supervisor: Yes, I also felt that when watching, it's hard, how do you respond to a robot?!

Mary: (laughing) Well, yes! It feels very cold and off putting. His robot way of responding, saying he has no feelings and doesn't care. But there's something...

Supervisor: Something?

Mary: Yeah, something more...

Supervisor: Yes, I think we might be missing something before he goes robot like. Let's go back – you express some feeling towards him, share what you're thinking, and you notice that he responds to your feelings and worries by becoming cold like a robot with no feelings. I think something might have happened before this. I think I might be working you hard here, but can you recall what he said to you?

Mary: Well, he did give me some credit, for contacting social care, you know, that I was doing my job.

Supervisor: Credit? Hmm, I can see how you got that idea but I'm not sure, well... watching from here, not receiving the full impact of the session, it didn't feel like credit to me.

Mary: I can't see it? Say more, what were you feeling when you heard it?

Supervisor: I don't know, this might be wrong, and please tell me if it doesn't fit with what you're experiencing.

Mary: Yes, of course.

Supervisor: I experienced his description of you 'just doing your job, following the rules and calling social care' well like him turning you into a machine, a robot who just follows the rule.

Mary: (gasp) Yes, that is what it feels like. Why couldn't I see that?

Supervisor: Useful question, let's also keep in mind it's easier sitting out here not receiving the full impact of his communication but what did you feel when he said, 'you were following the rules'?

Mary: I felt so stuck, anxious in that moment in the session, but now well, what I feel, if I am honest, is a little angry and afraid.

Supervisor: Oooh, can you say more about angry and afraid.

Mary: (hesitation) Well, a bit angry because I have done so much, I wasn't just following the rules but then also afraid that if I say something like this well... It would be conflictual maybe, blaming him.

Supervisor: Oh, yes might not be helpful for him to feel blamed. What on earth makes him turn you into a robot? If that is indeed what he is doing, what's the need?

Mary: Erm... guess if both of us don't have feelings, keeps everything safe. If I don't have feelings then it makes it easier for him to not have feelings about himself, he can keep putting himself in harm's way, but I keep bringing the feelings! It is a conflict!

Supervisor: Yeah, so it sounds as if you have an idea that he's trying to self-regulate or bring the arousal level down, following clear rules, no feelings, like robots.

Mary: Yes, that's helpful to think of it that way. And... I think I did notice this for a moment in the session, then panicked and got stuck, didn't quite know how to talk about this. I'm afraid he is going to drop out or erupt in anger. I think we frequently get stuck in this place. I'm feeling sad now thinking about it. I think it might feel so frightening for him, but then also comforting to know I care.

Supervisor: Hmm, this is hard stuff, you're working very hard to find that balance of naming and talking about something you think is happening but in a way that he can manage, so he can keep thinking and feeling together. Do you feel able to think about what you might say now? If you were back in that moment, when he is telling you that you are 'just following the rules'.

Mary: I think it depends, there are a few ways. If I feel he is in one of his more playful moods, I could respond by saying something like 'what so I am robot now, just following the rules?' Or I could say something about how maybe he is thinking about whether I am someone who cares and thinks about him or if I am someone who just follows the rules without thinking about him.

Supervisor: All of these seem useful.

Mary: Or I might be able to open the conversation up more generally. Let him know that I have noticed that something happens when we talk about feelings or rather when I express something about feelings and I am curious if he has noticed anything.

Conclusion

A mentalized mind is a creative mind, and a connected one. Fundamental to MBT-A supervision is the genuine belief and acceptance that we all can lose our capacity to effectively mentalize and particularly so when working with those who are emotionally dysregulated and presenting with risk to themselves and others. A mentalizing supervisory relationship aims to restore and facilitate our own mentalizing so that we can develop our skills in restoring our mentalizing when in the room with our patients. This, in turn, develops our patient's mentalizing capabilities, building resilience and flexibility and supporting their movement towards a healthy developmental path. With a collaborative spirit and shared understanding of the task of making the implicit explicit, the supervisory dyad works towards exploring the underlying thoughts, feelings and intentions motivating the behaviours of both clinician and adolescent and influencing their interactions.

References

Ackerman, S.J., & Hilsenroth, M.J. (2001). A review of therapist characteristics and techniques negatively impacting the therapeutic alliance. *Psychotherapy: Theory, Research, Practice, Training, 38*(2), 171–185. https://doi.org/10.1037/0033-3204.38.2.171.

Ackerman, S.J., & Hilsenroth, M.J. (2003). A review of therapist characteristics and techniques positively impacting the therapeutic alliance. *Clinical Psychology Review, 23*, 1–3.

Bevington, D., Fuggle, P., Cracknell, L., & Fonagy, P. (2017). *Adaptive Mentalization-Based Integrative Treatment: A Guide for Teams to Develop Systems of Care.* New York, NY: Oxford University Press.

Bevington, D., Fuggle, P., & Fonagy, P. (2015). Applying attachment theory to effective practice with hard-to-reach youth: The AMBIT approach. *Attachment and Human Development, 17*(2),157–174. DOI: 10.1080/14616734.2015.1006385.

Hilsenroth, M.J., & Diener, M.J. (2017). Some effective strategies for the supervision of psychodynamic psychotherapy. In T. Rousmaniere, R.K. Goodyear, S.D. Miller, & B.E. Wampold (Eds.), *The Cycle of Excellence: Using Deliberate Practice to Improve Supervision and Training* (pp. 163–188). West Sussex, UK: John Wiley & Sons Ltd. https://doi.org/10.1002/9781119165590.ch8.

Section III

Specific applications

Chapter 7

Working with adolescents who self-harm

Maria Wiwe and Trudie Rossouw

Self-harm in the adolescent population is a prevalent, difficult and complex problem that causes a lot of distress, not only for the young people struggling with this adversity on an everyday basis but also for their loved ones. In addition, the high degree of self-harming in young people is a challenge for schools and mental health services.

Studies demonstrate that the most frequent reason for self-harm amongst young people seems to be an attempt to get relief from painful thoughts and feelings (Gillies et al., 2018). Also, it appears that the more frequent the self-harming, the more severe the self-hatred in the young person as well as the higher the degree of suicidal ideation (Gillies et al., 2018).

Furthermore, strong associations are reported between self-harming behaviour in youngsters and depression and anxiety (Jacobson & Gould, 2007), substance use (Hilt, Nock, Lloyd-Richardson, & Prinstein, 2008) and borderline personality disorder (BPD) (Ferrara, Terrinoni, & Williams, 2012). Besides, in inpatient units, the rates of self-harm are as high as 50% (Nock & Prinstein, 2005). The crucial point to take from these studies is that self-harm is indicative of a mental health problem affecting the young person, and therefore self-harm is not carried out for the purpose of attention. Self-harm can be enacted with or without suicidal intent (Madge et al., 2008; Guan, Fox, & Prinstein, 2012). It is essential for clinicians to explore whether the self-harm is accompanied by suicidal intentions, as it is also essential to bear in mind that even when the suicidal thoughts are not present, youngsters dealing with self-harm frequently live in an inner world dominated by raw and forceful emotions preventing them from taking a healthy and constructive part in their adolescent lives (Rossouw & Fonagy, 2012).

This chapter has two sections: the first introduces antecedents of adolescents' mentalizing breakdowns and subsequent turbulence, in order to share an understanding of adolescent crisis and turmoil within a mentalization-based framework. The second consists of two excerpts from two different MBT-A treatments. Each of these clinical vignettes will present young people at different ages within the adolescent phase who struggle with self-harm.

Clinically, they present with emerging personality disorder, primarily with features of borderline and avoidant personality disorder.

Mentalizing breakdown leading up to self-harm in adolescence

As was described in the second chapter of this book, due to the neurobiological changes that are characteristic of the adolescent developmental phase, young people are especially prone to losing their mentalizing capability. In this particular developmental stage, adolescents are hypersensitised to social triggers such as facial expressions of other people, and especially to the facial expressions of other young people (Sebastian, Viding, Williams, & Blakemore 2010). This interpersonal hypersensitivity makes it harder for them to accurately read other people's minds, and so they easily end up misunderstanding others' intentions. A case in point is the fMRI-study conducted by Tahmasebi and colleagues (2012), suggesting that both angry and neutral faces are highly salient to adolescents, in ways that may differ by gender. Although this accounts for adolescents on the whole, young people struggling with mental health issues will inevitably become even more vulnerable to misinterpretation of facial expressions and subsequent mentalizing breakdowns. And as we all know, a neutral face can represent a variety of different mental states, whereas for adolescents it seems that it tends to be interpreted as rejection (Tahmasebi et al., 2012). As will be described below, rejection is one of the most difficult feelings an adolescent can encounter. It can be an extremely stressful experience which may lead to affective dysregulation and subsequent self-harming behaviour. Therefore, the mentalization model to understanding self-harm amongst young people naturally takes into account this age-specific interpersonal sensitivity.

The concept of the alien self

We just want to recap a few words about the alien self, which was described in Chapter 1. There we described how mentalization developed from the attachment relationship, based on the caregivers' ability to form attuned representations of the child's mental state in her or his mind, and through mirroring this representation back to the child, the child internalises this and it becomes part of the child's core sense of self. When things go wrong and the caregiver is overwhelmed with their own mental state (and remember, under the sway of overwhelming internal states all of us may fall prey to losing our ability to mentalize), the caregiver will not be able to mentalize the child or form an attuned representation of the child's state and is more likely to act under the influence of their own internal state. The child will internalise this unattuned mental representation, but as it is not really based on the child's mental state, it will start to form the building blocks of the "alien self"

(Fonagy, Gergely, Jurist, & Target, 2002). The description is very accurate as the internalised state is based on the caregiver's mental state and is not a reflection of the child's state at all.

As all of us would have had misattuned experiences growing up, we all have a degree of an alien self inside us. However, we are not dominated by our alien self. The difficulty comes when one is dominated by the alien self. The problem is compounded as the alien self is present in a dominant way when mentalization has broken down, therefore thoughts and feelings are experienced as facts (under the force of psychic equivalence, described in Chapter 1). The experience of the alien self is a sudden onset of intense negative feelings about oneself and a conviction that others see us in the same way.

Young people who often feel dominated by their alien selves usually have no sense of their own worth, skills, or talents, neither do they have any self-compassion. Instead, they are constantly anticipating being rejected and humiliated by others. The alien self consists of self-hatred and hopelessness and makes the youngsters feel like failures in all aspects of their lives (Rossouw, 2012). The alien self makes them lose sight of the possibility that they can achieve anything with their lives. Consequently, tormented by this vehement state of mind, the young person goes into a state of developmental arrest, and loses track of their expected developmental achievements, like for example attending school and socialising with their peer group. The mentalizing work is about helping them reconnect to their social world and get back on their developmental track.

Mentalizing model of self-harm

Being interpersonally sensitive in the sense that has been outlined above, a young person is particularly vulnerable to relational triggers evoking negative social emotions like, for example, rejection, shame or humiliation. The adolescent phase is the time in life when the most important thing is getting approval from peers and at the same time being at the peak of vulnerability to peer-rejection (Masten et al., 2009). Consequently, the everyday life of a teenager is basically a minefield for possible mentalizing breakdowns, which has the potential to decouple the adolescent from their social world. Hence the adolescent will lose contact with what is most important for them. Due to our own attachment history and the actual level of stress, we all have a 'tipping point' where we switch from a relatively mentalizing mode into a non-mentalizing mode (Fonagy & Luyten, 2009). A young person coping with mental health issues will be more vulnerable in this respect. The mentalizing model of self-harm elucidates the mental processes of the young person who turns to self-harm to regulate affects.

If we put ourselves in the mind of the adolescent, then we are in a world where one of the most important things is the way our peers see us and respond to us. Due to our hypersensitivity to social cues, we often are aroused and anxious about being rejected, judged or mocked. Much like a seesaw, as our anxiety levels go up, our ability to make sense of ourselves and our social world goes down. We, therefore, lose our ability to mentalize. Saying this in large academic words unfortunately does not convey the subjective experience very well. When we lose our ability to mentalize, not only do we lose our ability to understand social relations and ourselves, but we also suddenly feel overwhelmed with the return of pre-mentalizing thinking. Hence, under the influence of psychic equivalence, our thoughts start to feel like facts, escalating the anxiety we feel. At this moment, the adolescent's ability to create accurate representations of the mind of the other is eliminated. Additionally, the ability to acquire a clearer understanding of one's own contribution to the behaviour of others will break down, as well as the capacity for self-compassion and empathy for others (Rossouw, 2012). It is very common that in these states, we often see the activation of the alien self and the young person may find themselves overwhelmed with alien self-dominated thoughts, which express significant self-hatred. Due to the absence of mentalization, all thoughts are experienced as facts, which will lead to the young person feeling that they ARE bad, worthless or whatever other negative feelings they are having. Not only do they feel that about themselves, but as they are not able to mentalize others when they are in this state, they are also certain that others see them in the same light. This creates an unbearable feeling dominated by hostility inside and outside as well as a feeling of loss of everything that has been good or of value. Any form of action to get away from this unbearable state then feels like the only solution, which explains the rush to self-harm. It is for this reason too that self-harm provides some form of short-term immediate relief – it changes the unbearable mental state teleologically into a concrete state where there is a wound that can concretely be dressed.

Hypermentalization

Hypermentalization is an inaccurate form of mentalizing. It consists of psychic equivalence thinking and can often activate the alien self. As some clinicians may know, young people often refer to "overthinking" – this is to some degree a description of hypermentalizing. Hypermentalizing is ascribing in-accurate mental states to others and building upon that by adding more and more detail about the motives or feelings of others without sufficient evidence. Young people who hypermentalize very easily end up being highly aroused and, due to the alien self described above, soon experience an unbearable internal state from which they desperately try to escape by finding a concrete solution, such as self-harm. Our colleagues (Sharp et al., 2013) found that hypermentalizing was the hallmark mentalizing failure in young people with BPD, in comparison to young people who did not have BPD.

Therapeutic interventions

Under the force of the alien self, adolescents relate to themselves in strikingly dehumanised ways, with no sense of self-compassion and feeling utterly alone in the world. We learned in Chapter 1 about epistemic trust and the need for epistemic trust in order to be able to learn from others. If a young person is in a state of mind dominated by the alien self, with a lack of ability to effectively mentalize those around them, they are highly likely to be in a state of epistemic mistrust and therefore struggle to gain from the therapeutic encounter. In Chapters 3 and 4, we described the therapeutic technique in detail to be used when working with these young people. The underlying principle is to establish a therapeutic alliance with these youngsters and to maintain emotional contact, which is crucial for the adolescents to stay connected to the social world around them.

In their paper on the phenomenological experience of psychotherapy, Fonagy and colleagues (2019) described three aspects that lead to effective therapeutic change – (1) an epistemic match, (2) improving mentalizing and (3) re-emergence of social learning. The first refers to the young person's experience of being recognised – in other words, they feel understood and validated – they find a representation of their mental state in the mind of the therapist. This experience is a potent ostensive cue for the development of epistemic trust. Fonagy and colleagues (2019, p. 96) stated: *In brief, if individuals experience themselves as being understood, they will be inclined to learn from the person who has shown that he or she understands them. This will include learning about oneself, but also about others and about the environment in which one lives – most importantly, how to navigate the social and cultural environment with all its complexities and challenges.*

Understanding the experience of the young person and being supportive, empathic and validating, therefore, act as important ostensive cues for the work of restoring mentalization to follow – all of which will improve the young person's ability to mentalize when under strain and accurately appraise and understand those around them, which will be a strong antidote to hypermentalization.

Young people with self-harm present with higher risk and hence risk assessment and management of risk needs to form part of our sessions. Questions that are often raised are: How do you assess and manage risk without this interfering with the therapeutic work? How can assessing risk build epistemic trust? The answer is that we cannot really assess or manage risk without epistemic trust. How to conduct risk assessments with adolescents is beyond the scope of this chapter, as the focus of the book is on MBT-A. However, our view is that it is best to establish an emotional connection with a young person first and help the young person to feel understood before we conduct a risk assessment. The latter can be done in an empathic and understanding way too, which will further enhance trust, rather than as a tick box exercise.

In terms of risk management, if one feels that risks are such that an hospital admission is not necessary, then it will be good to discuss a safety plan with the young person and their families. The safety plan will include a discussion about the understanding of the trigger factors for the self-harm as well as ways in which the young person and their families can help them to stay safe. Examples of safety/crisis plans were discussed in previous chapters.

The bulk of the work with young people who self-harm follows the therapeutic techniques discussed in earlier chapters. It follows the dance of making emotional contact, providing support, empathy and validation as well as clarification, elaboration or challenge at times and mentalizing the moment when needed.

Below we present two clinical examples to illustrate this work.

Zoe, 13 years of age
Perceived burdensomeness

Zoe is struggling in many areas of her young life; she is dropping out of school, getting into severe fights with friends and family members along with frequent and intense cutting. Sometimes she uses alcohol in order to 'numb' herself from painful feelings.

In addition, during the assessment phase, Zoe was clear about not feeling understood by anyone. She often uses phrases like "I'm a burden to others" and "everyone would be better off without me". It is crucial for clinicians to be attentive to perceived burdensomeness amongst youngsters. Young people who see themselves as a burden to the people around them tend to believe that other people also view them this way (Buitron et al., 2016). Naturally enough, this is an extremely distressing predicament, but also a marker for a non-mentalizing mode (i.e. psychic equivalence, where the inner world equals the outer). Adolescents who have interpersonal relationships characterised by ongoing conflict may come to believe that they are a drain or a burden on other people in their lives. This belief of being a burden on others appears to play a role in the pathway from chronic interpersonal stress to suicidal ideation (Buitron et al., 2016; Puzia et al., 2014).

The excerpt below is from a session characterised by a high level of emotional stress. Zoe's mother has informed the therapist that Zoe did not attend school last week and that she has been cutting herself extensively. Since Zoe belongs to the group of younger adolescents (13–17-years-olds), parental work is more central compared to older adolescents. Zoe's parents did not attend every session, but in the session described below, Zoe's mother was present.

The emotional level tends to rise quickly in Zoe's family and the family members easily end up misunderstanding each other, the aim for the therapist is therefore not only to try to reinstall Zoe's mentalizing capability but also Zoe's mother's.

Zoe: (crawling up in the chair, hiding her face behind her

	hoody, screaming at her mother to leave the room).
Therapist (with a soft facial expression, turns to both Zoe and her mother Brenda):	Oh gosh, I can see you are both struggling now, I'm so happy you managed to get here in this struggle!
Zoe's mother Brenda (with her arms folded in a forced manner):	Tell me about it.

Zoe, still hiding her face, continues to scream and curls deeper into the chair.

Therapist:	Oh gosh guys, I'm really really sorry you feel this way, I can see you're both struggling, eeh or even the three of us, I'm really gonna need your help today to understand what is happening.
	Being aware of the strength in the attachment relationship between parent and child, the therapist knows that they both have a tremendous impact on each other's state of mind. Therefore, the therapist empathises in order to lower the emotional temperature in the room, knowing that high emotional pressure makes it more difficult for everyone to think and feel clearly. Aiming at stimulating Zoe's and her mother's own agency, she's being transparent about her own subjectivity.
Therapist:	Zoe, I just want you to know that I'm not mad at you, I'm not mad at your mum, actually I'm very proud of both of you for how brave you both are coming here to see me in this struggle.
	These young people are typically so poor at perceiving their own and others' mental statesthat making thoughts explicit, especially at the beginning of therapy, is critical to the work. The therapist therefore declares her intentions, in order to help Zoe understand that she is not judging her or her mother, but that her intention is to work alongside them. She is also aiming at empathising with two minds, she knows that she needs to get Zoe's mother's mentalizing on-line in order for Brenda to be able to mentalize her daughter.
Zoe:	I don't believe you, I know you hate us! I want mum out of here, I know she hates me, she just wishes she never had me!
Therapist:	Goodness gracious, how on earth would that be

	possible, that your mum wants you dead! Dearest Zoe, let us push the pause button, my brain is shutting down when I get too stressed and you know I'm not very helpful then, dear!
Zoe:	I don't want some stupid pause!
Therapist (teasing in order to stay emotionally connected to Zoe):	But I need one Zoe, look my brain is about to fly out of the window!

Zoe giggles.

Therapist (empathising, getting alongside):	And you know what, I really need a pause since I realise that if I were in your shoes now, I guess I wouldn't have even managed to get out of bed.
Zoe screams:	I'm only here cause mum made me!!
Therapist:	That is a determined and strong mum you've got there, and you came with her to see me, great work Zoe! *Therapist trying to connect Zoe to the world around her by alleviating her sense of threat.*
Zoe:	She sucks!

Zoe's mother Brenda rolls her eyes and sighs.

Zoe looks out from her hoody:	Look, look, she rolled her eyes at me, that's what I'm telling you, she hates me, she really hates me!!
Therapist looking puzzled:	Wow Zoe, that's really good, how you picked up on your mother rolling her eyes at you! I mean how quick and perceptive are you? I didn't pick up on that, I'm just too slow for you.
Zoe:	Yes! And she hates me when she rolls her eyes!
Therapist:	Oh gosh, she does? Help me Zoe, I feel completely lost, here.

Zoe and Brenda start screaming at each other.

The therapist stands up, puts her hands up in the air:	Stop, stop, stop! Both of you, come on guys, I can't think when you scream like that!
Therapist:	Zoe I really need your help here, you know,

	I can't follow your thoughts now. I mean, my brain just can't work out this leap from your mum eye-rolling you to hating you! How do you know that is what she is feeling?
Zoe:	I feel it!
Brenda:	Well, you're wrong!
Therapist (using her 'mentalizing hands' again in order to try to decrease emotional temperature):	Oh gee, let us pause again, don't forget about the sloth over here. I'm just wondering, I mean sometimes we do have these strong feelings inside of us and then we tend to believe that they are all true *(psychoeducation)*, do you recognise that Brenda?
Brenda:	Yes of course.
Therapist:	Good, good, I'm wondering if that is what Zoe is struggling with right now?
Zoe:	But I know it's true, I know she hates me cause I feel it.
Therapist:	You know Zoe, sometimes when I feel really crushed I also get convinced that it's true and that it can't be in any other way. *Therapist tries to present an alternative perspective by using herself as a model.*
Zoe:	Hmm.
Therapist:	And then when I feel calmer it's actually like a kind of fog lifting in my brain and I can sense that there might be more to it than I first thought. Do you recognise that?
Zoe:	No!!
Therapist:	I'm sorry Zoe, I'm being too pushy, I'll let you rest a little. I'll turn to your mum for a while. I wonder, can you help me out here Brenda, what do you think Zoe feels when you roll your eyes?
	The therapist assumes that Zoe's mind is still fixed in psychic equivalence and takes responsibility for being too premature with alternative perspectives. By shifting the focus to her mother she might be stimulating the curiosity in Zoe, helping her out of her rigid position.
Brenda:	I have no idea. She's clearly not listening that's the

	problem. And that is why I'm rolling my eyes.
	Listen out for words like clearly, just, should, must, always, never; they are all indicating that mentalizing has gone out of the window.
Therapist:	Oh I see, so am I getting this correct, when Zoe is not listening then you roll your eyes?

Brenda is nodding.

Therapist:	What do you see on Zoe that tells you she's not listening?
Brenda:	She just keeps turning her face away from me, like I'm not her mum that she should listen to, and then it always ends up with her cutting herself.
Therapist:	I see, so when Zoe turns away, tell me again, how does that leave you feeling?
Brenda:	Eeh, well actually, like I'm a piece of garbage.
Therapist:	Oh, that sounds really difficult, Brenda. Zoe turns away and then you feel like you're a piece of garbage, then what happens? Zoe?
Zoe:	She totally freaks out!
Therapist:	Oh gosh, what do you mean by "freaks out" Zoe, what do you see in your mum then, Zoe?
Zoe:	She looks mad and screams at me.
Therapist:	Do you know how you look when you look mad as Zoe described you, Brenda?
Brenda smiles:	I guess, Zoe's dad says that I look like I could kill someone, eeh, and don't worry I wouldn't though.
Therapist:	Oh that's reassuring! So what do you believe is happening inside Zoe, when she sees that look in your face?
Brenda:	I don't know, I mean she must know that I don't hate her.
Therapist:	Zoe, could you tell us what you feel when your mum looks like that in her face?
Zoe:	I feel scared.
Brenda:	Well, Zoe knows she shouldn't be scared of me, I'm her mum for Christ's sake.
Zoe:	I am though!

Therapist *(psychoeducational):*	Hey guys, you remember it's about those really strong feelings inside of us again, like for example fear, it kind of takes over everything, it happens to me sometimes, for sure. So even though we basically don't need to be scared in that particular moment, we are scared anyhow, you know what I mean?

Both nodding.

Therapist:	I might be totally in the wrong here, I'm just curious if that is what is happening for Zoe then?
Brenda:	But I'm her mum, she should know that I'm not a threat to her.
Therapist:	Hold on Brenda, bear with me a little, Zoe could you help us out here, what in your mum's behaviour or in her face actually scares you?
Zoe:	I don't know, she kind of looks hateful.
Therapist:	Is that the look that your dad refers to when he says he thinks your mum looks like she could kill someone?
Zoe:	I think so.
Therapist:	What is behind that look, do you think Brenda?
Brenda:	Gee, I mean I know I can look kind of harsh, but I think I'm just desperate.
Zoe:	If she's desperate then she hates me!
Therapist:	Zoe, help me out here, you know I am this old sloth, and there's this leap again! This time my old and slow brain can't work out the jump from being desperate to hating someone. How do you do that?
Zoe:	I just know it! I'm such a misfit! She wants me to be like my sis, going happily to school every day. She doesn't see I'm actually trying really bloody hard to be normal! *A young person with vulnerable self-esteem is prone to experiencing intense socially negative emotions when feeling misunderstood. The experience of being misunderstood may trigger a collapse in his or her sense of self, which may be accompanied by intense fear of abandonment, leading to internal panic and resulting in acting out behaviour such as self-harm or suicidal ideation.*
Brenda gasps:	Oh, honey!

Therapist:	You're doing really well Zoe, really well, what you're saying is so important. Before we have a closer look at that, I'm wondering what your mum feels when she says 'oh honey'?
Zoe:	She's sad, I make her sad.
T:	Should we check in with her?

Zoe nods, looking at her mother.

In summary, the primary aim is to connect emotionally with the adolescent in distress in order to restore the adolescent's mentalizing capability. A young person spinning in a non-mentalizing mode, crushed under the force of the alien self, will inevitably feel deeply alone and disconnected from her social world. Not only can this situation be dangerous in terms of suicide attempts as a way to get out of this intolerable state of mind, but it also makes the youngster vulnerable to falling off their developmental track, which typically includes attending school and building a social network. In order to be able to do that, the young person needs to be emotionally connected enough to her social world. This can be established through improving mentalization, leading to a more accurate view of herself and a greater ability to imagine the minds of others.

Nadia, 18 years old
'Overthinking' about being hated

Like Zoe, Nadia is struggling with difficulties in multiple areas of her life; apart from her struggle with considerable self-harming behaviour, she has stopped attending school and communicating with friends. At the same time, her mind is incessantly preoccupied with her friends' whereabouts and she spends an excessive amount of time on social media platforms. In withdrawing from her social world, although still watching her friends on pictures and postings on various social media, she ends up feeling intensely alone, isolated and a failure.

During her assessment phase, Nadia and her therapist identify experiences of feeling left out and of rejection as Nadia's main triggers for mentalizing breakdowns. Nadia herself recognises time spent on the internet observing other young people doing what they are 'supposed' to do, to be a main trigger for emotions like the above mentioned. She talks about examining those pictures and reading all the added comments triggers her into overthinking, where she ends up hating herself immensely. The term 'overthinking' is often used by adolescents to describe hypermentalizing.

Seated in her chair in the treatment room, Nadia is wiggling her body back and forth, as she mumbles: I can't handle it, I can't handle it, I want to die, please let me die.

The therapist places herself onto the floor besides Nadia. Looking worried and stammering a bit, she says: Gee, oh Nadia, I'm so sorry you feel this way and I think I need to sit down as well. Listen to me Nadia, I don't want you to die, I would be totally crushed if you did. Tell me, what happened?

Nadia, still looking down, wiggling herself: I don't know, I have no idea. I just know that I really want to die. I need some peace and quiet.

Therapist:	Oh dear Nadia ... I'm so impressed that you actually got on the bus to come over here and see me when you're in this state of mind. I'm proud of you. *Since Nadia is in a state of mind where the degree of self-hatred is extremely high, the therapist needs to embody a counterpart to the alien self, by being affirming, warm and compassionate.*
Nadia:	I'm hateable and such a freak.
Therapist:	What happened Nadia? How come you feel like this?
Nadia looking down, biting her nails very hard:	I don't know. I hate myself.

Therapist, in a gentle voice: don't hurt yourself by biting yourself – let's just talk and try and make sense of what you are feeling.

Nadia stops biting:	Okay then, but I don't know anything.
T:	That's ok, tell me more about that, the 'I-don't-know' place? What do you think pushed you into that place?
Nadia:	I don't know, I mean I hate it for sure and I hate that everyone wants me to know, I just know that I've cut myself, which proves I'm such a failure. God, I hate myself, the whole world hates me!!
Therapist:	Oh gee, I can't see how anyone would hate you?! I certainly do not hate you! I'm not the least cross with you for cutting yourself, I'm not judging you, Nadia, okay?

The therapist explicitly tries to alleviate the burden of psychic equivalence.

Nadia looking up:	Okay, thanks.
Therapist smiling:	Oh you're most welcome, I'm just wondering if something happened that made you feel awful about yourself and then you might have thought that you didn't have any other option than to cut yourself?
Nadia:	Hmm, yeah, I felt awful.
Therapist:	What happened Nadia, what happened?

Nadia:	I don't know.
Therapist:	That's alright, we'll just take it slow, one step at a time. I'm really curious about those awful feelings. You know I have this hypothesis that your feelings at that point were so powerful that they might have pushed you over the edge to cutting. What do you think about that?

> *The therapist engages in the not-knowing stance (see Chapter 3) and transparently presents her hypotheses, inviting the adolescent to share their interest in the mental processes.*

Nadia:	I don't want to think about that.

> *Nadia is still stuck in a position of psychic equivalence.*

T:	Oh gosh, I can relate to that, you know I wouldn't want to go back either, sometimes I avoid revisiting such spots in my mind. And then I also know that if I don't, nothing will ever get any better. So come on, let us do it together, huh?
Nadia:	I can't go there, it's too awful, I know they all hate me....

Basically it was nothing, eeh, whatever, I was in my room, as usual, and I scrolled through my Instagram and then I saw this picture of Louisa and Shannon, and they just looked super-happy and super-cool and I mean we actually used to hang out the three of us but not anymore and I know they used to be kind of cool as to not posting stuff on the two of them on Insta without me and then they suddenly stopped being nice and all and just posted happy pictures of the two of them, all the time, and I know that is because I didn't go to Louisa's birthday party last year. It obviously pissed them off! I mean she was turning 16, which I do know is an important birthday, I mean it's not like I don't know that, but I was very depressed and I just couldn't drag myself out of bed and mum was screaming at me, trying to force me to go, telling me I would lose all of my friends if I didn't. Well, mum was right, because now I'm completely alone and it's obvious they posted that picture thinking of me, to kind of show me that I'm not a part of them anymore since I failed to show up at Louisa's party. *As previously mentioned, in hypermentalizing the youngster's analytic ability (i.e. inability) goes into a 'spin' where feelings and thoughts 'jump' far too many steps ahead from reality.*

Therapist:	Hang on Nadia, can we slow down a bit? You're too fast for me and I really want to make some sense in order to understand what was going on for you when you saw the picture of Louisa and Shannon.

> *Exploration of what the young person feels as well as clarification of what happened in the relevant interpersonal context provides the building blocks of mentalizing the moment. To be sure to reach the heart of the matter, the principle of slowing down the process is vital.*

Nadia: Nah, it's alright really it doesn't matter, it's probably nothing, it's just my stupid thoughts, which don't mean anything anyhow.

Therapist: No, I don't agree, I think your thoughts mean a lot, they are important, they are very important to me and they are important every time you come here, I do want to know.

Nadia: Aah, but I don't know. It sucked. It broke my heart and now my mind is just an empty hole. Nadia starts to cry. I don't know, it kind of went black in my head and suddenly I saw myself actually leaving my room and the house, who could ever believe I would do that *(laughing a little)*, going to Tesco's to buy razor blades. And then I cut myself in the street in the middle of the day. I feel so stupid about that now, I'm such a freak.

T: You are not a freak, you are in pain and I understand it.

Conclusion

Getting alongside the young person, the clinician has to show enough interest and curiosity in the subjective state of mind that preceded the self-harm, to explore the subjectivity that could not be coped with the moment when the adolescent abandoned her capacity to think and feel about herself and others. The work is often an ongoing battle against the alien self, which creates high states of arousal and pushes young people into impulsivity. We need to continuously try to slow things down, pause to think and clarify our understanding to kickstart mentalization and humanisation and connect the adolescent to her social world.

References

Buitron, V., Hill, R.M., Pettit, J.W., Green, K.L., Hatkevich, C., & Sharp, C. (2016). Interpersonal stress and suicidal ideation in adolescence: An indirect association through perceived burdensomeness toward others. *Journal of Affective Disorders, 190,* 143–149.

Ferrara, M., Terrinoni, A., & Williams, R. (2012). Non-suicidal self-injury (NSSI) in adolescent inpatients: assessing personality features and attitude toward death. *Child and Adolescent Psychiatry and Mental Health, 6*(1), 12.

Fonagy, P., Gergely, G., Jurist, E.J., & Target, M. (2002). *Affect Regulation, Mentalization, and the Development of the Self.* London: Karnac Press.

Fonagy, P., & Luyten, P. (2009). A developmental, mentalization-based approach to the understanding and treatment of borderline personality disorder. *Development and Psychopathology*, *21*(4), 1355–1381.

Gillies, D., Christou, M.A., Dixon, A.C., Featherston, O.J., Rapti, I., Garcia-Anguita, A.,?… Christou, P.A. (2018). Prevalence and characteristics of self-harm in adolescents: meta-analyses of community-based studies 1990–2015. *Journal of the American Academy of Child and Adolescent Psychiatry*, *57*(10), 733–741.

Guan, K., Fox, K.R., & Prinstein, M.J. (2012). Nonsuicidal self-injury as a time-invariant predictor of adolescent suicide ideation and attempts in a diverse community sample. *Journal of Consulting and Clinical Psychology*, *80*(5), 842–849.

Hilt, L.M., Nock, M.K., Lloyd-Richardson, E.E., & Prinstein, M.J. (2008). Longitudinal study of nonsuicidal self-injury among young adolescents: Rates, correlates, and preliminary test of an interpersonal model. *The Journal of Early Adolescence*, *28*(3), 455–469.

Jacobson, C.M., & Gould, M. (2007). The epidemiology and phenomenology of non-suicidal self-injurious behavior among adolescents: A critical review of the literature. *Archives of Suicide Research*, *11*(2), 129–147.

Madge, N., Hewitt, A., Hawton, K., Wilde, E.J.D., Corcoran, P., Fekete, S.,?… Ystgaard, M. (2008). Deliberate self-harm within an international community sample of young people: comparative findings from the Child & Adolescent Self-Harm in Europe (CASE) Study. *Journal of Child Psychology and Psychiatry*, *49*(6), 667–677.

Masten, C.L., Eisenberger, N.I., Borofsky, L.A., Pfeifer, J.H., McNealy, K., Mazziotta, J.C., & Dapretto, M. (2009). Neural correlates of social exclusion during adolescence: understanding the distress of peer rejection. *Social Cognitive and Affective Neuroscience*, *4*(2), 143–157.

Nock, M.K., & Prinstein, M.J. (2005). Contextual features and behavioral functions of self-mutilation among adolescents. *Journal of Abnormal Psychology*, *114*(1), 140–146.

Puzia, M.E., Kraines, M.A., Liu, R.T., & Kleiman, E.M. (2014). Early life stressors and suicidal ideation: Mediation by interpersonal risk factors. *Personality and Individual Differences*, *56*, 68–72.

Rossouw, T. (2012). Self-harm in young people. Is MBT the answer? In N. Midgley & I. Vrouva (Eds.), *Minding the Child: Mentalization-Based Interventions with Children, Young People and Their Families* (pp. 131–144). London: Routledge.

Rossouw, T.I., & Fonagy, P. (2012). Mentalization-based treatment for self-harm in adolescents: a randomized controlled trial. *Journal of the American Academy of Child and Adolescent Psychiatry*, *51*(12), 1304–1313.

Sebastian, C., Viding, E., Williams, K.D., & Blakemore, S.J. (2010). Social brain development and the affective consequences of ostracism in adolescence. *Brain and Cognition*, *72*(1), 134–145.

Sharp, C., Ha, C., Carbone, C., Kim, S., Perry, K., Williams, L., & Fonagy, P. (2013). Hypermentalizing in adolescent inpatients: treatment effects and association with borderline traits. *Journal of Personality Disorders*, *27*(1), 3–18.

Tahmasebi, A.M., Artiges, E., Banaschewski, T., Barker, G.J., Bruehl, R., Büchel, C.,?… Heinz, A. (2012). Creating probabilistic maps of the face network in the adolescent brain: a multicentre functional MRI study. *Human Brain Mapping*, *33*(4), 938–957.

Chapter 8

Working with gender diverse young people and their families

Ioanna Vrouva, Jason Maldonado-Page, and Nicole Muller

Introduction

> *"It is the first time in my life I cannot see a picture. I simply cannot imagine how I will look like without my breasts. When I get a mirror after the operation, I can see how it is. I know I want this, but it also feels like a wild step. I let them change my body, but I don't know what will happen with me emotionally. Can I be satisfied? Will I feel more like the real me? I don't know".*
>
> Jacob, 19 years old, transgender man

As discussed previously, adolescence often signifies a period of emotional turbulence, uncertainty and distress about the changing body, the developing mind, old and new relationships, all of which weave together to create the young person's developing identity. Working with gender diverse young people and their families presents clinicians with familiar tensions inherent in working therapeutically with adolescents, but, like Jacob, clinicians too may need to grapple with some perplexing questions for the first time.

Drawing on an amalgamation of anonymised clinical experiences in the United Kingdom and the Netherlands, this chapter presents conversations with gender diverse young people and their families. The pronouns used in the clinical examples sometimes match the young person's assigned gender at birth and sometimes not, to reflect the fact that for some young people, preferred pronouns (and decisions about transitioning) may change over time (Churcher Clarke & Spiliadis, 2019).

Personal reflections

In writing this chapter, we were keen to share our thoughts and dilemmas with openness, as working with gender diverse adolescents and their families can bring up strong emotional reactions. The way of working described in this chapter may be interpreted differently, depending on readers' personal and professional experiences, and may be appraised through a different lens in the future, as the field continues to develop, and we make no claims that our approach is the right or only way to answer some of these incredibly complex questions.

Working with this group has made us reflect on our own gender identity development. Looking back at our own adolescence, we could all relate to questioning our gender identity at certain points, feeling distress around aspects of our pubertal development, struggling to fit into heteronormative or otherwise restrictive cultural gender norms often modelled by our parents, and experiencing sometimes intense anxiety about finding somebody to accept and love us and our body. As teenagers, we did not use the internet, and wondered what it would have been like to have online or other access to peer support groups or public narratives about the meaning of our experiences as signs of gender dysphoria (the diagnostic term used in DSM-V [American Psychiatric Association, 2013]), which would require medical interventions to be resolved.

The mental health field has an invidious history in relation to the pathologising stance it has taken in the past concerning different sexualities. As authors, we feel committed to supporting diversity and helping young people develop a sense of personal history, through reflecting on the multiple meanings and functions of their thoughts, feelings and actions.

Working in this highly contentious field, there were times when we felt concerned about being experienced as not 'affirmative' enough, unnecessarily cautious, withholding, or even 'transphobic'. These can be distressing professional experiences, and we found it useful to monitor these pressures on our own mentalizing. At those times, we tried to seek further understanding of ours and the young people's experiences, often reflecting on them together in the consulting room. By pressing a mentalizing "pause" button (Bateman & Fonagy, 2006), we tried to imagine and better understand some of the struggles and feelings of the young people and families we work with in the here and now, and aimed to be genuinely empathic and supportive. The mentalizing stance also helped us become more aware of the mentalizing and non-mentalizing processes that exist between young people, their families, their peer group, the clinicians, and the teams with which clinicians work.

A note on embodied mentalizing in adolescence

The onset of puberty brings with it many physical changes, which occur in different bodies in different ways, at different times and rates (Waddell, 2005). These physical changes thus have both a universal and an individualised component.

How each adolescent will negotiate these challenges and work out a sense of embodied, gendered self also depends to a large extent on the adolescent's ability to think about both their mental states and body at the same time, described as embodied mentalizing (Fonagy & Luyten, 2009; Luyten, van Houdenhove, Lemma, Target, & Fonagy, 2012). Embodied mentalizing describes the ability to see the body as a seat of emotional experiences, together with the capacity to reflect with openness on both the body's influence on the mind, as well as the mind's impact on bodily experiences and sensations. Hence, mentalizing and being mentalized have been described as full body/ mind experiences (Marchetti, Massaro, & Di Dio, 2017).

Challenges in working with gender diverse young people and their families

In recent years, the rate of young people questioning their gender identity has risen exponentially (Di Ceglie, 2018). Clinicians supporting these young people face a multitude of challenges, with developmental, empirical, clinical, professional, cultural, ethical and therapeutic dimensions. From a developmental perspective, as alluded, distress around body development at the onset of puberty, as well as a level of uncertainty regarding one's sexuality/sexual orientation and gender are often typical of the process of adolescent identity formation, experienced by many young people regardless of their assigned and self-identified gender.

Empirically, the factors contributing to the persistence and desistance of gender dysphoria are still largely unknown. Because of this uncertainty and evolving evidence base, clinicians are left to make recommendations, sometimes based upon anecdotal clinical experience or untested or partially tested theories (Marcus, Marcus, Yaxte, & Marcus, 2015).

When working with gender diverse young people with significant associated difficulties, such as social difficulties or mental health struggles, it can sometimes be very difficult to unpick where these different parts of the self may overlap and intersect. Sometimes young people with complex experiences and problems may attribute all their struggles (which can understandably make them feel hopeless and even suicidal at times) solely to the mismatch between their gender identity and their body.

Supporting the parents of gender diverse young people can also be complex. Seeing their child in distress can instil fear and panic in caregivers, which can often make them either completely reject their child's non-typical gender identification, or alternatively be drawn towards a possibly premature resolution (Wren, 2019). Parents may also feel guilty or disloyal to their child unless they fully affirm and advocate for the child's wishes. In contrast, some other parents may feel paralysed by religious or other cultural expectations about how their children should present themselves and behave, depending on their assigned genders. Finally, in some families, unmentalized trauma (Silverman, 2015) can, at times, become transferred and expressed through the parent's relationship to the child's body, and complex safeguarding concerns may emerge.

From a professional perspective, the new Memorandum of Understanding on Conversion Therapy (UK Council for Psychotherapy [UKCP], 2017, p. 1), understandably describes conversion therapy as "unethical and potentially harmful" (ibid. p. 1), while also suggesting that "some people might benefit from the challenge of psychotherapy" and that … "clients make healthy choices when they understand themselves better" (ibid. p. 1). These recommendations *leave* a large *grey area* as to the self-understanding that clinicians can aim for, especially given the shifting dynamics of adolescent identity development. Widening the lens to reflect on wider cultural challenges, many young people still live in marginalising and disrespectful social environments, characterised by homophobia, misogyny, and intolerance of gender neutrality and fluidity (Wren, 2019).

Online platforms have enabled young people to access information about transgender issues and the associated activism, helping them feel less ashamed and isolated. However, cyberspace can also become all-consuming, allowing or even implicitly encouraging a level of self-diagnosis to address the nature of young people's distress (Lemma, 2018) with premature certainty. Young people have described such experiences of labelling themselves as being "lost and found at the same time" (Marcus et al., 2015). Peer relationships offer invaluable opportunities for exploring and expressing one's developing identity, but peer pressures and the possibility of a gang-like mentality can also be a concern, with the danger of the development of the adolescent's individuality becoming derailed by the need for uniformity and fitting in (Churcher Clarke & Spiliadis, 2019).

In this context, a linear medical pathway can sometimes become, in young people's (and their parents') mind, the only acceptable way of managing their experience of difference and/or distress. On this teleological mode (described in Chapter 1), only concrete acts, e.g. a referral to a specialist service or a referral to the endocrinology clinic, may come to 'count' as evidence that the clinician cares and wants to help.

The dilemmas around how to respond to requests for even earlier medical intervention can bring to the fore significant ethical challenges. The process of informed consent regarding treatments that can have life-changing effects and side-effects on healthy young people's bodies can be highly complex, and clinicians then have to manage difficult tensions between wanting to respect the young person's autonomy versus feeling responsible for protecting them from potential future harm (Wren, 2019).

Noticing mentalizing difficulties and enhancing mentalizing strengths when discussing gender

The MBT framework helped us appreciate gender diverse adolescents' (and their families') varying ability to reflect on and make meaning of their and other people's experiences. When starting to work in this field, clinicians can get caught up in shifting language, and many young people describe the "correct" terminology and language with strong conviction. For instance, young people may correct their family members, peers, or a professional, by saying, "*I am not a Trans girl, I am a girl*". In response, it helps to empathise with the distress they seem to be experiencing and show an interest in understanding what this means for the young person. The clinician can invite the young person to help them (or the parent, sibling, etc.) understand how they see the difference between the two terms and how each term makes them feel, and in what way it matters to them to be referred to in this particular way.

Once, talking to a young person's parent, a clinician mistakenly referred to the young person as "*her*" instead of using the young person's preferred pronoun "*him*". The young person became instantly offended and somewhat aggressive, describing this misgendering episode as "*unacceptable*" and "*unforgivable*". Whilst initially surprised by the intensity of the reaction, the clinician tried to apologise to the young person authentically, but also remain curious about why this mistake had upset the young person so much. The therapeutic alliance was restored by acknowledging the young person's distress and revisiting this mistake in a different session. Exploring the meaning this had for the young person (namely that he did not "pass" well enough as a boy, his fear of humiliation, and a painful sense of not being accepted by others) helped the young person feel understood. Only then did it become possible to mentalize how the young person would be able to work out when somebody makes an unintentional mistake, rather than using language to reject or humiliate him.

Often young people's narratives reveal a difficulty in acknowledging the links between the external reality of the body and one's gendered sense of self, and clinicians are faced with the less mentalizing mode of psychic equivalence (described in Chapter 1). Therefore, during the assessment, it is important to discuss the "inside" of thoughts and feelings and the "outside" of external appearance and the body, especially given the distress so many young people experience about not "passing" as the gender they identify with, and their expectation that changing the outside will also change the inside.

At other times, young people's accounts of their embodied identity may sound barren of personal meaning and disconnected from their thoughts and feelings. Here the clinician may be at risk of feeling the pressure to know and validate, e.g. making statements like "*how hard it must be to be trapped in the wrong body*", before truly understanding what this experience is like for each young person; in other words, there is the risk of unknowingly interacting in *pretend mode* (described in Chapter 1). An indication that young people and their families are functioning in pretend mode can involve talking about complex experiences in simple narratives, such as a mother concluding that a Trans boy has been feeling much better after binding his chest, without at the same time sensitively wondering how previous trauma may have also contributed to her child's feelings. The MBT clinician may choose to use their own thoughts and feelings in this conversation to stimulate mentalizing, reflecting on how the mother sounds clear in her mind about her child's experiences. In contrast, for the clinician, it is still difficult to understand what it may be like to be in the young person's shoes, having to bind and hide the chest every day, and what feelings this brings up for this young person.

The following questions can aid mentalizing when asked in a genuinely empathic way that stimulates curiosity in the young person. "How does your appearance resemble how you feel inside, and how is this linked to gender stereotypes? How do you think other people look at you, and what is it that you want them to notice and understand about you? What does it feel like when others wonder whether you are Trans when they see you? Which parts of your body generate the most difficult feelings for you, and how do you understand this? How have you come to know that the bullying/abuse/other trauma you experienced has something/nothing to do with how you feel towards your body?"

Working with gender diverse young people also involves holding a balance between trying not to normalise pathological behaviour versus not pathologising normal behaviour. This is especially challenging because what is 'normal', and what is not is always complex and difficult to define. Furthermore, it is important to hold the balance between helping young people reflect on their internal experiences and helping them think about the thoughts and expectations of others. Often gender diverse young people can get caught up in thinking about others and how accepting and supportive they are of the young person's gender identity, while at the same time struggling to attend to their own experiences, often characterised by confusion, sadness and mourning. As described below, these experiences can be acknowledged and mentalized, once young people have started feeling safe in the therapeutic relationship.

Camilla is 16 years old and her parents wonder if she has autistic traits. In the MBT-A assessment, she slowly opens up and tries to understand what in her life has made her so withdrawn; she tries to reflect on her sad feelings, mourning the idea of being 'normal'.

Camilla tensely explains to her therapist that she is always afraid of what will happen at the airport when she goes on holiday. Because she looks like a boy, she is always directed to the men's area, but when airport workers notice she does not have a male body, they are always shocked and do not know how to react. Suddenly, Camilla starts crying softly and reflects that this feeling of not being 'normal' is very familiar, always looking for a group to belong to at school, being afraid of being laughed at, or sent away. 'Children can be so cruel', she reflects. To keep safe and not disappoint her parents, she has learned not to express her feelings, but to place them somewhere far away. When she fell in love with a girl she really liked, she started wondering again what this meant about her sexuality and if this was 'normal'. And now in this relationship with her girlfriend, she feels so ashamed about her body, not wanting to shower together or to have sex in a bright room, because then her girlfriend can see the body of a girl, while Camilla feels like a boy. The space she inhabits feels so lonely. Camilla desperately wants to be 'normal' and thinking she will never be normal makes her deeply sad. She is hoping to embark on a medical transition and feels jealous of boys with a well-functioning penis. In the assessment phase, she feels the impact of not being understood for so long. She realises it feels good to share her feelings with her therapist, trying to become more aware of the impact of all these experiences and how they have influenced her experience of herself, and her social life.

To promote mentalizing of the mind/body links within the whole family, we have sometimes invited the adolescent's parents to bring in photos of themselves when they were the age of their child. Parents were asked to examine their photos and to share what was seen and unseen, while their children were encouraged to be curious and ask questions. The parents were instructed not to answer as adults, but as their adolescent self might have answered. This helped parents connect with their own adolescent experiences, and many would share stories of shame and awkwardness, as well as challenges with their changing bodies. This exercise brought humour into the therapeutic room, and adolescents would often be really interested and surprised that their parents had had similar experiences. Emotional stories were elicited, many of which parents had never shared before with their child. For example, a mother of a Trans boy, who was hoping to have medical interventions to look more masculine and muscular, shared her painful experiences of being bullied as an overweight teenager, and what had helped her overcome them. The photograph exercise helped create a transitional space, where adolescents could trust their parents as people who could possibly understand the challenges they were facing. However, sometimes parents would speak about how their child's lived experience still felt unknown to them, despite their efforts to understand.

In these situations, we would bring an empty chair into the room. Following the Gestalt empty chair technique (Perls, Hefferline, & Goodman, 1951), we would ask parents to sit in the chair and would encourage them as best as possible to become their child, to think from their perspective and to embody their emotional posture; we would then interview them. The interview technique was similar to the Internalised Other Interview (Burnham, 2006), and the MBT-F idea of literally stepping into another family member's shoes (Asen & Fonagy, 2017), with the main task being to help parents mentalize their child's lived experience. Young people would witness this and would then be given the opportunity to connect with what they had heard. This technique was also used with young people to mentalize their parents' position, and to mentalize the competing needs of siblings, as a way of allowing for things to slow down, and for family members to connect on their shared and different experiences.

It feels encouraging to see gender diverse young people demonstrate stronger mentalizing capacities over time. This usually involves a willingness and a capacity to put themselves in other people's shoes (e.g. *"my mum has known me as "Katie" for 14 years, I get it why she slips sometimes and that it isn't intentional"*), a capacity to tolerate difference in thinking (*"I understand why people were a bit confused when I came out as Georgia at school, as I'd always tried to appear very masculine"),* the courage to express uncertainty (*"I'm not sure why I've been feeling this way or what it means exactly"),* and difference within the peer group (*"my Trans friends think that cisgender people don't understand, but I have felt at times understood, and at other times misunderstood by people and this doesn't always have to do with whether you're Trans"),* an ability to imagine that mental states such as feelings about the body may be different over time (*"I know I'd like to have surgery in the future, but I also know what I want might change and that'd be OK, too"),* and a capacity to engage with exploration in a curious, open, and non-defensive way. As noted elsewhere (Bateman & Fonagy, 2006), high-lighting and reinforcing positive mentalizing is just as important as noticing mentalizing struggles.

Enhancing mentalization when working with families

The following extract describes the beginning of a first session with 13-year-old Alex (previously Alexandra), his parents Bill and Jane, and two therapists, TT1 and TT2.

T1:   *Welcome everyone! We're both curious about what it was like coming to our meeting today.*

Mum: *Alex was very excited. She was up most of last night, talking to her friends online, (addressing Alex)- weren't you?*

        (Alex looks unhappy and goes silent)

T1:   *Alex, you look upset. Can you share with us what happened?*

Alex: *She always calls me "she". I've told HIM (emphatically, pointing at mum) a million times and HE just doesn't listen.*

Dad: *Alex, this is disrespectful, don't you think?*

Alex: *That's what Mum just did to me!*

T2:   *Sorry to interrupt; we can only begin to imagine what it may be like for you all coming to our meeting today, perhaps with very different feelings and hopes and worries. We'd really like to hear and understand everyone's ideas. (Turning to Alex): Alex, we usually ask people to tell us their preferred pronouns when we meet here. What are yours? I use she/her pronouns.*

T1:   *And I use he/him pronouns.*

Alex: *(Looking happier) I go by he/him, that's what all my friends use now.*

Dad: *But you're still a "she" at school.*

T1:   *Sorry to interrupt again. I tend to do that in sessions, but what are your pronouns? (turning to mum and dad)*

Dad: *Um I suppose the normal ones he and him. I suppose...*

Mum: *Err, she and her...*

        (Jane and Bill looking confused)

T1:   *Thank you. We like to ask everyone as we don't want to make any assumptions in here. We also know that sometimes these pronoun preferences may change over time, so please let us know if that happens. Right, Alex you were about to say something when I rudely interrupted – sorry about that again.*

Alex: *I'm a boy everywhere, that's who I really am, I simply haven't come out at school properly yet. (Jane and Bill exchange concerned glances)*

T1:   *Bill, Jane, Alex, sounds like we'll need your help to catch up, please bear with us, at this stage can we check if everybody's OK if we two use Alex's preferred pronouns here in this meeting?*

Mum: *It's up to you. I don't mind.*

T1:   *We would like to use Alex's preferred pronouns as a way of respecting Alex's wishes about the language that he feels most comfortable with, and if Alex feels comfortable, we are likely to have a more open and useful conversation, and understand Alex a bit more, that's where we're coming from. We certainly aren't here to tell you who Alex is, or what will happen in the future, this is for Alex to figure out, and (turning to Alex) figuring out our identity does take time.*

Mum: *That's fine, but just to make it clear, Alex isn't having any pills or medications to change her body.*

        (Alex looks exasperated)

T1:   *Hmm, it looks like you came here with big worries in mind, Jane. (Turning to Alex): Alex, I notice you look unhappy again, and I think I can now guess why, but can I take us a step back? When your mum said you were looking forward to this meeting, did she get it right?*

Alex: *Yeah, I was looking forward to it, as I really hope to get on T (testosterone) and start my transition.*

Dad: *We're never gonna give our permission for that.*

        (Alex getting tearful and addressing his Dad)

Alex: *You'll NEVER understand!*

        (Mum is welling up; Dad keeps his head down)

T2:   *Alex, so sorry to see you upset, and looking at your parents, they too look quite sad right now. Can you help us out, what do you think upset each of you?*

Alex: *I don't know, and don't care to be honest.*

T1:   *May I make an observation? When we feel hurt, it's difficult to be kind and interested in each other. Even when we do care. I may be wrong, but the sense I get sitting with you three today is that there's a lot of care and goodwill among you, and also a lot of upset feelings too…*

        (therapists looking at each other)

T2:   *I was thinking something similar; it sounds like there's a lot to think and talk about, about a lot of different hopes and worries too. (Turning back to the family). Shall we go around and agree that each of us shares their hopes and worries, just for this meeting? (Alex nodding). Can I go first? (family slightly surprised).*

Dad: Go on.

T2:   *I hope you will leave this meeting today feeling respected and knowing that we want to understand properly. I worry also that we might say something that makes somebody uncomfortable. If we misunderstand at any point, can you please let us know? Sometimes we may use a word or ask a question that will make you think: "they really didn't get it" or you might feel uncomfortable. Can you please tell us if that happens?*

 (Family nodding)

T1:   *Whilst we will do our best to try and understand, sometimes we may find ourselves being "clumsy rather than clever"* [referencing Burnham & Harris, 1996] *in how we say or phrase things or our questions. Sometimes we may need to have some challenging conversations, not because we don't believe you or because we know what's best for you, but exactly because we don't know and we really want to learn as much as possible about your experiences and how you and your family see things. So, hopes and worries, Alex, are you happy to go next?…*

The above extract illustrates the mentalizing pressures within the family system. Often, in similar situations, parents' mentalizing can get compromised by their concerns and worries, unless these can be explicitly verbalised, and understood, whereas Alex's transition plans and certainty about the future may limit his ability to mentalize not only his parents' intentions but also his own potential uncertainty or feelings of ambivalence.

Practitioners familiar with MBT-F (Asen & Fonagy, 2011; Keaveny, Midgley, Asen, Bevington, Fearon, et al., 2012) and/or systemic ways of working (Dallos & Vetere, 2009; Hedges, 2010; Maldonado- Page & Favier, 2018) will readily recognise some key procedures and processes that clinicians try to engage with right from the start: the use of curiosity, humour, the use of self to facilitate engagement and epistemic trust (Fonagy & Allison, 2014), and pausing interactions that are likely to lead to an escalation of conflict in the session. Mentalizing tends to suffer during heated arguments, or when the attachment system is activated (Bateman & Fonagy, 2004), and the clinicians are aiming at a calmer conversation, to enable mentalizing to come back on-line (Keaveny et al., 2012).

Furthermore, clinicians are consciously adopting a curious, not-knowing, non-expert stance, mentalizing the moment, and holding the balance between the adults and the adolescent, their different hopes and worries. Making the most of the benefit of having a co-worker, at the end of the extract, the clinicians introduce two slightly different but complementary ideas, leaning to different sides of the therapeutic boat, to prevent it from capsizing. They make explicit both their wish to respect and offer a safe space, but also the need to engage in some potentially challenging conversations. Readers with no gender-specific expertise will hopefully feel reassured that they can use their existing skills to initiate conversations with gender diverse young people; and paradoxically, the less knowledge one claims they have on the subject, the easier it is to hold a mentalizing stance.

Enhancing embodied mentalizing

Looking in the mirror before and after an operation can be a significant experience for transgender young people, which can become difficult if their fantasies and wishes before surgery are different from what they see in the mirror. Sometimes, in thinking about surgery, a transgender adolescent can often operate in pretend mode, disconnecting the experience of the body from how they feel inside. To reactivate mentalizing, it can be really helpful, if the therapist tries to explicitly mentalize bodily and/or sexual aspects concerning the transition.

The following extract is a conversation with Jacob, the 19-year-old transgender man we met at the beginning of this chapter.

J: *Everybody has a different reaction. So, I don't know how much scar tissue I will have. I will have to wait and see how my body will adjust.*

T: *Yes, you cannot know beforehand. But when I listen to you talking about this, I feel your emotions are far away. Am I right?*

J: *Yes, that is true. Thinking about scars gives me strong emotions, but I don't want to be emotional. Especially when scars are big. You can imagine someone has been in pain. There is a story behind it. But it can also be touching, something beautiful. That is also possible.*

T: *Would you dare for a moment to try and feel and think how it would be for yourself to have scars?*

J: *I think I will see them as beautiful. It has been such an enormous tribulation and it will remind me every day when I see these scars. I did challenge myself. It tells my story, my battle. Knowing the operation will be done this upcoming month, I feel so many different feelings. I know I have to accept them, but it is so hard. But I guess it will be different after my operation. Maybe I can find some peace. I don't know if I will ever find peace.*

T: *How does it make you feel now?*

J: *You know, I can always see pictures of everything, but with this I can't. It is the first time in my life I cannot see a picture. I simply cannot imagine how I will look like without my breasts. When I get a mirror after the operation, I can see how it is. I know I want this, but it also feels like a wild step. I let them change my body, but I don't know what will happen with me emotionally. Can I be satisfied? Will I feel more like the real me? I don't know...*

T: *Yes, I feel for you. It must be is so difficult for you!*

J: *Yes. I try to be realistic about it. It has a good side but also a difficult side. But it must be so liberating not to wear this constricting binder. I feel its pressure the whole day. I sometimes have difficulty breathing because of this thing.*

T: *So many different feelings. I hear a trembling in your voice?*

J: *Yes, you know while talking about this so explicitly I can, for the first time really feel my fear, and I know I want this, but I am so afraid as well…*

Conclusion

The above extract illustrates that taking a mentalizing stance that also keeps the body in mind helps to provide a safe context for sensitive conversations, which are neither experienced as overly affirmative and unquestioning nor threatening and interrogative. Exploring the complexity of feelings and keeping an open mind as to future outcomes depends largely on forming and maintaining an open therapeutic relationship, based on an empathic alliance and with a continuous effort to stay connected with the young person's felt experiences in the here and now (Rossouw, 2012).

Working with gender diverse young people and their families requires a commitment to exploring and understanding the young person's internal world and their experiences of their body, helping significant others understand the young person, and reflecting openly on one's own thoughts and feelings as a clinician. This way of working can by no means answer all complex questions but can allow the clinician to approach dilemmas openly with the young person and their family in a supportive, sensitive and meaningful way.

References

American Psychiatric Association. (2013). *Diagnostic and Statistical Manual of Mental Disorders (DSM-V)*. Washington, DC: American Psychiatric Pub.

Asen, E., & Fonagy, P. (2011). Mentalization-based therapeutic interventions for families. *Journal of Family Therapy, 34*, 347–370.

Asen, E., & Fonagy, P. (2017). Mentalizing family violence, Part 2: techniques and interventions. *Family Process, 56*(1), 22–44. 10.1111/famp.12276.

Bateman, A.W., & Fonagy, P. (2004). Mentalization-based treatment of BPD. *Journal of Personality Disorders, 18*, 36–51.

Bateman, A.W., & Fonagy, P. (2006). *Mentalization-based treatment for borderline personality disorder: A practical guide*. Oxford: Oxford University Press.

Burnham, J., & Harris, O. (1996). Emerging ethnicity: A tale of three cultures, *Meeting the Needs of Ethnic Minority Children: A Handbook for Professionals*. London: Jessica Kingsley.

Burnham, J. (2006). Internalized other interviewing: Evaluating and enhancing empathy. *Clinical Psychology Forum, 140*, 16–20.

Churcher Clarke, A., & Spiliadis, A. (2019). 'Taking the lid off the box': The value of extended clinical assessment for adolescents presenting with gender identity difficulties. *Clinical Child Psychology and Psychiatry, 24*, 338–352.

Dallos, R., & Vetere, A. (2009). *Systemic Therapy and Attachment Narratives: Applications in a Range of Clinical Settings*. London, England: Routledge.

Di Ceglie, D. (2018). The use of metaphors in understanding atypical gender identity development and its psychosocial impact. *Journal of Child Psychotherapy, 44*(1), 5–28.

Fonagy, P., & Allison, E. (2014). The role of mentalizing and epistemic trust in the therapeutic relationship. *Psychotherapy, 51*, 372–380. 10.1037/a0036505.

Fonagy, P., & Luyten, P. (2009). A developmental, mentalization-based approach to the understanding and treatment of borderline personality disorder. *Development and Psychopathology, 21*, 1355–1381.

Hedges, F. (2010). *Reflexivity in Therapeutic Practice*. Basingstoke: Palgrave Macmillan.

Keaveny, E., Midgley, N., Asen, E., Bevington, D., Fearon, P., Fonagy, P., Jennings-Hobbs, R., & Wood, S. (2012). Minding the family mind: The development and initial evaluation of mentalization-based treatment for families. In N. Midgley & I. Vrouva (Eds.), *Minding the Child: Mentalization-Based Interventions with Children, Young People and Their Families* (pp. 98–112). London: Routledge.

Lemma, A. (2018). Transitory identities: some psychoanalytic reflections on transgender identities. *The International Journal of Psychoanalysis, 99*(5), 1089–1106. 10.1080/00207578.2018.1489710.

Luyten, P., van Houdenhove, B., Lemma, A., Target, M., & Fonagy, P. (2012). A mentalization-based approach to the understanding and treatment of functional somatic disorders. *Psychoanalytic Psychotherapy, 26*(2), 121–140.

Maldonado- Page, J., & Favier, S. (2018). An invitation to explore: A brief overview of the Tavistock and Portman Gender Identity Development Service. *Context: The Magazine for Family Therapy and Systemic Practice in the UK, 155*, 18–22.

Marchetti, A., Massaro, D., & Di Dio, C. (2017). The bodies "at the Forefront": Mentalization, memory, and construction of the self during adolescence. *Frontiers in Psychology, 8*, Article ID 1502.

Marcus, L., Marcus, K., Yaxte, S.M., & Marcus, K. (2015). Genderqueer: One family's experience with gender variance. *Psychoanalytic Inquiry, 35*(8), 795–808.

Memorandum of understanding on Conversion Therapy in the UK (version 2). (2017, October). retrieved from: http://www.pinktherapy.com/portals/0/Mou2_final.pdf

Perls, F., Hefferline, R., & Goodman, P. (1951). *Gestalt Therapy: Excitement and Growth in the Human Personality*. New York: Dell.

Rossouw, T. (2012). Self-harm in young people. Is MBT the answer? In N. Midgley & I. Vrouva (Eds.), *Minding the Child: Mentalization-Based Interventions with Children, Young People and Their Families* (pp. 131–144). London: Routledge.

Silverman, S. (2015). The colonized mind: Gender, trauma, and mentalization. *Psychoanalytic Dialogues, 25*(1), 51–66. 10.1080/10481885.2015.991246.

Waddell, M. (2005). *Understanding 12–14 Year Olds*. London: Jessica Kingsley.

Wren, B. (2019). Ethical issues arising in the provision of medical interventions for gender diverse children and adolescents. *Clinical Child Psychology and Psychiatry, 24*(2), 203–222.

Chapter 9

Conduct disorder – working with externalising behavioural problems in teens and their families

Svenja Taubner and Sophie Hauschild

Externalising disorders are among the most common behavioural problems in children and adolescents (e.g., Frick & Kimonis, 2005). Concerning teenage offenders, conduct disorder (CD) is amongst the most prevalent (Burke, Mulvey, & Schubert, 2015) with a high risk of chronification and the development of Antisocial Personality Disorder (ASPD; Ridenour, Cottler, Robins, Compton, Spitznagel, & Cunningham-Williams, 2002). In this chapter, we present a newly developed mentalization-based treatment for CD in adolescence (MBT-CD), which is currently being tested in a feasibility study.

Conduct disorder

The essential feature of CD is a repetitive pattern of behaviour that violates fundamental rights or major age-appropriate societal norms or rules (American Psychiatric Association, 2013): Patients need to meet three of 15 criteria in the domains of aggression against humans and animals, destruction of property, deceitfulness or theft, and serious violations of rules. Prevalence rates vary between 2–9% (Costello, Mustillo, Erkanli, Keeler, & Angold, 2003; Wagner, et al., 2017). High comorbidities are frequent, especially with Attention-Deficit-Hyperactivity-Disorder (Sigfusdottir et al., 2017), but also with, e.g., posttraumatic stress disorder (Allwood, Dyl, Hunt, & Spirito, 2008). CD is a risk factor for the development of ASPD (Ridenour et al., 2002) and may lead to anxiety disorders, depression, drug abuse and bipolar disorders (Kim-Cohen et al., 2003). In sum, the high risk of developing a chronic mental illness following CD shows the need to establish an early diagnosis and effective treatments to externalising problems to prevent severe adult psychopathology.

Mentalizing and conduct disorder

From the developmental psychopathology and psychoanalytic point of view, any psychopathology is regarded as an adaptation to mainly attachment-related problems. However, later in life, functional "solutions" may not fit well with the demands of current situations and may cause suffering for both the individual and others around him or her. About 70% of children show forms of aggressive behaviour with a peak in aggressiveness at the age of two years (Tremblay, Hartup, & Archer, 2005). This is followed by a steady decline in aggressiveness in the majority of children, which leads to the hypothesis that children do not learn to be aggressive, but instead, most children unlearn aggression in the service of an evolutionary helpful optimal adaptation to the cultural context (Fonagy, 2008).

Fonagy, Gergely, Jurist, and Target (2002) have proposed a model in conceptualising inhibited mentalizing as an adaptation to cruelty in attachment relationships. Inhibition of mentalizing serves as protection because children no longer need to think about a perpetrator's frankly malevolent motives when they are simultaneously vulnerable to and existentially dependent on the same individual. If others' actions are not mentalized, however, the understanding becomes "concrete"; that is, it is restricted to an understanding in terms of physical or observable reality: The social environment is no longer interpreted from the "intentional stance," but from a "physical stance" (Dennett, 1987). In this case, an angry voice can be perceived as being only loud, and a threatening gesticulation is seen only as a raised arm (Hill, Fonagy, Lancaster, & Broyden, 2007).

There is accumulating evidence of substantial mentalizing problems in young people and adults with a combination of histories of maltreatment and severe interpersonal aggression (e.g., Chiesa & Fonagy, 2014). Antisocial behaviour has been consistently shown to be associated with deficits in mentalizing (Newbury-Helps, Feigenbaum, & Fonagy, 2017), especially in violent subgroups (e.g., McGauley, Ferris, Marin-Avellan, & Fonagy, 2013). Similar patterns were found for adolescents (Cropp, Taubner, Salzer, & Streeck-Fischer, 2019; Möller, Falkenström, Holmqvist Larsson, & Holmqvist, 2014; Taubner & Curth, 2013; Taubner, Wiswede, Nolte, & Roth, 2010). Mentalizing also was found to possibly buffer psychopathic traits (Taubner, White, Zimmermann, Fonagy, & Nolte, 2013) and to be an important protective factor against violent behaviour in adolescence (Taubner, Zimmermann, Ramberg, & Schröder, 2016).

Mentalization-based treatment for conduct disorder (MBT-CD)

MBT-CD is based on key principles of MBT for Adolescents as well as ideas from the treatment of patients with ASPD. The current programme of MBT-CD lasts six to 12 months and consists of a psychoeducational workshop, 30 individual sessions, and ten family sessions. Importantly, MBT-CD is adjusted to the little motivation and help-seeking when starting therapy and thus starts with an engagement programme.

Problematic externalising behaviour is regarded as a result of ineffective mentalizing and a failure to "unlearn aggression". This core idea is formulated in joint therapy goals and an early treatment focus. At the beginning of therapy, patients and their families go to a psychoeducational workshop, which offers information about core concepts of MBT-CD as, e.g., adolescence, mentalizing and emotions. Individual sessions start with a thorough assessment of mentalizing capacities by developing a mentalizing profile; family sessions start with assessing different perspectives of every family member on "the problem" and developing a shared crisis plan. Individually with the adolescent, motivational interviewing (Rollnick & Miller, 1995) is provided to assess the pros and cons to the most problematic behaviour that sets the ground to formulate therapy goals. If necessary, skills are provided to support affect regulation and stabilise disruptive behaviour. Additionally, an emotion escalation sheet is worked out to explore under which circumstances emotions get uncontrolled and to re-establish responsibility for behaviour. Furthermore, the therapist explores additional social risk factors that may undermine treatment and address them actively (e.g., substance abuse). The initial phase ends with an individualised case formulation that summarises and contextualises how the problem behaviour is related to ineffective mentalizing and outlines expected treatment outcomes. This case formulation constitutes the focus of treatment.

After the initial more structured phase, the therapist follows the individual process, intending to engage the patient and family in mentalizing and breaking coercive "loops" of non-mentalizing between family members faced with seemingly uncontrollable and non-understandable behaviour. The therapist uses the classic not-knowing stance and intervention techniques such as empathic validation or the mentalizing loop. Family sessions follow the format of MBT-Family (Asen & Fonagy, 2012). After the end of therapy, three booster sessions are arranged to stabilise therapeutic success (Figure 9.1).

Stance in MBT-CD

Modifications of the core MBT model have an impact on the therapeutic stance with regard to the low motivation, hidden antisocial behaviour, low trust, and special characteristics of the switch-point in this population, e.g., collapse of mentalizing capacity when experiencing shame. In general, it is advised to treat adolescents with CD individually and not in groups because they are in danger of learning from their deviant peers more than from their therapists. Adolescents and their families do not necessarily have high motivation to start therapy and need special engagement from the therapist and sometimes external motivation from other services (school, juvenile justice). The majority of adolescents with CD have developed deactivating strategies to cope with attachment needs and thus, offering treatment presents a threefold problem. First, it is perceived as standing against their wish for maturation and autonomy; second, they prefer not to be in close relationships; and third, they fear a loss of "street credibility". One way to motivate these adolescents is to regard problems as a task for the whole family, to be

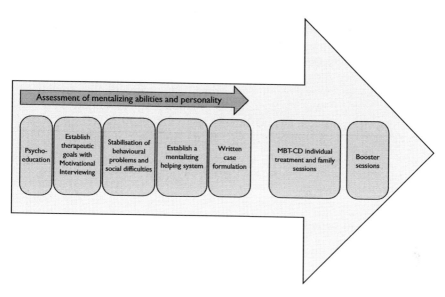

Figure 9.1 The process of MBT-CD.

very interested in their personal view and to side with their experience actively. However, adolescents with CD might not open up in therapy, appear not interested, deny problems and have problems to express themselves in words. This might lead to impatience in the therapist and possibly patronising behaviour if the patient is provokingly uninterested in the emotional consequences of offending behaviour or acts in an anxiety-provoking way towards the therapist (e.g., by bringing a knife to therapy). This can lead to a vicious circle of unempathic or rejecting feelings in the therapist as well as shaming behaviour with a high risk of drop-out. Therefore, for the therapist, keeping a mentalizing non-judgmental stance and being aware of his or her own switch point is crucial for successful treatment. Due to a high risk of acting out outside of the therapy sessions, close collaboration with other services and the family is needed. This more systemic thinking has the advantage of an integrative view of the patient, keeping a close eye on the crisis plan and can also help to establish a mentalizing helping system (Bevington, Fuggle, & Fonagy, 2015). It is recommended to engage with something the adolescent is passionate about, including playful elements and creative ways to establish joint attention (e.g., drawing). Such ways of engagement can help re-establish curiosity for mental states outside the core problem behaviour. Moreover, it enables the therapist to stay carefully attuned to the affect focus and the therapeutic relationship. Furthermore, anxiety levels in adolescents and their families are sometimes higher than therapists expect and patients show. Therefore, it is essential to keep in mind the technique of empathic validation. However, empathic validation needs to be used cautiously by not expressing too much compassion or pity for the adolescent, especially concerning their own potentially traumatic experiences (e.g., maltreatment). This avoids making the patient feel helpless or "like a victim" which is sometimes experienced as aversive. Furthermore, affect identification should take into account that some basic emotions like anxiety are sometimes not tolerated by the adolescent and a first step to deal with these forms of "uncomfortable feelings" might be to find expressions, e.g., "tense" or "worried", which tap into the quality of experience more than naming it as anxiety. This is well in-line with the not-knowing stance to explore the quality of experienced feelings together, without the therapist imposing their own words for emotions.

Case vignette – Susan

With the following case vignette, we aim to give insight into the specific challenges in using MBT with this group of patients. Susan, 16 years old, had repeatedly committed violent crimes during a period of several months before she first came into therapy. At this point, more than 15 criminal complaints had been filed against her. Starting therapy saved her temporarily from being sentenced to do time in a women's prison. Instead, she was on probation, and the court ordered continuing therapy. In Susan's eyes, her violence was always justified. She saw herself as the protector of the people important to her. When someone insulted or threatened a family member or core member of her peer group, she would respond with violence to "teach" them to show respect. Susan quit school several months before starting therapy.

Susan had a little sister with similar problems, who was vital to her and who was one of the persons, Susan was most eager to defend against any attacks. Their parents appeared attached and loving. However, they also expressed severe difficulties to set boundaries and appeared anxious about the siblings' oppositional behaviour and violence. As a consequence, they treated Susan like a little child who did not know what she was doing and could not be considered fully responsible for her actions. The therapist assumed that this was a constant devaluation of Susan, kept her from taking responsibility for her life and fuelled her self-hatred at the same time. A repeated conflict arose around getting up for school or community service (a court requirement for both siblings) when Susan successfully opposed to getting up and regularly missed her appointments. This was also true for the first five therapy appointments that were all cancelled with somatic complaints as justifications for not showing. When she finally arrived in treatment, the therapist met a friendly, shy girl dressed like a boy. She connected with the therapist and was happy to report about her talents (e.g., basketball,) and plans for the future (working with disabled children!) but remained distrustful and very oppositional about her duties. She expressed the wish not to end up in prison and to stop physical violence.

Half of her gang was already imprisoned, and the therapist regarded her at high risk.

MBT-CD interventions

Contrary moves and foci of intervention

The therapist developed Susan's Mentalizing profile (Fig. 9.2) to understand her mentalizing difficulties better and accordingly set session foci for contrary moves to resolve rigid patterns and activate aspects of effective mentalizing.

Susan's capacity for mentalizing the Self can be described as low: She had no words for her internal world other than quite general statements as, e.g., just wanting to relax. She could barely connect her actions with her thoughts or feelings except for her general feeling of being treated unjustly and the intention of protecting people close to her. Possibly consequentially, Susan did not experience herself as an active agent in her own life. Focusing on others, her mentalizing capacity can be described as medium. She was somewhat more concerned with other people's inner worlds, e.g., caring for her father, who was not able to withstand quarrels in the family without having severe headaches. However, she often misattributed hostile intentions to others, e.g., she assumed her mother wanted "to annoy her" when her mother pushed her to do something.

Her mentalizing was quite focused on cognitive (medium) instead of affective (low) aspects: She could imagine different perspectives to some extent; however, an empathic "feeling with" or feeling what others feel, i.e. affective mentalizing, was severely impaired. Furthermore, she could not name emotions and did not know the meaning of many emotions or affective states, such as defiance.

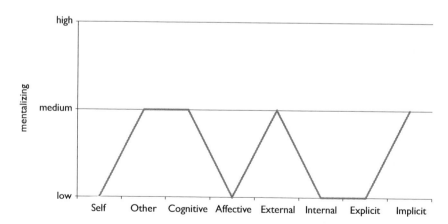

Figure 9.2 Susan's mentalizing profile.

Consequently, whenever the therapist introduced a name for an affect, she double-checked if Susan would understand the meaning of the word.

Susan screened her world for visible "signals" and evidence (external: medium), giving her too clear a view into other people's mental states, while she barely seemed to consider not visible thoughts, feelings or intentions of others (internal: low). When asked about others' states of mind, her general answer was: "How should I know?!".

Susan was mostly in a state of implicit mentalizing (medium), which is characterised by quick and reflexive assumptions leading to automatically associated (re)actions: She assumed an attack whenever someone said or did anything that could be interpreted negatively to her family or friends, and then – almost like a reflex reaction – would physically attack them. Her explicit mentalizing was low, as the conscious and slow processing of mental states was barely possible at the beginning of therapy. See Figure 9.2

Given this profile, the therapist decided to focus on self, affective, internal and explicit mentalizing during the sessions.

Supporting agency instead of controlling behaviour

Susan only had two ways of dealing with conflicts: oppositional avoidance and physical violence outside. While she knew that the judicial complaints against her were consequences of her violent conflict resolution strategy, she felt she was right, as she only ever attacked people who were mean to others, and never "without reason". Thus, in her automatic mentalizing, she was unable to question her mental states or to take new perspectives. While having the conviction of total control, the therapist could watch her having problems to control her anger. At the beginning of therapy, the therapist felt several times threatened that Susan would get up and hit her when being mad about the therapist's comments, but instead, Susan related to her therapist in an avoidant way, which was also difficult to deal with. The parents were pushing the therapist also to try to convince Susan to fulfil commitments outside therapy (visit school) or to write reports that she was unable to do community hours because of her mental problems. The therapist feared to have enmeshed conversation with Susan about her not fulfilling her duties (like at home). She also felt helpless (like the parents) about Susan's total opposition to any duty, including getting up in the morning. Thus, there was a typical high risk of having non-therapeutic patronising interactions. Thus, the therapist decided to focus on joint attention issues like motivational interviewing and talking about non-conflictual topics like romantic love and basketball to first establish curiosity in mental states. It is an important aspect of the stance in MBT-CD that the therapist refrains from controlling behaviour or feeling responsible for the patient's actions and instead tries to support agency and actively sides with the patient's mental world.

Motivational interviewing on "using violence"

The first Motivational Interviewing (Rollnick & Miller, 1995) dealt with the pros and cons of using violence as a conflict resolution method. Motivational Interviewing is a humanistic technique that focuses on the exploration of motives to sustain or change a specific behaviour in a non-judgmental and validating manner, which fits well with the MBT stance. First, the therapist asked Susan, on a scale of 1 to 10, how important it was for her to change her behaviour, i.e. to stop using violence as conflict resolution. She answered that her motivation to stop violence was five, which came as a surprise to the therapist, and she praised the answer accordingly as very positive. Secondly, the therapist asked how confident she felt that she could change her behaviour. Susan felt somewhat insecure about whether she could manage and gave a two on this scale. Here the therapist suggested exploring the difference between the wish to change and the subjective inability to do so in more detail. It turned out that her behaviour was mostly quite controlled, but she had anger issues. She was capable of deciding to use violence or not, and thus, the focus was mentalizing motives to use violence. The interview (see Table 9.1) revealed that to Susan, using violence was a very effective way (100%) to reinstall respect in others who insulted people close to her. While talking would not help, she argued, people would stop insulting her friends and family when she physically attacked them and importantly, would not do it again. The cons of violence, e.g., prison and her parents' disapproval, seemed to hardly affect her emotionally. In her version of events, she first started to act violently when her sister was on crutches, and a boy physically attacked her at school. Both girls seemed to have no trust in relying on teachers for their physical and mental safety, and thus Susan hit the boy and learnt an effective way of protecting her sister and herself. From her point of view, her violence was altruistic and defensive only. The therapist got the impression that she felt like Robin Hood, defender and protector of the weak in a world full of hatred and hurting. See table 9.1

Case formulation

In their 7th Session, the therapist gave Susan a Case Formulation in the form of a letter. The formulation summarises the therapists' understanding of Susan concerning the link between her symptoms and mentalizing. It serves to engage the patient in a discussion about possible treatment foci, with the aim of therapist and patient reaching an agreement regarding what they want to work on in the subsequent sessions. Susan did not want to read the formulation in front of the therapist and complained that the letter was too long. She then read only the first and the last paragraph but seemed to like it and promised to read it all later. The therapist introduced the letter by saying that it contains what she had understood so far but that she is also quite unsure about

Table 9.1 Motivational interviewing with Susan on using violence as conflict resolution strategy

	Pros	Cons
Using Violence	• Gaining the victim's respect • Lack of respect is countered immediately • No feeling of guilt, always justified! • It's controlled, not an emotional reaction • 100% effective • Easy, I am good at it • Important that family and friends believe me; police and the justice system do not matter	• Low reach (you cannot kill everybody) • It's automatic (like a Boxing-Automat), no decisions possible • Criminal complaints, prison • Parents don't approve • Parents suffer because of it • Does not change what others think • Risk of getting beaten up
Not using violence	• No criminal complaints • No prison	• People could continue not showing respect • Talking is ineffective • Threatening is also ineffective • Being weak

many things and tried to address some open questions in the following session. For the first time in weeks, Susan finally got very engaged and reported about recent events and how difficult feelings kept her from falling into sleep.

Dear Susan, for a few weeks now, you and your family come to see me. In the beginning, you said that you would like to change and be less involved in fights. Later, you added that you also didn't want to go to prison. At the moment, your desire for change seems to have become weaker; you sometimes seem annoyed and just want to get some rest. You told me that your family and friends are very important to you. However, it sometimes sounds like your parents are really worried about you having to go to a closed institution. I wonder how confident you feel about choosing another path, or whether you have already given up inside and therefore so often put up resistance. I believe that (fortunately) it all still lies in your own hands. Also, from my point of view, your life is not ruined, like you once said. I was very moved that you think like that.

Both in everyday life and in therapy, you sometimes show a rather rough, disinterested and tough side. Perhaps you worry that other (vulnerable) sides of you would be exploited by others to your disadvantage. What can we do to make you develop more trust in therapy? Please always tell me if something bothers you. Maybe I didn't understand you well, and so you also started to withdraw in therapy? I can only guess that you might be afraid of new situations, maybe you feel sad sometimes and then you might not find sleep? I would like us to be able to talk about this so that I can support you better in coping with these "weak" feelings.

From your point of view, the trigger for your violent actions is that you want to protect your family and friends. I can well imagine that it was difficult for you at school, and I am sorry that you were not sufficiently protected in various situations. Today, however, I sometimes have the feeling that you overinterpret the "danger" from others and then feel too certain about being right. Others may feel offended that you do not question your actions much and that you don't apologise or regret anything. At the same time, you have a very strong sense of justice and are very angry when others do not follow the rules (e.g., your parents). I guess you sometimes find it hard to apply the same standards to yourself and others. For example, you want to be treated like an adult, but you don't keep a lot of agreements or duties. Then it might be easier to stop thinking about things and retreat instead. I'd like to understand better why you're currently in withdrawal and don't dare to walk new paths (e.g., going back to school). It seems to me as if you don't know where you want to go at the moment and then you are simply defiant against what others want from you. I imagine this to be very exhausting in the long run.

I am happy that the appointments are working so well and that we are in good contact now and again. You are a great girl, an amazing sister and a talented basketball player! I would like to support you in finding out where you want to go and in finding a good way to deal with both "strong" and "weak" feelings.

The following session summary illustrates how the mentalizing loop is used to explore the focus behaviour in MBT-CD. Susan told the therapist she was banned from the drug store in her hometown. This was the last store she had still been allowed to enter. Her sister had been smoking pot in front of the store. The store manager told her sister to stop and then called the police. Susan reported this quickly, and ended with "So we were banned, but **I** didn't do anything". The therapist slowed down the process by bringing herself back into their present interaction ("This is way too fast for me") and engaged Susan in the process of micro-slicing the interaction with the police and the store manager using the technique "stop, rewind and explore". In doing this, Susan explored that her "doing nothing" meant that she wasn't smoking pot like her sister, however, when the store manager stepped up "too close" to her sister and told her to stop, Susan told him to take a step back, which he did. The therapist used the "Stop and stand" technique at this moment to stress that this was a rare occasion that Susan was actually successful with words instead of actions. Contrary to other sessions, Susan became very precise in describing the process of deciding if she should hit the manager or not. Here, the therapist engaged her in exploring feelings and thoughts during the scene. At first, she was in rage ("I saw red") but then she checked with her friend who shook his head and with her sister who also signalled to retreat. She herself also came to a conclusion to rather talk than hit because she thought about her probation. The therapist praised these ways of engaging in reflection even though her emotions had been strong. This might have been an effect of therapy: enabling her to use a mentalizing buffer between feelings, thoughts and actions. It turned out that the manager had brought one of her peers to prison by informing the police about his theft. Susan held a huge grudge about this. The manager tried to ban all teenagers from the shop, but Susan was able to restrict the banning to herself and her sister. The therapist stressed again that she had successfully changed something by her words only. Susan smiled but regarded this as an exception and claimed that usually, words do not solve problems. However, she felt a bit proud. By exploring and micro-slicing such events, eventually mentalizing can be established in situations where no mentalizing was possible before, which may lead to a new perspective. Furthermore, agency and responsibility for her actions are reinforced.

Family sessions

Family sessions are an essential part of MBT-CD because there is a need to establish a mentalizing communication within the family to open a virtuous cycle of social learning outside of therapy. In the first family session, Susan (S) and her mother (M) and father (F) talked about difficulties at home which arose in the morning, when Susan's mom tried to wake Susan's younger sister Chiara. Chiara did not want to get up for her community service. Susan, always protecting her sister, just reported that at 7 am her sister started screaming because her mother was trying to wake her, and Susan started defending her sister. During the family session, the mother was getting quite agitated when talking about how this scene. At the same time, Susan became more and more absolute in her statements. The therapist (Th) used the technique "Mentalize the moment" to explore the internal states of the mother and Susan at that moment and initiated the "noticing and naming" of this typical, non-mentalizing family interaction. She introduced the metaphor of a lion attack to describe Susan's switch point and reflex reactions. Importantly, the therapist kept displaying curiosity in the face of Susan's and her mother's psychic equivalence as well as normalizing Susan's defensive reaction given the fact that her automatic interpretation of the situation was a life-threatening one. The following transcript illustrates the session process.

M: It's also about the fact that Chiara has to do it on her own, but Susan always protects her, and tells me "Let her sleep, she got to bed late! She can do community service tomorrow."

S: Yeah, but it's not just about protecting her, I also want my rest and silence in the morning.

Th: Stop, stop, stop... And what is going on within you (to mother) in that moment? When that happens, and two girls are against you?

M: Well, I try to explain to Susan, that this isn't going to work...

Th: Ah OK, so you manage to do that... And what is going on inside of you (to mother)?

M: I feel rage.

Th: Ah rage, OK... because I just thought...

M: Helpless as well.

Th: Yes, that's what I thought just now, it could also make one feel quite helpless.

M: Yes, helpless. And then I'm thinking, Susan knows it better; she knows that her sister needs to do the community service, otherwise she is going to jail, and I just want her sister to not go to prison, and yet, Susan is so unreasonable and supports her sister's behaviour. [...]

Th: OK. And you (to Susan), what is going on inside of you in that moment? Do you realise what is going on in your mother then?

S: Yeah. But inside of me – I just want to sleep.

Th: Oh my.

S: That's why I say these things. But I also always say to my sister when she's awake, "if you don't do your community service, you're going to jail".

Th: So you're on your mother's side.

S: Yes. I always say that.

M: Well, yes, but I think what you're saying right now isn't quite the truth, Susan. Because in these moments you're awake. You don't say these things to get your rest but to protect your sister. You see her being tired and angry and not feeling well and then you defend her against your better judgment. To the bone.

Th: Mh. I think you (to Susan) have an unfavourable role in this. You're not helping anyone, not yourself, or your sister or your mother.

M: That's also why she keeps getting into bad situations, and how she got all of the complaint filed against her: because she protects her sister.

S: Well, yeah, but we can discuss this a thousand times. I told you in the loony bin, I am telling you now, and I will tell you this whenever, wherever: This is how I am. That's it. Nobody's going to change that. (very angry)

F: But you know, that you don't need to protect her...

S: I don't give a shit.

Th: But that's why I am curious what is going on inside of you in that moment, because I think "just wanting to sleep" doesn't quite capture it. (not-knowing stance)

S: She's my sister. That's it.

Th: Mh... But I think what might be going inside of you is you interpreting the situation a certain way. And I don't know if you can think clearly in this moment. (addressing non–mentalizing)

S: No idea.

Th: Maybe it is like a reflex? Because now you're saying, she needs to do her community service.

S: Well yeah, she has to.

Th: But at this moment, when you defend her, this thought is gone...?

S: Yes, because she also has to sleep.

M: Protector at any cost.

Th: Yeah... It sounds like as if in that moment, you're really convinced that your sister is in danger. As if you needed to save her life or something?

S: What? In danger because of my mother? Of course not, she's my mother, I don't need to be afraid of her...

Th: OK. I mean, to me it sounds a little bit like it, when you're saying these things, kind of dramatically...

M: Well yes, for me, this is what it feels like...

Th: As if your mother was a lion about to eat your sister and you're there to protect her from that

S: I don't know, maybe it is like that. No idea.

Th: Yes, but then I get why you are saying these things in such an absolute way, everybody would react like that: when there is a lion around, you need to act fast, otherwise you're lost. But of course, you're also telling me now, that there is no lion, just your mother. (validating and normalising).

Feasibility trial and first conclusions

Currently, we are investigating and refining the MBT-CD treatment programme in a feasibility study. Herein, we study the acceptance of MBT-CD by adolescents and families considering the reach of potential participants, their willingness to participate, drop-out rates and drop-out reasons. Based on ongoing reviews considering, e.g., the families' drop-out reasons, we continuously adapted the treatment programme (e.g., by reducing the psychoeducational sessions from six single sessions to a two two-hour-workshop). Also, we hope that this trial will offer new insights into the association between mentalizing improvements and symptom reduction with MBT-CD. The other important focus is building collaborations with agencies such as schools, youth services and psychiatric or psychotherapeutic clinics, which so far proved to be a major factor in enabling dissemination. So far, the mentalizing stance seems fruitful in work with these highly impaired and distrustful adolescents to re-establish trust and curiosity in mental states and by this change antisocial cognitions and behaviour.

References

Allwood, M.A., Dyl, J., Hunt, J.I., & Spirito, A. (2008). Comorbidity and service utilization among psychiatrically hospitalized adolescents with posttraumatic stress disorder. *Journal of Psychological Trauma*, 7(2), 104–121. https://doi.org/10.1080/19322880802231791.

American Psychiatric Association. (2013). *The Diagnostic and Statistical Manual of Mental Disorders: DSM 5*. Arlington, VA: American Psychiatric Publishing.

Asen, E., & Fonagy, P. (2012). Mentalization-based family therapy. In A.W. Bateman & P. Fonagy (Eds.), *Handbook of Mentalizing in Mental Health Practice* (1st ed., pp. 107–128). Washington, DC: American Psychiatric Publ.

Bevington, D., Fuggle, P., & Fonagy, P. (2015). Applying attachment theory to effective practice with hard-to-reach youth: The AMBIT approach. *Attachment and Human Development*, 17(2), 157–174. https://doi.org/10.1080/14616734.2015.1006385.

Burke, J.D., Mulvey, E.P., & Schubert, C.A. (2015). Prevalence of mental health problems and service use among first-time juvenile offenders. *Journal of Child and Family Studies*, 24(12), 3774–3781.

Chiesa, M., & Fonagy, P. (2014). Reflective function as a mediator between childhood adversity, personality disorder and symptom distress. *Personal Mental Health (Personality and Mental Health)*, 8(1), 52–66. https://doi.org/10.1002/pmh.1245.

Costello, E.J., Mustillo, S., Erkanli, A., Keeler, G., & Angold, A. (2003). Prevalence and development of psychiatric disorders in childhood and adolescence. *Archives of General Psychiatry*, 60(8), 837–844. https://doi.org/10.1001/archpsyc.60.8.837.

Cropp, C., Taubner, S., Salzer, S., & Streeck-Fischer, A. (2019). Psychodynamic psychotherapy with severely disturbed adolescents: Changes in reflective functioning. *Journal of Infant, Child, and Adolescent Psychotherapy*, 18(3), 263–273. https://doi.org/10.1080/15289168.2019.1643212.

Dennett, D.C. (1987). *The Intentional Stance*. Cambridge, MA: MIT Press.

Fonagy, P. (2008). Persönlichkeitsstörung und Gewalt. Ein psychoanalytisch-bindungstheoretischer Ansatz. In F. Lackinger & W. Berner (Eds.), *Psychodynamische Psychotherapie bei Delinquenz: Praxis der übertragungsfokussierten Psychotherapie* (pp. 326–365). Stuttgart: Schattauer.

Fonagy, P., Gergely, G., Jurist, E.L., & Target, M. (2002). *Affect Regulation, Mentalization, and the Development of the Self*. New York: Other Press.

Frick, P.J., & Kimonis, E.R. (2005). Externalizing disorders of childhood and adolescence. In J.E. Maddux & B.A. Winstead (Eds.), *Psychopathology: Foundations for a Contemporary Understanding* (pp. 325–351). Lawrence Erlbaum Associates Publishers.

Hill, J., Fonagy, P., Lancaster, G., & Broyden, N. (2007). Aggression and intentionality in narrative responses to conflict and distress story stems. An investigation of boys with disruptive behaviour problems. *Attachment and Human Development*, 9(3), 223–237. https://doi.org/10.1080/14616730701453861.

Kim-Cohen, J., Caspi, A., Moffitt, T.E., Harrington, H., Milne, B.J., & Poulton, R. (2003). Prior juvenile diagnoses in adults with mental disorder: Developmental follow-back of a prospective-longitudinal cohort. *Archives of General Psychiatry*, 60(7), 709–717. https://doi.org/10.1001/archpsyc.60.7.709.

McGauley, G., Ferris, S., Marin-Avellan, L., & Fonagy, P. (2013). The Index Offence Representation Scales; a predictive clinical tool in the management of dangerous, violent patients with personality disorder? *Criminal Behaviour and Mental Health: CBMH*, 23(4), 274–289. https://doi.org/10.1002/cbm.1889.

Möller, C., Falkenström, F., Holmqvist Larsson, M., & Holmqvist, R. (2014). Mentalizing in young offenders. *Psychoanalytic Psychology*, *31*(1), 84–99. https://doi.org/10.1037/a0035555.

Newbury-Helps, J., Feigenbaum, J., & Fonagy, P. (2017). Offenders with antisocial personality disorder display more impairments in mentalizing. *Journal of Personality Disorders*, *31*(2), 232–255. https://doi.org/10.1521/pedi_2016_30_246.

Ridenour, T.A., Cottler, L.B., Robins, L.N., Compton, W.M., Spitznagel, E.L., & Cunningham-Williams, R.M. (2002). Test of the plausibility of adolescent substance use playing a causal role in developing adulthood antisocial behavior. *Journal of Abnormal Psychology*, *111*(1), 144–155.

Rollnick, S., & Miller, W.R. (1995). What is motivational interviewing? *Behavioural and cognitive Psychotherapy*, *23*(4), 325–334.

Sigfusdottir, I.D., Asgeirsdottir, B.B., Hall, H.A., Sigurdsson, J.F., Young, S., & Gudjonsson, G.H. (2017). An epidemiological study of ADHD and conduct disorder: Does family conflict moderate the association? *Social Psychiatry and Psychiatric Epidemiology*, *52*(4), 457–464. https://doi.org/10.1007/s00127-017-1352-6.

Taubner, S., Wiswede, D., Nolte, T., & Roth, G. (2010). Mentalisierung und externalisierende Verhaltensstörungen in der Adoleszenz. *Psychotherapeut*, *55*(4), 312–320.

Taubner, S., Zimmermann, L., Ramberg, A., & Schröder, P. (2016). Mentalization mediates the relationship between early maltreatment and potential for violence in adolescence. *Psychopathology*, *49*(4), 236–246. https://doi.org/10.1159/000448053.

Taubner, S., & Curth, C. (2013). Mentalization mediates the relation between early traumatic experiences and aggressive behavior in adolescence. *Psihologija*, *46*(2), 177–192. https://doi.org/10.2298/PSI1302177T.

Taubner, S., White, L.O., Zimmermann, J., Fonagy, P., & Nolte, T. (2013). Attachment-related mentalization moderates the relationship between psychopathic traits and proactive aggression in adolescence. *Journal of Abnormal Child Psychology*, *41*(6), 929–938. https://doi.org/10.1007/s10802-013-9736-x.

Tremblay, R., Hartup, W., & Archer, J. (Eds.). (2005). *Developmental Origins of Aggression*. Guilford Press.

Wagner, G., Zeiler, M., Waldherr, K., Philipp, J., Truttmann, S., Dür, W., & Karwautz, A.F.K. (2017). Mental health problems in Austrian adolescents: a nationwide, two-stage epidemiological study applying DSM-5 criteria. *European Child and Adolescent Psychiatry*. Advance online publication, https://doi.org/10.1007/s00787-017-0999-6.

Chapter 10

Working with at-risk mental states in adolescence

Mark Dangerfield

Andrew walked into my office at the Day Hospital with a threatening and defiant attitude. He had spiky hair and wore a sleeveless T-shirt that showed off his physical strength in the form of thickly muscled arms. He looked at me and asked if we had teachers at the Day Hospital. I said yes, we had a teacher working with us. He then said, "Well, you should know that I beat teachers up". Andrew had been expelled from the third school in two years, as a result of what was described as severe behavioural disorders. He had no friends and walked around his neighbourhood with a German shepherd, having organised his identity around this image of a tough guy that wanted to frighten everybody. In my mind, this was only external armour, covering a very fragile self and intense feelings of persecution.

Andrew had suffered severe neglect from birth, living in a disorganised and chaotic relational environment, abandoned to emotional effects that were not worked through. The predominant relational style in his family was based on a dynamic that triggered confusion, denial, dissociation and threat. Throughout his childhood, his emotional experience was not recognised or contained but despised. This state of affairs laid the groundwork for damaged and disorganised thought processes, his capacity to modulate emotions and his mentalizing abilities seemed significantly impaired, resulting in a lack of integration of mental structure and in the at-risk-of-psychosis mental state he presented.

In order to survive, Andrew had developed maladaptive coping mechanisms that hid a highly damaged mental space. His mind was dominated by the experience of absence, emptiness, confusion, threats, despair and abandonment that could not be worked through, and unnamed pain that could only be evacuated in a teleological mode through acting out. Under these conditions, what was truly despairing for Andrew was not being able to trust anyone. Amongst the vast amount of contradictory feelings he seemed to experience, one of the most despairing was that of not having anyone and also the expectation that this was his place in the world: "I have no one and will never have anyone". Understandably, he had organised a fragile identity around the image of a tough kid, with his strong body as armour holding him together and allowing him to approach others, despite the intense persecutory anxieties he experienced. He didn't have any close friends and didn't trust anyone. His appearance and initial contact were intimidating, although, behind this image, I found myself imagining a lost and very frightened child.

Andrew presented a clinical picture which, from a phenomenological perspective or when looked at through a categorical lens, met criteria compatible with emergent conduct disorder, oppositional defiant disorder and intermittent explosive disorder. However, when considered from a dimensional perspective (Lingiardi & McWilliams, 2017; Tizón, 2018a, 2018b, & 2019) the clinical picture becomes more multi-layered and complex, allowing us to understand his emotional and relational life in a more detailed way. This has important implications for treatment modality, as certain modifications of technique in the psychotherapeutic approach are very useful and pertinent when working with at-risk and non-help-seeking young people. Furthermore, if we consider this situation through the understanding of the inconsistent, unpredictable and neglectful caregiving – including family, school and other care systems–, Andrew's difficulties in modulating his emotional life and his very deficient relational and mentalizing skills can be understood as failures in his developmental process, something that also has important implications in the design of the therapeutic process and the understanding and formulation of the presenting symptomatology.

The MBT model provides both theoretical and clinical constructs that help us address the complex picture that these young people present. It also offers an approach that not only allows individual but also systemic considerations in the therapeutic process. Some concepts, such as epistemic trust, parental embodied mentalizing and mentalized affectivity, as well as some contributions of the AMBIT model, are key to describing my work with adolescents presenting at-risk mental states.

Regarding the title of this chapter, when I speak about at-risk mental states (ARMS), I am referring to the term used by mental health professionals to describe young people who are experiencing early, low-level signs of psychosis. The National Health Service in the UK describes three groups of young people who may be said to present ARMS. First, those who have been functioning less well over the last 12 months. This would include individuals who have withdrawn from school, college or work or have not been able to spend time with family or friends. Second, people with short-lived or milder symptoms of psychosis within the last three months, and third, persons who experience brief or limited intermittent psychotic symptoms. These are psychotic-level symptoms that have naturally ceased within seven days.

After working at a Day Hospital for adolescents for nearly ten years, I moved on to manage a pioneering clinical service in Spain: ECID, a mental health outreach team for adolescents of the Vidal and Barraquer Foundation in Barcelona, based on the Adaptive Mentalization-based Integrative Treatment (AMBIT, Bevington, Fuggle, Cracknell, & Fonagy, 2017; Bevington, Fuggle, & Fonagy, 2015; Bevington, Fuggle, Fonagy, Target, & Asen, 2012). Described more fully in Chapter 12, AMBIT is a mentalization-based model for teams working with young people who have multiple and complex difficulties. AMBIT broadens the field of intervention by providing tools to stimulate mentalizing, applying principles and practices based on four different levels: working with young people and their families, working with teams, working with our network and supporting teams to adopt a learning position regarding our own practice.

At ECID, we primarily work with adolescents presenting ARMS; either those who have dropped out of school and life and retreated into their homes or even bedrooms, connected to the world only through video games and the Internet, or adolescents who have dropped out of school, are also non-help-seeking, and are on the street engaging in risky behaviours. Despite the different clinical picture, both groups share the same fragile self, lack of emotional and relational resources to face life and impoverished mentalizing capacities. They live trapped in states of epistemic hypervigilance or epistemic mistrust, something that is related to their understandable non-help-seeking attitude. In this context, I have found in the MBT focus a wonderful umbrella under which to adapt my therapeutic stance and be able to reach them where they are. It involves scaffolding the treatment by modifying the approach to facilitate a secure base built on epistemic trust. The goal is a relationship in which the young person can revisit the developmental process that leads to the sense of agency and trust which in turn facilitates mentalizing (Malberg, 2013a, 2013b & 2019). The overall aim of this intervention is to provide a different model of relationship for both the adolescent and the systems around them, in order to facilitate a generalisation of a different emotional experience in the context of the young person's relational environment – family, peers and others – as the condition that determines the therapeutic effect of the intervention.

Relational trauma and psychopathology in adolescence

There is strong evidence showing that adverse childhood experiences are extremely common in people who develop serious mental disorders (Artigue, Tizón, & Salamero, 2016; Cutajar et al. 2010; Dangerfield, 2012; Fuller-Thomson & Lewis, 2015; Read, Van, Morrison, & Ross, 2005; Sorensen et al., 2010; Teicher, Samson, Anderson, & Ohashi, 2016; Varese et al., 2012). There is also clear evidence regarding the fact that people who have suffered adverse childhood experiences (ACEs) are often reluctant to reveal their histories of abuse, and that mental health professionals also tend to be reluctant to assess them (Read, Hammersley, & Rudegeair, 2007; Dangerfield, 2012 & 2017).

Data collected in recent years on the work with this group of young people (Dangerfield, 2012 & 2017) supports the existing evidence that demonstrates the relationship between suffering ACEs and a greater psychopathological risk, as well as the relationship between ACEs of adolescents with the fact that their parents also suffered ACEs in their own childhood. This fact helps us understand the intergenerational transmission of relational trauma and its repercussions at a behavioural and psychological-relational level.

Regardless of the manifestations at the clinical-phenomenological level, we can understand the ACEs suffered during childhood often as pre-conceptual traumatic experiences (Grimalt, 2012; López-Corvo, 2013 & 2014), which have caused significant damage to the organisation of the emotional sphere, affecting the ability to modulate emotions, to make sense of one's emotional experience and mentalizing capacities. This is also explained from the known fact that "the link between attachment and mentalizing is clear" and that "attachment contexts provide the ideal conditions for fostering mentalizing" (Fonagy, Lorenzini, Campbell, & Luyten, 2014).

Working with young people who have been exposed to toxic stress is a tough and complex task, especially for what it means in having to take care of their intense non-mentalized anxieties and damaged emotional sphere: a very intense, wordless suffering that predominates in their psychic life. They desperately need help, but it is common to see how contact with their emotional needs is very threatening, as it destabilises their fragile survival system, an understandable adaptive response to a neglectful and abusive environment. Tolerating dependence and the need for affection is very often experienced as catastrophic for them, due to the lack of trust in a sufficiently available and reliable relationship. It is very common to observe how they experience contact with another human being as something that implies the fear of a traumatic repetition of the experience of abandonment, contempt and abuse. It is not safe to approach another person's mind if we haven't had an experience of predictable and consistent attachment. In this relational context, the more neutral and distant position predicated on a classical psychodynamic stance fails and there is a need for a developmentally informed lens. A more active therapeutic attitude is needed in order to establish basic trust in the relationship with young people who had such early deficits of having been held in mind predictably and consistently. As Slade (2014) describes (p. 253): "the dynamic relationship between the experience of threat and attachment shapes the development and maintenance of essential relationships, the organisation of psychic structure, and the nature of defences and adaptation. This element of attachment theory … is particularly relevant to the clinical situation. It helps us imagine moments of fearful arousal in our patients' pasts, attend to their manifestations in the present, and understand current suffering in light of the long-term sequelae of adaptations that were crucial to survival. Finally, it helps us find language that brings alive or mentalizes these aspects of the patient's early experience such that transformation is possible".

Deficits in parents' mentalizing inhibit their capacity to provide an experience of mutuality and thoughtful curiosity about their children's internal experience of relationships. The parents' inability to regulate their own affective states creates an unpredictable and inconsistent relational environment for them to grow up in. The cycle of generational transmission of relational trauma becomes evident and is facilitated in this context.

Mentalizing development and the concept of the "alien self"

Mentalizing is a capacity that is very easily overwhelmed and is never entirely stable, consistent or one-dimensional (Fonagy & Allison, 2011). When we receive an emotional impact that disrupts our ability to mentalize, we resort to an attachment figure to recover, find containment and confidence, or the reliable internalised relational experiences that accompany us from within and that can also allow us to find some containment.

Early experiences of marked mirroring facilitate the development of mentalizing and what is known as the secondary representation of the child's experience in their own mind (Bateman & Fonagy, 2004). This gradually repeated experience will form the child's nuclear self (Fonagy, 2000), that leads to an internal representation of themselves as an intentional being and as an agent, which is generalised to the representation of others, leading to the development of a mentalizing model of the world. This model helps the child perceive the relational world with meaning and in a predictable way and respond to the complexities of social reality with resilience (Fonagy, 2000).

If this process does not develop in a minimally adequate way, as in the group of at-risk adolescents that we are talking about, this process can lead to the development of an "alien self" (Fonagy, 2000), also described in Chapter 7. In a situation of a carer who is overwhelmed by their own suffering and responds in a hostile or fearful way to the child's discomfort, we could imagine the young child's experience could be described as follows: "If my carer misperceives my internal state, if they get scared or angry about my discomfort, what I will see and experience is the fear or anger in the other. So, the experience that I internalise is the experience that my discomfort scares or annoys the other whom I desperately need, which leads to the internal experience that I am fearful or I make the other angry, when what is really happening to me is that I am alone and terrified". When this adverse relational pattern is constant, the child internalises this neglectful or abusive relational experience as a nuclear aspect of their sense of self, when it is in fact a state of the caregiver that becomes an "alien state" of the child. The child's real state is that they are alone and terrified, experiencing unbearable, overwhelming anxieties that cannot be processed. This concept of alien self refers to the process in which the caregiver's representations of the child are based on erroneous attributions, something that will promote the child's internalisation of misadjusted representations of themselves. If repeated experiences of this type predominantly mark the relationship with the caregivers, there will be a situation where the child's mind is dominated by an "alien self" (Rossouw, 2012).

This highly pathogenic feature emerges as the child is experiencing a moment of emotional discomfort when what will be triggered in their mind is the maladaptive relational pattern of a mean and hostile response to their moment of discomfort, something that will only increase the suffering and trigger an escalation of despair, loss of mentalizing and teleological and psychic equivalence modes in an extreme level resulting in high risk of destructive acting out.

This happens because the internal experience of the alien self is similar to the experience of an internal tormentor: constant self-criticism, self-loathing, absence of internal validation and expectation of failure. The self is hated and, through the projected lenses of the "alien self", the external world can be perceived as potentially hostile, humiliating and persecuting (Rossouw, 2012). At the same time, the internal representations are inconsistent with their own experiences. Representations of others will also be misadjusted and lead to the experience that the relational world is meaningless and unpredictable. It follows that the "alien self" prevents the development of mentalizing (Rossouw & Fonagy, 2012) and is an important element to understand central aspects of the difficulties of at-risk adolescents.

In adolescence, diminished mentalizing capacities lead directly to greater difficulty in finding meaning in the behaviour of others, a greater difficulty in understanding one's own feelings, greater anxiety, increased feeling of threat, loss, anger and despair. There is a higher presence of paranoid feelings and fear of losing significant others. But one of the feelings that is the source of intense suffering and a greater risk of both self-destructive and hetero-destructive actions is feeling bad, feeling destroyed from within. It is very common to meet young people who feel overwhelmed by an intense hatred towards themselves and thoughts such as: "I am horrible, I hate myself, I should be dead, nobody will miss me…". As a consequence, the young person needs to regain control over the spiral of confusing and catastrophic anxieties that invade them, so they resort to acting out as a desperate way of feeling that they can recover some sense of agency over their own life.

When mentalizing is lost there is a feeling of fragmentation, loss of coherence and loss of the feeling of agency over one's life. The search for the attachment figure does not contain, due to the severe neglect or abuse prevailing in the relationship or simply because of its absence. The internalised relational experiences do not offer containment either since there is an insufficient presence of minimally containing experiences and a predominance of the alien self that increases despair. This situation stimulates violent actions, a violence that can be understood as a shield against these catastrophic anxieties, as a kind of illusion of regaining control over catastrophic experiences and not only as an evacuation of discomfort that cannot be processed in another way.

Any mechanism that makes fragmentation stop is valuable for the adolescent, such as moving towards massive projections on external reality, the massive use of psychic equivalence that generates a highly threatening experience. Persecutory anxiety is something mentalizable since there is a persecutor, while the most primitive and catastrophic experience of the absence would be the non-mentalizable emptiness, the non-mentalizable pain from which one can flee, returning to the sensory sphere, clinging to the sensations as a form of psychic survival (Coromines, 1991, 1994).

The young person with mentalizing deficits who does not feel understood may feel like the world is against them, something that attacks and destroys their sense of self that, furthermore, is in the process of formation. This destroys what they are and unleashes psychotic anxieties, an unbearable reality that pushes the adolescent to retreat from the world or to act out destructively: the clinical presentations of the young people we work with.

Clinical case

To illustrate what I have been describing, I will go back to Andrew and a situation that occurred a few months after we had started our work together. Despite the initial difficulties and thanks to the intensive relationship we could have at the Day Hospital, we were able to establish a trustful relationship, in which he tolerated having conversations with me.

I will introduce some technical aspects of the mentalizing stance defined as a table with four sturdy legs that support and facilitate the therapeutic process. These are: curiosity made explicit, terminating non-mentalizing, holding the balance between the different dimensions of mentalizing – as described in previous chapters – and highlighting the moments in which the patient mentalizes.

The situation I will describe took place six months after he was admitted. It was the first day of what we called "classroom activity" after two months without it. After less than five minutes, I heard a loud noise coming from the corridor. I recognised Andrew's voice in rage, completely overwhelmed, in the middle of an explosive outburst, screaming all sorts of nasty insults at the teacher and kicking and punching a door and the wall. I was afraid that he might hurt himself, as he had broken different parts of his hand in other similar episodes. Two colleagues were also there, but I asked them to keep away, as I didn't think physical containment would be helpful at all.

P: *Leave me alone, Mark! Don't touch me! Don't fucking touch me!*
T: *Andrew, I am not going to touch you.*
P: *Fuck that bitch! I'll kill her, Mark! I'm gonna fucking kill that motherfucker!*

He was kicking and punching the wall and a door, dominated by extreme teleological and psychic equivalence modes. My main concern was that Andrew might badly injure himself again.

T: *Andrew, I am afraid you might hurt yourself and I don't want that to happen.*
P: *That bitch! Fucking bitch! I'm gonna beat the shit out of that fucking bitch!*

He kept on kicking and punching the wall.

T: *Andrew, I am worried because I think that you could seriously hurt your hands if you punch the wall.*

P: *Fuck it, fuck it! I don't fucking care!*

T: *I do, Andrew. I do care. I don't want you to hurt yourself.*

As I made my mental state quite explicit firmly and clearly, Andrew tolerated me getting closer, although still completely overwhelmed. When someone is not mentalizing, we should not force them to mentalize, because they cannot listen to us. We can't address non-mentalizing with mentalizing. Instead, we must indicate that we are by their side, validate their emotional state by both verbal and non-verbal means, showing that we are with them and that we support them. As the emotional storm passes, we can try to recover mentalizing in other areas. Following these principles and with the idea of trying to shift the focus to an area where it may be more feasible to recover mentalizing, while also moving away from the focus of persecution, I say:

T: *Andrew, why don't we just leave this place? Why don't we leave now? Why don't we just walk out to the garden, just you and me?*

P: *OK! Let's get the fuck out of here!*

Here, I intend to try to actively shift the attention focus, trying to move his mind–and him– away from what had triggered the emotional storm and dysregulation. This has to do with the idea of building epistemic trust through joint attention and affect regulation (Midgley, Ensink, Lindqvist, Malberg, & Muller, 2017), as the first step in the process of helping re-establish mentalizing. We can also understand his reaction as triggered by his intolerance to the frustration of being confronted with schoolwork, and how this may have triggered the alien self within, something that leads him to a massive attribution to the teacher of this destructive and profoundly unfair aspect of himself in this extreme psychic equivalence mode, that he then manages in a teleological way as he has always done. However, my intention of moving him away seems successful, as he agrees to come outside with me, although swearing and kicking doors and the wall as we go.

This technical aspect is also connected to interrupting non-mentalizing. The therapist has an active role here, especially if it is a known pattern of the young person or family. In situations of emotional dysregulation like this moment with Andrew, it is important to find ways to stop and actively try to focus on less conflictive areas to diminish the risk of destructive behaviours.

In less intense moments of dysregulation, in order to interrupt non-mentalizing, I find it useful to blame it on myself, with a self-deprecating sense of humour suggesting that I am confused or not following. With these adolescents, this is less persecutory and is also helpful to communicate our mental state in the current moment.

Following this encounter in the clinic, Andrew and I leave the building and walk around the garden. He leads us towards a nice place in the garden with a bench and trees around that offer welcome shade on this hot summer day. He sits down and I sit beside him, while he continues to utter insults with great anger towards the teacher and I try to validate his emotional state, trying to make him feel that I am next to him, in touch and available to receive his suffering and despair, validating his experience and noticing and naming what I am acknowledging of his current situation, both emotionally and physically. After a while, I try to stimulate mentalizing in another area that I think will be much more tolerable, and I opt for the sensory level we are both sharing, mentioning how hot it still is, and appreciating the shade. He listens to me and his despair and rage seem to decrease.

T: *Hey Andrew, how do you cope with this heat? Because I just feel I have had quite enough for this year.*

Here I actively invite him to mentalize about how he is experiencing this shared sensation, but first showing my own thought process about it and making explicit my curiosity about his mental state. Curiosity made explicit is another of the legs of the mentalizing stance, because, when working with this group of adolescents, there is nothing worse than pretending that we know what it is to be in their shoes. We must be humble, tolerant and make explicit our not-knowing stance. It is important to be able to tell them that we do not know how to read their minds and that we need them to help us understand them. We should never say anything to an adolescent without checking whether they believe that what we have told them is relevant to them at that time or not.

P: *Yeah… I don't like it either… and so fucking sticky… fucking heat… and look… mosquitos, too… like this fucking mosquito here now wanting to bite us…*

Notice how he adds another sensory quality to what he is feeling: the sticky effect of the intense humidity. Then he sees a mosquito, which will become a valuable co-therapist.

T: *Gosh, you are right. And it's a tiger mosquito isn't it? What do you think?*

I invite him to mentalize about the mosquito. Again, in such a situation, what counts is the process and not so much the content of our interaction.

P: *It sure is man! Those are the worst kind.*

Focused on the mosquito, Andrew begins to calm down. When working with at-risk adolescents like Andrew, getting closer to thinking about central aspects of their past and present history, approaching emotions and emotional need is unbearable and even catastrophic, due to the internalised relational experiences of abandonment, neglect and/or abuse, which lead them to expect the same from the therapeutic relationship. For this reason, what we consider as the main goal is the need to give ourselves time to try to develop mentalizing in areas where it can be more tolerable. This can be achieved more easily if we start where their psychic developmental process was detained, starting from the most primitive level: mentalizing the sensory level. In other words, mentalizing the new emotional experience shared with the therapist from the most primitive level.

From a technical perspective, this supports the idea of facilitating a process in which the therapist will be available, and will notice and name what is happening, in order to stimulate mentalizing from this level of development.

Andrew shifts from a moment where he was overwhelmed and totally unable to mentalize, to a state in which he has regained the capacity for mentalizing, something that I explicitly acknowledge, highlighting the moments in which Andrew mentalizes. A fundamental concept to understand therapeutic work is epistemic trust (Fonagy & Allison, 2014), described in detail in other chapters of this book.

As I see that we are making progress, and have decreased the state of emotional dysregulation accordingly, I try to open the focus of shared attention. I am curious about what he has done this weekend. He tells me that he hasn't done much and I ask him if he has seen anyone.

P: *Well... you know... I was going to meet with Kate and Maria (girls from the Day Hospital) but Kate said no...*

T: *Oh, and how did you feel about that?*

P: *It sucked, man!*

T: *I imagine, yes. But, could you help me see what "it sucked" means for you? To see if I can understand you better.*

P: *It sucked means it sucks, Mark! ... What the fuck?! ... That I got fucking annoyed, that I didn't like that to happen because I wanted to see her on Saturday and I didn't.*

Despite the initial reluctance, Andrew can develop the emotion that he just described. We can refer to the concept of mentalized affectivity (Jurist, 2005), as an important one that underpins a technical stance in the process of affect regulation where we try to facilitate a revaluing of affects, and not just modulating (Fonagy, Gergely, Jurist, & Target, 2002). The reflection on the affective experience –identifying, processing, and expressing affects– has the goal of developing a new meaning that Andrew can manage to express. I intervene validating and checking what I am understanding. We move on and I ask what he thinks had to do with the fact that Kate said no to him.

P: *She said she was angry with me... and that she didn't want to see me because of that... fucking angry with me! Why the fuck?!*

T: *Well, that's a good question, Andrew. What do you think made her angry?*

P: *She said she was angry because I said something about a guy that she is also seeing... that guy is a jerk! A fucking jerk!*

T: Oh, I see...

P: *Yeah, I know that motherfucker... he lives in my neighbourhood... an asshole... and I know that motherfucker has been playing around with other girls... and I didn't want her to get in trouble with him... so I told her...*

T: *Right, fair enough, so you just wanted to warn her about this guy, right?*

P: *Yeah Mark, that's what I fucking did!*

T: *Ok, and what did you say to her?*

P: *We were texting... and I wrote a message... look... I've got the conversation here... she says she is going to see this guy and I say: "you're dragging yourself around like a bitch with this jerk!"*

This is Andrew's usual manner of talking, without much awareness of the emotional impact his words have on others.

T: *I see... well, and then she got angry after reading this message of yours.*

P: *Yes, she just said that's enough, she was not going to see me that day and ends the fucking conversation, man!*

T: *Right, so she got angry. But, can you understand why she got angry over what you said?*

P: *But, Mark, man... she knows me... she knows I talk like that!*

T: *You're right... but even so, maybe there are things that we can imagine might hurt her. Because I have the impression that you don't want to hurt her. Is that right?*

P: *Of course! Of course I don't want to hurt her.*

T: *But look, let's see if we can find another way of saying things, I mean, you know what we've talked about, how the way we say or do things to others might impact others, how it will make them feel. We've been working on this, haven't we?*

P: *Yeah... yeah...*

T: *And on how sometimes we can find different ways of saying the same thing, sort of giving the same message but in a different way... in a way that we can imagine won't hurt the other person so much... you know, when we've been talking about putting yourself in the other person's shoes.*

P: *Yeah... yeah... so? How would you say this to her Mark? How would you warn her about this jerk?*

T: *Don't you want to give it a try?*

P: *No, I don't... go on Mark... you say it!*

I think that Andrew is showing honest curiosity about what I might have in mind, he is interested in my way of expressing this. So I think it is important to respond.

T: *Ok, something like: Kate look, I'm really fond of you and I don't want this guy to hurt you, so please be careful, because I know other girls who have been hurt by this guy.*

P: *Motherfucker! That's a good one man! ... Yeah! But fuck! This is exactly what happened before with the teacher... fuck me, it's the same thing... it's what happened just now... I said things in a way that got her angry...*

T: *Look Andrew, I think that what you are doing now is very valuable. You are very capable of thinking in a way that helps you understand things that just happened. This is what we always aim at, this way of thinking that really helps you.*

Here I highlight the mentalizing that Andrew displays, another important leg of the mentalizing stance. We do it by focusing on the here and now, detecting, highlighting and valuing effective mentalizing: "I really like the way of thinking that you are being capable of showing right now. Look at how different it is from the way you were thinking just five minutes ago when you seemed so certain about what you were saying about such a person... instead, now you are wondering about how that person might feel when you do something like what you had done. Do you see the difference?". In my intervention, I focus on this particular quality of Andrew's mind when it appears. He then continues:

P: *Yeah man... but the thing is that when she (the teacher) gave me all that text I had to read, it was so fucking long, that I told her to fuck off, to get that fucking text away from me and shove it up her arse...*

T: *Right, ok, and then you said she got angry, something we might be able to understand.*

P: *Yeah, yeah... of course...*

T: *So, can you think of another way you could have said this to the teacher?*

P: *Yeah... I could say: don't give me such a long text because I haven't read anything for two months... let's start with something shorter!*

T: *That's very good Andrew, very good indeed. And how do you think the teacher would feel if you said it like that?*

P: *Ok... she wouldn't get angry with me... yeah... things would go better...*

We see in the sequence how Andrew has been able to identify a relational pattern in which he elicits rejection from others in two different situations. My goal wasn't initially to try to mentalize the situation with the teacher that had emotionally dysregulated him, but it is very valuable that he can do it himself, once his despair has been contained and we are able to regain a mentalizing mode.

Conclusion

Adverse relational experiences have led at-risk adolescents to the closure of a learning path, damaging their ability to learn through interpersonal experiences and becoming more inflexible and rigid in the face of change (Bateman & Fonagy, 2012). We face this obstacle in our therapeutic work with them since it sets the scene for the relationship to fail, one in which the young person very often does not ask for help, but rather might actively reject it. It may be common for clinicians or teams to try to introduce some change in the young person's way of thinking or feeling. Instead, we should first ask ourselves what we should change in our own minds, in our own teams and networks to be able to reach this young person who does not expect anything good from a relationship with an adult, even less so if this adult is a mental health professional. The relational experience can have a therapeutic effect because it favours a change in the adolescent's availability and mental attitude towards relationships, so that they can be more open to being influenced by benign and benevolent relationships that they could already have in their surroundings, but were unable to see and benefit from.

The MBT approach implies offering ourselves as a model that makes our implicit thought processes explicit. In this way, we offer a model of someone who is not perfect, of someone who is aware of the fact that there are limits to our knowledge and is safe in acknowledging it: "I am curious because I know I do not know". We also offer a model of interest in one's own and others' mental states, making reflections on how we might feel or what we think about a certain situation and asking ourselves out loud how the other person might feel and think. At the same time, we are making explicit our curiosity, awareness of the impact of emotion, awareness that the patient's mind is opaque and shaping the ability to take different perspectives. Above all, we try to promote an atmosphere of epistemic trust that restores the young person's capacity for agency and hope.

References

Artigue, J., Tizón, J., & Salamero, M. (2016). Reliability and validity of the list of mental health items (LISMEN), *Schizophrenia Research*, *176*, 423–430.

Bateman, A., & Fonagy, P. (2004). *Psychotherapy for Borderline Personality Disorder: Mentalization-Based Treatment*. Oxford: Oxford University Press.

Bateman, A., & Fonagy, P. (2012). *Handbook of Mentalizing in Mental Health Practice*. Washington, DC: American Psychiatric Publishing.

Bevington, D., Fuggle, P., Cracknell, L., & Fonagy, P. (2017). *Adaptive Mentalization-Based Integrative Treatment: A Guide for Teams to Develop Systems of Care*. Oxford University Press.

Bevington, D., Fuggle, P., & Fonagy, P. (2015). Applying attachment theory to effective practice with hard-to-reach youth: The AMBIT approach. *Attachment and Human Development*, *17*(2), 157–174.

Bevington, D., Fuggle, P., Fonagy, P., Target, M., & Asen, E. (2012). Innovations in practice: Adolescent mentalization-based integrative therapy (AMBIT) – a new integrated approach to working with the most hard to reach adolescents with severe complex mental health needs. *Child and Adolescent Mental Health*, *18*(1), 46–51.

Coromines, J. (1991). *Psicopatologia i desenvolupaments arcaics, Assaig psicoanalític*. Barcelona: Barcelona Espaxs.

Coromines, J. (1994). Possibles vinculacions entre organitzacions patològiques de l'adult i problemes del desenvolupament mental primary. *Revista Catalana de Psicoanàlisis*, *XI*, núm. 1–2.

Cutajar, M., Mullen, P., Ogloff, J., Thomas, S., Wells, D., & Spataro, J. (2010). Psychopathology in a large cohort of sexually abused children followed up to 43 years. *Child Abuse and Neglect, 34,* 81–822.

Dangerfield, M. (2012). Negligencia y violencia sobre el adolescente: abordaje desde un Hospital de Día. *Temas de Psicoanálisis,* n° 4, Junio 2012. (www.temasdepsicoanalisis.org).

Dangerfield, M. (2017). Aportaciones del tratamiento basado en la mentalización (MBT-A) para adolescentes que han sufrido adversidades en la infancia. *Cuadernos de Psiquiatría y Psicoterapia del Niño y del Adolescente, 63,* 29–47.

Fonagy, P. (2000). Attachment and borderline personality disorder. *Journal of the American Psychoanalytic Association, 48(4),* 1129–1146.

Fonagy, P., & Allison, E. (2011). What is mentalization? The concept and its foundations in developmental research. In N. Midgley & I. Vrouva (Eds.), *Minding the Child: Mentalization-Based Interventions with Children, Young People and Their Families* (pp. 11–34). London: Routledge.

Fonagy, P., & Allison, E. (2014). The role of mentalizing and epistemic trust in the therapeutic relationship. *Psychotherapy, 51,* 372–380.

Fonagy, P., Gergely, G., Jurist, E.L., & Target, M. (2002). *Affect Regulation, Mentalization, and the Development of the Self.* New York: Other Press.

Fonagy, P., Lorenzini, N., Campbell, C., & Luyten, P. (2014). Why are we interested in attachments? In P. Holms & S. Farnfield (Eds.), *The Routledge Handbook of Attachment: Theory* (pp. 38–51). New York: Routledge.

Fuller-Thomson, E., & Lewis, D.A. (2015). The relationship between early adversities and attention–deficit/hyperactivity disorder. *Child Abuse and Neglect, 47,* 94–101.

Grimalt, A. (2012). Traumes preconceptuals: l'assassinat de la menti el self oblidat. *Revista Catalana de Psicoanàlisi, XXIX(2),* 69–88.

Jurist, E. (2005). Mentalized affectivity. *Psychoanalytic Psychology, 22(3),* 426–444.

Lingiardi, V., & McWilliams, N. (Eds.) (2017). *Psychodynamic Diagnostic Manual, Second Edition: PDM-2* (English Edition). New York: The Guilford Press.

López-Corvo, R.E. (2013). Time distortion between "conceptual" and "preconceptual" traumas. *The Psychoanalytic Review, 100(2),* 289–310.

López-Corvo, R.E. (2014). *Traumatised and Non-Traumatised States of the Personality: A Clinical Understanding Using Bion's Approach.* London, Karnac Books.

Malberg, N.T. (2013a). Mentalization based group interventions with chronically ill adolescents: An example of assimilative psychodynamic integration? *Journal of Psychotherapy Integration, 23(1),* 5–13.

Malberg, N.T. (2013b). A caged life: A girl's discovery of freedom through the co-creation of her life's narrative. *Journal of Infant, Child and Adolescent Psychotherapy, 12,* 59–71.

Malberg, N.T. (2019). Psychodynamic psychotherapy and emotion. In L.S. Greenberg, N.T. Malberg, & M.A. Tompkins (Eds.), *Working with Emotion in Psychodynamic, Cognitive Behavior, and Emotion-Focused Psychotherapy* (pp. 13–52). Washington, DC: American Psychological Association.

Midgley, N., Ensink, K., Lindqvist, K., Malberg, N.T., & Muller, N. (2017). *Mentalization-Based Treatment for Children: A Time-Limited Approach.* Washington, DC: American Psychological Association.

Read, J., Hammersley, P., & Rudegeair, T. (2007). Why, when and how to ask about childhood abuse. *Advances in Psychiatric Treatment, 13,* 101–110.

Read, J., Van Os, J., Morrison, A.P., & Ross, C.A. (2005). Childhood trauma, psychosis and schizophrenia: A literature review with theoretical and clinical implications. *Acta Psychiatrica Scandinavica*, *112*, 330–350.

Rossouw, T.I., & Fonagy, P. (2012). Mentalization-based treatment for self-harm in adolescents: a randomized controlled trial. *Journal of the American Academy of Child and Adolescent Psychiatry*, *51*(12), 1304–1313.

Rossouw, T.I. (2012). Self-harm and young people: Is MBT the answer? In N. Midgley & I. Vrouva (Eds.), *Minding the Child: Mentalization-Based Interventions with Children, Young People and Their Families* (pp. 131–144). London: Routledge.

Slade, A. (2014). Imagining fear: Attachment, threat and psychic experience. *Psychoanalytic Dialogues*, *24*, 253–266.

Sorensen, H., Mortensen, E., Schiffman, J., Reinisch, J., Maeda, J., & Mednick, S.A. (2010). Early developmental milestones and risk of schizophrenia: A 45-year follow-up of Copenhagen Perinatal Cohort. *Schizophrenia Research*, *118*(1–3), 41–47.

Teicher, M.H., Samson, J.A., Anderson, C.M., & Ohashi, K. (2016). The effects of childhood maltreatment on brain structure, function and connectivity. *Nature*, *17*, 652–666. doi:10.1038/nrn.2016.111.

Tizón, J. (2018a). *Apuntes para una psicopatología basada en la relación. Vol. I: Psicopatología general*. Barcelona: Herder.

Tizón, J. (2018b). *Apuntes para una psicopatología basada en la relación. Vol. II: Relaciones dramatizadas, atemorizadas y racionalizadoras*. Barcelona: Herder.

Tizón, J. (2019). *Apuntes para una psicopatología basada en la relación. Vol. III: relaciones emocionalizadas, intrusivas, actuadoras y "operativas"*. Barcelona: Herder.

Varese, F., Smeets, F., Drukker, M., Lieverese, R., Lataster, T., Viechtbauer, W., Read, J., Van Os, J., & Bentall, R.P. (2012). Childhood adversities increase the risk of psychosis: A meta-analysis of patient-control, prospective- and cross-sectional cohort studies. *Schizophrenia Bulletin*, *38*(4), 661–671.

Chapter 11

MBT-A group therapy with adolescents with emerging personality disorders

Nicole Muller and Holly Dwyer Hall

The parallel use of an individual and group modality is a key part of the treatment package in MBT for adults with a personality disorder, with the group component recognised as a significant element of MBT programmes (Bateman & Fonagy, 2011; Karterud, 2015; Karterud & Bateman, 2012). The UK's National Institute for Health and Clinical Excellence (NICE, 2015) recommends therapy for people with personality disorder be delivered in at least two modalities, individual and group or family therapy.

Despite this, clinicians often feel reluctant to engage adolescents in group therapy citing concerns around group dynamics, the potential for sharing unhelpful behaviours and the adolescent's sensitivity to peer influence (Hutsebaut et al., 2011), making for unmanageable interactions. Indeed, groups can be highly charged environments stimulating complex emotional interactions requiring considerable effort on the part of therapists and participants to remain aware of their own mental states whilst also attending to others. Yet, it is within this rich and fertile social learning ground that mentalizing therapists can make use of an adolescent's intensified interest in peer relations to provide a '*relationally restorative and repairing experience*' (Malberg, 2010). By aligning ourselves with the adolescent's developmental task of establishing meaningful peer relationships and focusing on emotionally, developmentally and culturally relevant themes, the group setting has the potential to become a secure and safe peer environment. Here, members can risk exploring challenging interpersonal narratives and discover new ways of being.

This chapter describes the MBT-A Group model developed in the Netherlands for use with adolescents with emerging personality disorders between the ages of 13-23 years engaged in Individual and Family MBT-A sessions in community or inpatient settings.

Establishing the group composition – who and why?

Amidst rapid changes in physical, neurological, emotional and social development, the adolescent's personality is changing. Some degree of turmoil - increased moodiness, impulsivity and risky experimentation might be expected as adolescents negotiate their journey towards autonomy and self-discovery. For a small group, these problems reach clinical significance with adolescence widely re-cognised as a period of heightened vulnerability for the onset of major mental disorders (Paris, 2003). Adolescents with emerging personality disorders often present with a variety of characteristics and significant comorbidity (Becker, Grilo, Edell, & McGlash, 2000; Eaton, Krueger, & Oltmanns, 2011) but differ sig-nificantly in how they think, perceive, feel and relate to others. Difficulties are characterised by extreme mood swings, unpredictable behaviour, persistent un-stable or negative self-image, relationships typified by distrust, with significant problems in regulating emotions and impaired mentalizing (Muller, Ten Kate, & Eurelings-Bontekoe, 2017). These difficulties frequently lead to incongruous and controlling behaviours (acts of self-harm, violence, substance misuse) distressing the young person and those around them. MBT-A considers these maladaptive behaviours to be the result of the failure of mentalization impacting on the young person's capacity to regulate affect and are in part owing to neurodevelopmental changes temporarily compromising mentalizing (Fonagy & Luyten, 2009). For young people with emerging personality disorders, this phase-specific compro-mise exacerbates earlier existing developmental difficulties, further weakening mentalizing and mentalizing mediated affect regulation (Fonagy & Allison, 2014). MBT-A aims to develop a young person's awareness of mental states in them-selves and others, enhancing their capacity to mentalize. Within the group con-text, this translates to creating an environment in which it feels safe for adolescents to be curious with their peers about underlying motivations and factors inhibiting mentalizing capabilities and to grow confident in responding differently. This involves developing an awareness of how preconscious processes (implicit men-talizing), which holds the strength of early relational patterns, can influence our thoughts and behaviour and make these automatic assumptions explicit. The group aims to foster a respectful and genuine curiosity in understanding the connection between feelings, thoughts, and actions in the here-and-now.

The mentalizing stance in MBT-A groups

Empathising, managing conflict, tolerating criticism, fostering a non-judgmental environment and working relationally are important therapist activities for effective group psychotherapy (Leszcz, 2014). MBT-A therapists need to be present in mind, body and soul. Recognising that adolescents can struggle to read the emotional expression on faces (Tahmasebi et al., 2012) therapists need to feel comfortable noticing, naming, processing and expressing their own affective states whilst being benignly curious about others. '*I find myself feeling quite concerned for you when you talk about your binge drinking yet you seem very relaxed about this?*' By genuinely expressing what they perceive and experience, therapist, support adolescents to become aware of themselves and others, hence promoting curiosity and modelling thoughtful reflection.

The stance is active and direct, encouraging the emergence of group dy-namics; being sensitive to what is said, but also to what is unspoken. '*I notice we're talking quite a bit today but I get the feeling some of us might not be feeling heard.'* When used non-defensively, humour is a powerful tool, surprising the minds of others, reducing tension and increasing the bond amongst members. *'Seriously, you all think I'm that old. What, did you see me park the dinosaur out back?'* However big or small, therapists validate positive mentalizing attempts, helping to build a resilient group atmosphere and convey the importance of caring for oneself and others. *'I'm pleased everyone is here today. It can be hard to get here every week but when we do, we're building a supportive group.'*

Method and structure

Karterud (2015) has written about how cohesion is operationalised in MBT-Groups describing how therapists take responsibility for group processes by creating a context and continuity through their continuous thinking about the group, both in the group and before and after sessions. 'Managing authority' (Karterud & Bateman, 2012) is supported by having clear and specific aims which are understood and agreed before the group commences. Whilst maintaining a benign inquisitive stance, therapists will challenge non-mentalizing and attempts at damaging the group through hostility or denigration. By remaining in contact with the intense and troubling affects, the therapists, with much empathy, will be identifying, processing and helpfully expressing these emotions, 'mentalizing affectivity'. Here it is essential to have two co-facilitators who are able to support one another in recognising and managing non-mentalizing impasses without taking on the role of expert or exerting coercive control over the group. Through recognising our own contributions to such impasses, implicitly and explicitly monitoring our own mistakes, therapists reaffirm that mistakes offer an opportunity to revisit and learn more.

One of the therapists starts each group session with reference to the last session using this as an introduction to the present whilst also creating explicit continuity for the group. After looking back, group members check in with how they are doing and are asked if they want to share about the past week or if there is something they would like help with. Long silences are avoided as they are likely to raise anxiety and impair mentalizing. Therapists are actively curious *'I'm not sure what people are feeling about this silence. I was thinking it might be hard to speak after the difficult ending last week. Do you have any thoughts about this Joe?'* Ice breakers, structured skills-based activities, as well as expressive activities, might be used to engage members and stimulate mentalizing, particularly in the early stages of a group or with developmentally younger groups.

In some groups, therapists closely manage the time and attention between participants whilst others give more responsibility to group members with this changing over the life span of the group. Experienced group members might take on more responsibility, explaining the structure to new members and starting the session off by reflecting on the last session.

The interplay between individual and group sessions is important with individual sessions supporting the adolescent's group participation by providing a space away from the group to further reflect on their own contributions to non-mentalizing group interactions.

Before starting – securing the framework

Working with groups of adolescents with emerging personality disorder in intensive MBT-A programmes is often like working on the edge of life and death, on the edge of acting out or collaboration. Remaining connected in moments of crisis and seeking to *understand* behaviour and not act upon it is vital to success. Mentalizing is fragile and programmed to break down and when faced with an adolescent's rage or an overwhelming sense of hopelessness and suicidal ideation, it is hard not to feel equally overwhelmed and respond with concrete controlling behaviours.

Being aware of our own feelings in response to our patients requires therapists to have trusting relationships with colleagues and the institutions within which we work. There needs to be a commitment to creating and maintaining a receptive, responsive and mentalizing atmosphere to ensure therapists can effectively restore and maintain their mentalizing in the face of extreme challenges. Colleagues need to feel secure to talk openly with each other without fear of judgement or blame. Communication between individual, family and group therapists need to be formalised through regular weekly meetings with identified specific purposes. Here therapists can jointly manage risk and complex decisions.

Group setting and make up

Ideally, the two therapists will be a female-male couple with a maximum of eight members with the group taking place weekly at the same time and in the same room. The room is organised into a circle of chairs with absent members continuing to be held in mind by their chair remaining in the circle. Groups are open with a new adolescent entering when another member leaves, providing they have completed the MBT-A Group Information session. Group duration is between 6–18 months alongside weekly individual sessions with six monthly reviews evaluating goals and progress.

Group therapists double as participants' individual therapists, which helps to build continuity and cohesion. Groups benefit from having male and female participants with a diverse range of identified emerging personality disorders. This offers opportunities to develop new perspectives and skills; members typified with borderline traits might help those characterised with avoidant coping strategies to notice and express anger whilst also learning from their 'avoidant' peer how to momentarily step away from emotions (Muller et al., 2017). Drug and alcohol use is a common feature, and it is important to distinguish use and misuse from substance dependence which would preclude taking part in the group. For those who misuse, reduction of substance misuse has to be an agreed goal. Often, as treatment progresses and the young person's capacity to tolerate and consider mental states in themselves and others increases, alcohol and drug abuse becomes less of an issue.

Establishing an alliance for group work

It is essential that during the assessment phase therapists work collaboratively with the adolescent to develop a formulation and mentalizing profile that supports their understanding, motivation and participation in group treatment. This needs to incorporate the adolescent's current interpersonal difficulties in the context of their peer relationships and other social environments.

Kelly clearly states, *'I'm not doing the group part. I'm fine meeting you and the family stuff, but NO GROUPS!'* Matching Kelly's affect the therapist wonders, *'Wow! What is it about groups?'* Kelly explains, *'It starts ok, I like people, they like me, then I take on all their problems.'* Kelly shudders and scratches her arms. The therapist picks up on this, first noting *'how it seems to start well but then you feel their problems become yours and you have to sort it all out?'* Kelly agrees. The therapist continues, *'I noticed you scratching as if you were feeling something?'* Kelly nods, *'I feel like they get into me, I get infected.'* Empathising and inviting elaboration the therapist offers, *'Yuck, infected, what do you do?'* Kelly describes, *'I lash out, feel furious then they hate me, think I'm a fucking bitch but I need to protect myself.'* *'So coming into a group, it's like walking into a room of infected people you need to protect yourself from?'* *'That's why I'm not interested in your group!'* exclaims Kelly. The therapist affirms Kelly's brave description of how she experiences herself with others whilst also noticing her own response to this. *'I can see how you feel you're protecting yourself from this "infection". But when you were explaining this to me, I felt sad.'* Kelly looks surprised and suggests she's alright. *'Well, that may be, but I think it could feel lonely at times, keeping yourself away from others, especially when you've told me you like people.'* Kelly says she doesn't want to talk about this anymore. The therapist agrees, noting how hard she has stayed with thinking about something she finds difficult. In a further assessment session, Kelly and her therapist think about how they might notice this "infection" pattern should it happen in the group and what can be done to help. With this support, Kelly agrees to try the group.

MBT-A group information sessions

These group psychoeducation sessions aim to build on the assessment phase and prepare the adolescent for further group work by developing their understanding of their own mentalizing strengths and weaknesses. It also acts as a more structured introduction to a group setting. Using a range of texts, exercises, video clips, structured activities and discussion, the group aims to introduce the concept of mentalizing and its importance in everyday life and how treatment can support the development of mentalizing skills. Groups typically cover the following: how to tell when we are mentalizing; what non-mentalizing looks like; skills and attitude involved in mentalizing, curiosity, openness and a willingness to reflect; how mentalization can break down under stress and when the connection to ourselves and important others feels threatened; how early experiences can influence our mentalizing and the characteristics of an emerging personality disorder and how enhancing mentalizing can help.

Mentalizing techniques and interventions in MBT-A groups

The technique of 'Parking' is a way of marking or noticing someone who is not able to connect to what is happening in the here-and-now. It is helpful for managing arousal, challenging non-mentalizing moments and holding the group on a mentalizing trajectory when someone has been "parked" it is important to come back to them as soon as possible.

> *The group is exploring an awkward moment from last week, one of the therapists is acknowledging to group member Chris that she had been thinking about their exchange last week. Kimberley, arriving late, bounces in, 'hey! you dyed your hair green Chris!'. 'Just wait a minute', offers the therapist 'I was in the middle of a conversation with Chris.' Kimberley's face darkens and she zones out disappearing behind her hair. The therapist notices and names, 'I think you're zoning out. Hang on, we'll come back to you shortly.' The other therapist tries to maintain eye contact with Kimberley, supporting her to remain present.*
>
> *The group explores the impact of the last session trying to include Kimberley, whilst acknowledging Kimberley's inability to connect, 'I can see you seem "out" Kimberley', can we pause, search and rewind to try and understand what happened for you to feel "out". Do you know when you were still in with us?' Kimberley says nothing and the therapist recruits others into the mentalizing task, helping Kimberley. Janice asks, "when you saw Chris' green hair you were totally in the room?' 'Yes', Kimberly says. Janice continues, 'then she (pointing to the therapist) firmly said, 'wait a minute. I think that's when you zoned out.' 'Yeah!', Kimberley replies relieved to feel understood by her peer. The therapist asks, 'did my tone of voice feel harsh?' Kimberley nods, 'Yes, I'm a perfectionist and when you criticised me, I thought I'm wrong. I'm nothing. I want to disappear.' Marking Kimberley's rising affect the therapist answers, 'No wonder you were having trouble being in the room, if you felt you were being criticised'. In validating Kimberley's feelings of shame and sense of being wrong, the therapist gets alongside her, giving room for angry feelings but not agreeing it was her intention to leave Kimberley out. Kimberley's arousal decreases and she makes eye contact.*

The other therapist thinks Kimberley might feel connected again and takes a not-knowing stance, checking and clarifying, 'Kimberley you seem to be back with us, no longer "out"?' Kimberley nods yes and the therapist asks if they can explore this "out" feeling a little further, seeking collaboration and modelling skills in noticing one's own capacity to manage arousal. Kimberley says 'yes'. The therapist asks the group how others might have heard the tone of voice of his colleague? This is working towards triangulation, 'asking another person in the group to give his view on the problems described by others or on the interaction between others, either from his own perspective or from his understanding of their perspective' (Bateman, Kongerslev, & Bo, 2019). There are a variety of responses, such as *'it was relaxed', 'I thought Kimberley was trying to stop the conversation and the therapist was angry about this'.* The group talks and Kimberley remains connected and clarifies she didn't want to *'stop the conversation'* but thinks she was *'feeling nervous about being late and was trying to join in'. 'That's really helpful,'* remarks the other therapist supporting Kimberley's mentalizing of herself. He then wonders how his colleague feels upon hearing Kimberley's worries about entering the group. *'I can see how you might have felt I was being harsh, I was quick to respond,'* she offers. Supporting his colleague to get her mentalizing back on track, the therapist asks *'any thoughts about this quick response?' 'I think I was feeling anxious to resolve some of the difficulties from last week. It stopped me from also considering what it was like for you Kimberley, arriving late.'* Here, therapist use of self enables the therapist to reflect on her own mentalizing breakdown making explicit her understanding of herself.

Employed in a non-blaming manner, these techniques foster a safe group environment for members to work in the here-and-now and maintain an affective focus whilst exploring relevant interpersonal difficulties. Group members become more aware of the affective states underlying their actions, the potential impact on others and importantly, that these can be understood in the context of supportive relationships.

Expressive activities

Expressive activities have a long history of use in MBT models and can be integrated into the group structure to adapt to the group's mentalizing abilities. Guessing games, discussing video clips, role-plays and artmaking are but a few ways in which creative interventions have been employed to promote thinking about mental states. In early psychoeducation groups, these activities are often used to illuminate the dynamic nature of implicit and explicit mentalizing and how easily we can make assumptions based on behaviour.

Therapist one sits on the floor with their head down, therapist two stands with their back to therapist one, they move a little, turn and look at each other without speaking. A few group members laugh, someone utters, 'this is pathetic.' Gently ignoring the initial non-mentalizing comment therapist one asks, 'What do people imagine is happening here?'

Tanya (shouting out):	*'It's me and my mum!'*
Susan:	*'Oh god, that's weird, I was thinking the exact same thing'.*
Therapist two:	*'What about you and your mum?'*
Tanya:	*'It's like when I cut, she's angry, sick of me so she doesn't look at me.'*
Therapist two:	*'Susan, what about you?'*
Susan (quietly):	*'Mmm, I think it's a mum and daughter, they've argued and are ignoring each other.'*
Therapist one:	*'It seems you are both getting feelings of anger and upset from this picture but different ideas about why. Any other thoughts?'*
Candice:	*Sad, like you're friends and want to talk but can't.'*
Therapist two:	*'Earlier, someone had a quick response, "pathetic", John I think you might have commented.*
John (somewhat unsettled):	*Yeah, I mean you guys standing there, felt like school and that's shit.*
Therapist two:	*'Fair enough, you feel we're like teachers! This activity is partly about explaining our understanding of how people make sense of one another's behaviour.*
John (smiling):	*'Yeah, I get it, a picture is worth a thousand words.'*
Therapist two:	*'Yes, (smiling) now, you might find this a little "teacherly" but I'm curious, how you think each of us finds those words, how do we quickly come to an idea about what is happening?'*
John (thinking):	*'What's happened to us, you know like if you've been bullied you just expect to be bullied by everyone, you can't stop seeing it.'*

In this early MBT–A group session, the therapists attempt to strike a balance between attending to the here and now process (validating John's feelings of being in class and experiencing the therapists as authority figures) whilst also more directly keeping to the task of engaging the group in developing their understanding of mentalizing. Their playful intervention promotes curiosity and shows their willingness to engage. It helps to establish a collaborative stance and hold the balance between perceived adult authoritative roles and child positions. The therapists can tolerate looking *'pathetic'* and with the focus on their 'scene', group members feel less inhibited and able to respond.

Expressive activities create a safe distance for the exploration of feelings, which might otherwise be experienced as overwhelming. Group members are able to generate something of their internal self, externally where it can be safely reflected upon. Here, adolescents can find tangible evidence of feelings and processes which can feel elusive and difficult to define, with the expressive activity supporting the movement from implicit knowing to explicit reflection. The use of alternative mediums encourages perspective-taking and challenges behavioural patterns as the adolescent risks exploring with a different avenue of expression. When explicit mentalizing capacities are diminished, the opportunity to put on paper, use clay or building blocks to capture some of the young person's thoughts and feelings, can empower the young person positively impacting on their sense of self-agency. If the expressive activity helps to stimulate mentalizing whether by supporting attention control, regulating affect or encouraging conscious reflection, acting as an intermediate step between implicit and explicit mentalizing, then it would be considered on the model.

'Yeah, I know exactly what you mean' – working with pretend mode

At times there can be a tendency for agreement amongst members, appearing to respond empathically, *'oh yes, I feel exactly the same'*. Such statements are often accompanied with lengthy descriptions which fail to capture any affect or make sense of what might be happening on a felt level. Missing is a genuine curiosity with excessive use of words creating an emotional distance leading to feelings of emptiness and meaninglessness. Here, the therapeutic task is to challenge the non-mentalizing without further splitting cognition and affect, slowly creating awareness and tolerance for affective states. This can involve starting with the body, noticing sensations, mentalizing at the sensory level, gradually building up a mentalizing picture through noticing and naming and being genuinely curious about what we ourselves and others might be feeling. As a therapist using our own feelings and expressing these in the context of trying to understand another can enable others to get in touch with their own feelings and 'breakthrough' Pretend Mode. Sometimes this can involve raising a bit of anxiety and heating up the arousal level to bring emotional states to the forefront (Muller & Midgley, 2020).

The group is painfully silent upon hearing group member John has been hospitalised following a serious overdose. The therapists experience the silence as impenetrable and attempts to evoke thoughts and feelings are met with 'I don't knows' followed by 'we all feel sad'. Unable to tolerate and notice their feelings they move into a seemingly thoughtful mentalizing exchange wherein they trace John's behaviour in the previous group, making spurious connections to his suicide attempt. This feels empty and disconnected. Then they decide 'we'll visit individually on different days.' 'Yes, good idea, he needs company', Tom comments. The group calmly plans how to help John feel less alone with little curiosity of their own internal states or how John might experience their intervention or indeed if he feels alone and unwelcome. 'Hold on' offers one of the therapists, 'my heart is racing with your thoughts and plans but I don't understand what I feel about what John did or why?.' Group members uneasily look up… The other therapist supports and clarifies,'it's great people are thinking about making John feel welcome but it feels like we're missing something, how we feel about what has happened and… what John might make of people visiting him. The other therapist offers how it is hard to put an activity into words.

Over the next 20-minutes group members use chalk, pencils, crayons, markers, clay and LEGO to create an image of 'how I am feeling now'. During this task there are 'sighs' and sounds of frustration. The sensory act of making something seems to give relief from distressing feelings, as black chalk is forcefully spread across a page. The therapists encourage people to notice how their bodies feel and what thoughts or feelings arise. 'This is depressing, I just feel sad', 'I'm gutted, I don't understand' with the creative process allowing some noticing and expression of affect.

The images are viewed individually, promoting shared joint attention on something else, holding powerful feelings and relational dynamics. Eye contact increases and therapists encourage members to be curious about the images. Kelly, looking at Cathy's image: 'I like the colours, the blended black and red. It kinda feels angry, no, maybe dark. Is that you with the hands in front of your eyes?' Cathy says yes and 'feels ashamed'. One of the therapists asks about this. Cathy red in the face, 'I feel jealous, wish it was me, you probably think I'm stupid.' 'No,' says Kelly supportively, 'you feel what you feel', then offers how she feels 'angry, like he's 'infecting' the group, I'm worried he'll bring me down.' The complex hidden affects and relational dynamics are safely finding form and expression, bringing heart and mind together and creating opportunities for the impact of John's suicide attempt to be further thought about.

'It's obvious you think I am no good' – working with psychic equivalence

Feeling misunderstood can be painful and isolating. Sometimes the feelings we have inside, particularly the negative ones, feel all too real and our interactions with others only seem to confirm this internal view. When operating in the non-mentalizing mode of psychic equivalence, there is little tolerance of alternative perspectives. Therapists can feel they have very little room for manoeuvre, aware of how easily the adolescent might be further unsettled. The therapeutic task is to get right alongside the adolescent offering empathic validation in the hope of stimulating some curiosity and difference.

Fourteen-year-old Fatima comes from a family characterised by fighting, where 'It feels like being in a constant war - If you are not with me, you are against me.' In the group, she empathises with others and tries to connect by underlining the bits in their stories she can recognise. The therapists have recognised this pattern of relating emerging in the group with members finding it difficult to create a space for difference, often agreeing with Fatima. Having in mind that Fatima comes from a family where it is dangerous to feel different, one of the therapists tries to help Fatima notice this pattern, 'It is interesting Fatima your way of connecting to others in the group is to share what you recognise in their stories. Is that right?' Fatima agrees. The therapists ask other group members if they also recognise this way of connecting with others in themselves. Rob says he does and also how he sometimes feels scared to think differently from Fatima, he feels she can be so fierce. Rob's statement elicits a profound reaction with Fatima screaming, 'I think you are an insensitive asshole Rob! You don't belong in this group!' The therapists work to validate the different emerging perspectives and feelings, trying to keep a safe atmosphere. Trying to regulate the growing arousal they use the technique of siding, whereby they side with the feelings of both Fatima and Rob whilst also taking the focus away from them and onto the therapist's imagined experience of the interaction. *'It's okay Rob to express your fears and Fatima, also for you to express your anger and maybe hurt? But if I was Rob, I might feel attacked by your raised voice and then I am no longer able to listen. What Rob has said really touched you, I want to be able to understand both your and Rob's feelings.'* The therapist's intervention aims to protect both Rob and Fatima. The other therapist asks group members what they make of these interactions. They express support for Fatima, leaving Rob in an uncomfortable position. The therapist tries to understand their responses whilst also validating Rob for daring to speak out. *One of the therapists tentatively wonders out loud what the effect of being raised in a family which Fatima has previously described to the group as 'like being in a war zone' might have had on Fatima. The therapist suggests that it might be important for Fatima to find similarities to stay out of the warzone and how this might be happening in a way in this group session, differences might mean people are against one another. Fatima hears this comment as 'you think I don't have an opinion of my own, I just go where the wind blows me' and feels criticised. In following sessions, Fatima's feelings of being criticised convince her that 'you, (therapist one) and Rob are against me and I am no good in your eyes'. The group joins in with Fatima believing Rob and the therapist are against Fatima and are fearful to voice any differing opinion should Fatima turn on them. The group is becoming a war zone.*

In supervision, the therapists are helped to identify their own feelings of fear, anger and hopelessness impacting on their mentalizing. They painfully note how this led to a premature and potentially controlling intervention, trying to make Fatima see the repeating pattern in her behaviour and the impact on the group. They had not adequately empathised and elaborated on Fatima's feeling state. The team agreed it was important to explore this with Fatima in her individual session and for the therapist to take responsibility for their part in the misunderstanding.

Fatima didn't arrive for upcoming sessions. The therapist texted Fatima encouraging her to keep contact, explaining how she could understand why Fatima might stay away but that the therapist wished to see her and work things out. Fatima arrived for a subsequent individual session still ready to go into a battle. The therapist quickly apologised to Fatima for the upset caused. Fatima continued to shout and accused the therapist of being like her father, criticising her. The therapist endured Fatima's feelings of anger, holding in mind how Fatima was possibly frightened, unable to explicitly mentalize with the therapist she felt was at war with her. After a while Fatima started to cry, saying she felt so rejected in the group. She spoke of being surprised the therapist had apologised and how this made her feel differently about herself. The next group session Fatima was able to connect to herself and others in a slightly different way. She was less aroused and able to connect with Rob saying, 'I don't understand you but maybe I can learn.'

'The group should be two years!' – working with a teleological stance

Adolescents in a pre-mentalizing teleological stance have expectations concerning the agency of others but this is restricted to observable behaviour. A therapist's benign concern and motivation to be helpful requires concrete acts like the extending of sessions to confirm care and interest. Often emotions are hard to recognise, feelings are confused with thoughts, and actions occur without thinking in an attempt to shift intolerable internal states. Within a group setting, conversations might focus on who did what and behaviour is explained in terms of physical circumstances, 'she left the group because she's tired!'. It can be hard to resist the urge to respond with action and therapists can feel they never give enough. Therapists need to manage these counter-transference responses and focus efforts on noticing the underlying emotional states, differentiating feelings from thoughts and reflecting on the interpersonal experience.

Nineteen-year-old Kelly is approaching the end of her time in the group having made good progress. Diagnosed with emerging borderline personality disorder at the age of 17, Kelly's early life was blighted by periods of severe neglect as her mother battled with depression and addiction. 'Kelly the carer' can be hypervigilant to other's minds often to the neglect of her own resulting in her feeling forgotten.

Kelly has been putting pressure on the therapists to "manage time better" and has enlisted group members to convince the therapists that the group should run for 2 years. She's arrived at the group with a well written letter to the clinic director and wants the therapists to sign the letter. Both therapists feel pressure to agree fearing Kelly might quickly feel hurt and end prematurely. They decide to share the dilemma with Kelly and the group.

'I feel real pressure to agree. Kelly, I can see it means so much to you, the letter is beautifully written'. 'Thanks,' says Kelly adding, 'but?' sensing the therapist has more to say. 'Yes, there is a but, I'm not sure I understand what I am agreeing to, but feel if I don't agree you will feel hurt.' Kelly quickly retorts, 'We're telling you the group isn't long enough.' There is a murmuring of agreement and Tom suggests 'Just bloody well sign it, I mean is it really so hard?' Taking a risk one of the therapists playfully challenges, 'And then what?' 'What' asks Kelly. The therapist explains, 'what if after 2 years it still doesn't feel enough, should we just keep extending it?' The group pauses but Kelly confirms, that's exactly what should be done!' Others now seem less certain. Noticing this, the therapists recruit Tamara who has a somewhat confused look on her face. 'Tamara, any thoughts about this?' Tamara hesitates, 'I don't know...umm... Kelly I want you to stay, but the group can't go on forever, I mean you're going to college, I don't want to be here forever.' 'What the fuck, Tamara' replies Kelly. The therapist encourages Kelly to pause, looking as though she is about to leave, 'Whoa, wait Kelly, please I'd like you to stay... what is it you've heard Tamara say?' 'I don't know' says Kelly, flustered

but remaining seated. The therapist asks others what they think and John (who has a strong connection with Kelly) offers, 'Tamara's trying to point out the positives but maybe Kelly you're just feeling shit about leaving, and babe I don't want you to go either.' There are a few laughs and Kelly looks a little tearful, 'I'm not going to get pissed off… sorry Tamara, we're ok?' Tamara nods, 'Yeah we're ok.' Susan talks about feeling frightened thinking about when she will have to leave and how she will miss Kelly. The group is moving out of a teleological stance and making tentative steps towards naming underlying feeling states and reflecting on interpersonal experiences in the context of Kelly leaving. After the group Kelly asks for an earlier individual session describing how she is 'freaking out.' The therapists agree that this would be helpful, responding to Kelly's growing awareness of how difficult she is finding leaving the group.

Ending therapy

As the previous vignette shows, ending therapy can be a difficult and emotive experience. It is not uncommon for the group to express low mood and feelings of sadness, as they begin to mourn the loss of a group member. The re-emergence of earlier non-mentalizing patterns are likely as newly formed attachment bonds are strained under the process of separating and saying goodbye.

After identifying a date for the last group session, the adolescent preparing to leave, and the therapists discuss this within the group. Adequate time needs to be given to the process of 'working through' the ending, enabling the departing individual and remaining group members to consider the various feelings emerging in this process.

In supporting leaving members to reflect on their time in the group, they are asked to write a card to their fellow group members. These cards remain in the group therapy room, enabling remaining and new members to read the goodbye messages of the previous group members. This chapter concludes with the goodbye letter 19-year-old Annju wrote at the end of treatment, which describes how this expressive activity can stimulate patient reflection on their therapeutic process.

> *Hello everyone,*
> *Today is my last day, that's a really weird thing to say.*
> *My road to recovery was a very long emotional one but I finally did it.*
> *I want to thank you for giving me the space to exist, it helped me give myself the space to exist.*
> *Recovery is long and hard.*
> *It starts with admitting that you have a problem and choosing to get better.*
> *I know there are a few of you who are scared of feeling/feeling pain but if I've learned one thing, it's to let yourself feel everything that has been building up. If you keep pushing it down, it could stand in the way and you have the right to feel*

it all.

It may be scary and hurtful but it will get better. There is a light at the end of the tunnel.

I believe in you.

Another thing is to become your own best friend. I know it's easier said than done but trust me, it helps a lot.

Thank you for helping me in the last stage of my recovery.

You guys were a big help and have taught me a lot.

Don't give up on yourself.

I know you can do it

and always remember how lucky you are to have yourselves.

References

Bateman, A.W., & Fonagy, P. (2011). *Handbook of Mentalizing in Mental Health Practice.* Washington, DC: American Psychiatric Publications, Inc.

Bateman, A.W., Kongerslev, M., & Bo, S. (2019). Group therapy for adults and adolescents. In A.W. Bateman, & P. Fonagy (Eds.), *Handbook of Mentalizing in Mental Health Practice* (2nd ed., pp. 117–134). Washington, DC: American Psychiatric Association Publishing.

Becker, D.F., Grilo, C.M., Edell, W.S., & McGlash, T.H. (2000). Comorbidity of borderline personality disorder with other personality disorders in hospitalized adolescents and adults. *American Journal of Psychiatry, 157*(12), 2011–2016.

Eaton, N.R., Krueger, R.F., & Oltmanns, T.F. (2011). Aging and the structure and long-term stability of the internalizing spectrum of personality and psychopathology, *Psychological Aging, 26*(4), 987–993.

Fonagy, P., & Luyten, P. (2009). A developmental, mentalization-based approach to the understanding and treatment of borderline personality disorder. *Development and Psychopathology, 21*(4), 1355–1381. doi:10.1017/S0954579409990198.

Fonagy, P., & Allison, E. (2014). The role of epistemic trust in the therapeutic relationship. *Psychotherapy, 51*(3), 372–380. https://doi.org/10.1037/a0036505.

Hutsebaut, J., Bales, D., Kavelaars, M., van Gerwen, J., van Busschbach, J., & Verheul, R. (2011). Implementatie van een behandelmodel voor persoonlijkheidsgestoorde adolescenten: Successen, mislukkingen en aanbevelingen. *Tijdschrift voor Psychotherapie, 37*(3), 162–176. https://doi.org/10.1007/s12485-011-0030-5 Implementation of a treatment model for adolescents with emerging personality disorder: Successes, failures and recommendations.

Karterud, S. (2015). *Mentalization-Based Group Therapy (MBT-G): A Theoretical, Clinical, and Research Manual.* New York, NY: Oxford University Press.

Karterud, S., & Bateman, A. (2012). Group therapy techniques. In A.W. Bateman & P. Fonagy (Eds.), *Handbook of Mentalizing in Mental Health Practice* (pp. 81–105). American Psychiatric Publishing, Inc.

Leszcz, M. (2014). The effective group therapist. *Groepen: Tijdschrift voor groepsdynamica and groepspsychotherapie, 9*(2), 9–20.

Malberg, N. (2010). *Mentalization-Based Group Therapy for Adolescents (MBTG-A).* Unpublished Manuscript, Yale University.

Muller, N., Ten Kate, C.A., & Eurelings-Bontekoe, E.H.M. (2017). Internaliserende problematiek in de kindertijd als risicofactor voor de ontwikkeling van persoonlijkheidspathologie op latere leeftijd. In: E.H.M. Eurelings-Bontekoe, R. Verheul, & W. Snellen (Eds.), *Handboek persoonlijkheidspathologie (pp. 63–72)*. Houten: Bohn Stafleu van Loghum. (Internalizing disorders in childhood as a risk factor to develop personality disorder later in life, in the Dutch *Handbook of Personality Disorder*).

Muller, N., & Midgley, N. (2020). *The clinical challenge of mentalization-based therapy with children who are in 'pretend mode'. Journal of Infant, Child, and Adolescent Psychotherapy.* https://doi.org/10.1080/15289168.2019.1701865.

National Institute for Health and Care Excellence (2015). *Personality disorders: borderline and antisocial.* (NICE Quality Standard No. QS88). Retrieved from https://www.nice.org.uk/guidance/qs88.

Paris, J. (2003). Personality disorders over time: Precursors, course and outcome. *Journal of Personality Disorders, 17*(6), 479–488.

Tahmasebi, A.M., Artiges, E., Banaschewski, T., Barker, G.J., Bruehl, R., Büchel, C., Conrod, P.J., Flor, H., Garavan, H., Gallinat, J., Heinz, A., Ittermann, B., Loth, E., Mareckova, K., Martinot, J.L., Poline, J.B., Rietschel, M., Smolka, M.N., Ströhle, A., Schumann, G., & Paus, T. (2012), Creating probabilistic maps of the face network in the adolescent brain: a multicentre functional MRI study. *Human Brain Mapping, 33*(4), 938–957. doi:10.1002/hbm.21261.

Chapter 12

AMBIT

Haiko Jessurun and Dickon Bevington

Imagine ... it is a typical day at work. You have just settled in the staff room with a coffee. One of your colleagues, a social psychiatric nurse who has a lot of experience with 'turbulent' girls, badly wants to discuss the case of 15-year-old Sandra.

Sandra has lived in residential care for about a year now. It is still not feasible to have her living with her parents. She attends a school for children with special educational needs, but this is also problematic, and she skips classes a lot. She has been having treatment from the Eating Disorders Team but has been transferred recently to the team treating Trauma and Mood Disorders. Sandra found this change difficult, but the main point of concern, according to your colleague, is that the children's home where she lives thinks that she should now be admitted to the local psychiatric inpatient unit; they have concluded that this is now the only way to keep her safe and help her. Her school maintains that she is welcome as long as she adheres to certain well-defined conditions, although this is likely to be hard to achieve. The psychiatrist from the Trauma and Mood Team believes that it is essential that things are normalised; Sandra should just go to school, and an admission to hospital is out of the question.

The psychiatric nurse then speaks of the last meeting between her, School, Youth Protection (safeguarding) services, and staff from the home where she lives. Your colleague describes being attacked by these other professionals, especially by the management of the residential care home. What you notice, sitting there with your coffee getting cold, is that — apart from the obvious anger and frustration in your colleague — all kinds of comments are surfacing about how unprofessional the management staff of the residential care are being, and how the Youth Protection officer "has been sucked in by the system", and so on.

After about 15 minutes or so, you too are feeling tense and frustrated; you are certainly empathically engaged with the frustration and anxiety of your colleague, but on the other hand nothing much very helpful has happened for Sandra ...

The vignette above is a typical example of the 'dis-integration' of the care system around those challenging young people, who are frequently described as "hard to reach" by services, although in truth they might better be described as "under-served": the help that is offered to them (often in large, complex, and expensive 'doses') is rarely experienced as *helpful,* and their rejection of it is, in that sense at least, purposeful and adaptive.

AMBIT has been developed over the past 15 years through an iterative open-source, and "deployment-focused" (Weisz & Simpson Gray, 2008) process involving several hundred multiple real-world services working with these clients (high complexity, high risk, low "engagement") to find a solution to the challenges that such young people present, with mentalization as the oil that greases the cogs involved. AMBIT is less a concrete (teleological) organisational model and more a systematic approach to the development and adaptation of systems of help around troubled adolescents and their families so *that these can be experienced as more helpful*, and thus be better used and more effective (Bevington & Fuggle, 2012; Bevington, Fuggle, Cracknell, & Fonagy, 2017; Bevington, Fuggle, Fonagy, Target, & Asen, 2013; Fuggle et al., 2014). How might an array of professionals in a locality, drawn from different training backgrounds, employed by different teams and agencies, with different commissioned priorities, who have different levels of experience, and of power, arrange themselves around a young person and their *pre-existing helping network* in a way that can be trusted, and thus used, and thus hold the hope of efficacy, and which might also be *sustainable*?

Epistemic trust and 'hard to reach' young people

AMBIT has been developed for young people whose severe psychiatric, social, educational, and other complex intersecting problems, including multiple adverse experiences, have called forth adaptive responses that have been labelled as "epistemic hypervigilance"; a sustained and pervasive tendency towards mistrust in the *social value* of any of the learning, experience, knowledge or advice that workers or helpers may hold and offer to them by way of help. Paradoxically, while the doors to help seem firmly closed to professional helpers, they can appear frustratingly (or worryingly) open to the representatives of the darker side of society: drug dealers, gang leaders, delinquent peers and adults who might want to exploit them. Something about these darker characters (who the young person may, in truth, identify as their existing *network of 'help'*) seems much easier for them to understand and accept uncritically. Research into Epistemic Trust suggests that this is 'won' when the young person experiences themselves as being seen (re-*cognised*) and understood; mentalized accurately, as it were. Compared to the 24-hour availability of the drug dealer, and the secure expectancies a young person might have about what this person will deliver in terms of mental state outcomes, the hapless mental health worker has their work cut out. Ideas about the General Psychopathology Factor ("P-Factor", Caspi et al., 2014) have led to the proposal that this transdiagnostic approach to the risk of chronicity and treatment resistance in an individual may in fact be a proxy measure for this disposition; one of poor or low adaptability of a person's *Epistemic Trust*. Evidence-based treatments may work well (however severe the symptoms) for individuals with a *low* P-factor but appear to "bounce off" those with *high* P-factors because of their fundamental inability to trust the value of the help on offer so that in their minds it makes sense to keep the door to help shut fast. Aside from the simpler outcomes of symptom reduction, school re-engagement, etc., an AMBIT-influenced service may see its more fundamental task as being able to address this *chronic Epistemic Hypervigilance* in their clients – to address their clients' relationship to help itself.

Complexity

The young people we are referring to have long histories and may have already experienced multiple different elements of care or help: systems that do not always appear to "agree". This often mirrors their experience of their own families, where mother and father may have fought in front of them (not uncommonly triggered by different ideas about what would constitute 'good parenting'). Their families of origin may not be very stable, nor able (because of the parents' own problems, or lack of abilities, or because of poverty) nor willing (because of the parents' own earlier adverse experiences of professional care) to accept any form of aid or use professional help. These young people may have had several psychiatric classifications, problems at school, social problems (peer group relationships) and antisocial problems (gangs and offending), so that police and drug services, or acute medical services who are called upon to address their self-injurious behaviours, are often a part of the mix along with social care, educational inclusion services, and forensic or youth offending services. As a direct result of these families' complexity, wealthy industrialised nations will often respond with a plethora of different services, and each one commissioned with a specialist brief to address specific disaggregated elements of the accumulated (perhaps agglomerated is a better word) burden of the young person's multiple problems. Each problem interacts with the others in evil synergies so that each makes the others harder to treat.

All these various services, 'care' or 'cure' systems, justice systems, social systems, local government, etc., become activated by one or other of the problems these young people present with and are motivated, inspired and energised to 'do their thing'. Paradoxically, the very complexity of these helping systems can amplify and indeed exacerbate the complexity and stasis. Services often have just one of these areas within their 'jurisdiction' (their "sphere of influence" which is the original meaning of the word 'ambit') and not uncommonly this leads to a stalemate around the young person or carers. A spectrum of services and organisations becomes involved, with different structures, different employees, different professions, codes of conduct, theoretical models, methods and training (neurobiological, sociological, cognitive behavioural, psychodynamic, systemic, etc.) Each training, of course, requires significant personal investment by the practitioners. Understandably, and often driven by the noblest of intentions, these differences invite disagreements or misunderstandings. In the context of high risk and high levels of personal engagement by individual workers who are driven to intervene with desperate trajectories, this adds *stress*. Workers under stress are inevitably prone to lose their own capacity to mentalize each other – they become more certain of their rightness or another agency's wrongness than is helpful. They become teleological, and power struggles are often enacted, covertly or sometimes overtly. Unfortunately, more often than experiencing our multiagency efforts as a benign transport into higher realms, our clients experience our efforts as contradictory, overwhelming, fractious, aversive, and at worst, intentionally unhelpful.

Workers *immune* to such stress would be inhuman, and probably unsuited to such work, but the paradox is clear: we work in conditions where stress is inevitable, and where despite our best efforts to mentalize, this capacity is rendered fragile.

Hectic help

Of course, most of these young people have a history in which their attachment systems have been compromised; they rarely have a model of secure attachment that they can use to support the task of building a helping therapeutic relationship with a professional. Just as their early caregivers were not able to adequately mentalize these young people, their own capacity to mentalize us, their workers, is also strained. The development of mentalizing capacity (see Chapter 1) is inhibited particularly if a child's attachment system is disorganised (Fonagy & Target, 2005). Young people may, despite this, manage *one* reasonably trusting relationship with a worker, but to create three or four, or more, with staff from different teams, is often much too much to ask. Moreover, Epistemic Trust shows no respect for a professional role, authority, or training – a young person may find it much easier to develop some epistemic trust in a low paid, systemically-overlooked residential care worker than in an expensive, highly qualified therapist with multiple degrees and diplomas!

The ambit: the importance of social networks

AMBIT can best be described as a set of principles and methods applied systemically that stimulate awareness of the above problems and help staff working with these kinds of clients to recognise more easily when and where the service systems dis-integrate (stop mentalizing each other), and then have tools to intervene to restore mentalizing. Importantly, AMBIT promotes an understanding of mentalizing that does not deny the prefrontal (neurodevelopmental) and dyadic (relational) aspects of mentalizing but emphasises mentalizing capacity as a measure of a person's *social connectedness* (at least as much as it is an individual or dyadic phenomenon). This refers to any individual, be they "worker" or "patient".

We argue that to ignore this phenomenon creates unhelpful pressures on individuals to hold themselves up as individual "mentalizing ninjas", while all the time the capacity they are trying to find and use (mentalizing) is dependent on them having access to a network of benign, mind-minded, minds. How so? The mother can only mentalize her screaming infant insofar as she has at least the idea of a network of other minds that can, would, or do *hold her own mind in mind*: her own mother, her partner, her friend, the health visitor, etc. - people who can construe and empathically represent (*re*-present) her own distress and exhaustion as understandable. Thus, in addition to "epistemic hypervigilance", another way to frame the General Psychopathology Factor referred to above is as a latent vulnerability that increases in direct relation to "*social thinning*" (McCrory, 2019), so that across time an individual, through neurodevelopmental vulnerability, trauma, or symptomatic illness, finds they have less and less access to benign and mentalizing minds.

Four quadrants: extending the focus on mentalizing across networks of help

AMBIT has its foundations in mentalizing and attachment theory (Bevington, Fuggle, & Fonagy, 2015), and thus there is a strong emphasis on the building of relationships, and the first one (inevitably) is the one with the young person. However, if it has anything substantively new to add, AMBIT seeks to shift attention toward equality of emphasis in its application toward the *workers* – across teams, and whole network or systems of help – as well as toward their *clients*.

In this field of work, there is perhaps a unique vulnerability to experiences of professional shame: "I feel anxious/upset/angry about this situation, not like my colleague H who always seems so calm; perhaps I'm a failure at this work?" Shame, in turn, tends to reduce help-seeking in a worker, rendering them even more vulnerable to isolation and further collapse of their fragile mentalizing capacity. We argue that a degree of anxiety in a worker is perfectly appropriate; to be expected, welcomed, even. To react otherwise in situations of such risk and complexity would suggest a degree of 'pretend mode' functioning. This necessity to protect and scaffold the workers' own mentalizing by strengthening their own networks is why AMBIT teams are trained to help develop and maintain a local culture that explicitly seeks to balance attention between three extra "quadrants" in our work, in addition to the more conventional focus on direct face-to-face "working with the client". These other three quadrants are represented in the AMBIT wheel (Figure 12.1):

- Working with the Team
- Working with wider Networks
- Learning at Work

Thus, AMBIT is a team approach, even though it emphasises strong individual "key" relationships where epistemic trust may arise. It is a framework for building helpful relations that are adaptive; building contextual support for *whatever* evidence-based practice(s) the team deploys, to give the best chance of

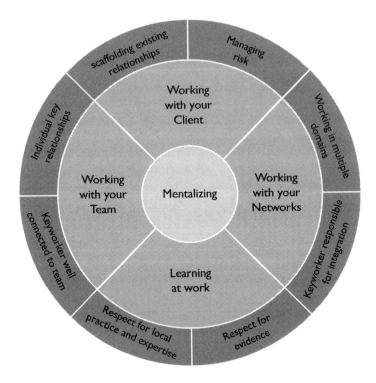

Figure 12.1 The AMBIT wheel (published in Bevington et al., 2017).

these interventions finding "epistemic openings" in their clients and supporting workers to live up to and sustain the kinds of secure expectancies that
they encourage clients to expect of them. Outside the four main 'quadrants' of
practice in which mentalizing attention (and a small number of disciplined
practices) is expected, there are eight elements of a 'principled stance', that
extend the "therapist's mentalizing stance" so as to consider *what else needs to be
held in balance* to navigate safely and effectively in this systemic context.

The AMBIT principles: 'grabholds' for workers in stormy seas

Each of the four quadrants is associated with a pair of principles, which are
always in tension with each other. Collectively these principles describe an
AMBIT stance that a worker tries to hold in balance. By design, the para-
doxical nature of these principles "describes the impossibility" of the work that
we try to do; when one principle is going right, its pair tends to go wrong. If

this description resonates with a worker's lived experience of the work, then perhaps some (epistemic) trust is evoked.

The eight principles and four quadrants are shown above in figure 1 and are briefly discussed per dialectical pair.

Working with your TEAM

– *Individual "key" relationships with a worker*
– **Keyworker well connected with the team**

The primary professional in contact with the client is referred to as the 'keyworker' in AMBIT, not necessarily being a formal role; it may simply be the worker who is currently "key" in the mind of the young person – with whom there is some epistemic trust – and in a network, this person may change over time. This person must first create some authentic contact, in which the young person experiences him/herself as being adequately understood. As a result, a keyworker will often be *'out there'* and will often feel isolated in contexts which we accept are stressful. The equal and "opposite" principle emphasises that such workers must remain "well-connected" to their team. The AMBIT approach aims to support generating and maintaining best (mentalizing) practice within such emotionally tense contexts, in which explicit mentalizing will be inhibited (Fonagy, Gergely, Jurist, & Target, 2004) unless the worker avoids isolation. A *"well-connected team"* holds an enculturated set of social disciplines that are based on mentalizing (ways of asking for help, ways of reaching out to one another) to support each other's individual work, minimising the risk of isolation or the pressure to be a "solo mentalizing ninja".

In the early stages of engagement, the keyworker may often have quite a central role in providing care and treatment/help for the young person and their existing helping network. In cases where the keyworker acts as a case manager, they may sometimes be the only direct contact with the young person and family. Direct approaches by additional workers, however well-intentioned, may in the early stages overwhelm the young persons' capacity for affiliative bonding. The keyworker in that sense constantly tries to view the helping network *through the eyes of the client* and to act in ways that help to shape, sequence, and adapt it productively. Keyworkers are encouraged to broadcast to their client an understanding of their *own connections,* particularly the help they receive from their own team, thus modelling to their clients that help-seeking is universal, and that 'this worker is supported, connected and able to trust the advice of his colleagues'. In this way, over time, implicitly and then explicitly, the invitation to the young person is to think about how their own helping network (beyond this worker) might be adapted and helped to become more useful, sustainable, and ultimately to be experienced as more *helpful.*

Working with your CLIENT

– Scaffolding existing relations
– Managing risk

The keyworker knows that they will not be helping the young person forever, but for young people who are wary of letting professionals into their lives, this might not always be so easy to mentalize. A fear that workers may be dangerously "adhesive" may be a common reason for "hard to reach" young people to keep workers at arms' length. Transparency about the *temporary* nature of this helping relationship, can (paradoxically) sometimes be critical to success in engaging a young person, alongside shared goal setting. Curiosity about identifying and understanding sources of help already available via the young person's *existing* network of help, likewise, creates a stance of humility and authenticity. The keyworker helps a young person to mentalize their *existing* helping network (as a direct parallel to showing them the team that supports the keyworker, and the benefits of being able to "phone a friend".)

Of course, in the case of young clients from extremely challenging backgrounds, many of their existing "helpers" are far from helpful in the eyes of a worker: dealers, gang leaders, etc. Obviously, these are not relationships that need scaffolding (!), but in the early stages of engagement, it is critical that these relationships are first *mentalized*, and not dismissed out of hand. A drug dealer is available to a young person 24–hours a day and offers secure expectancies of what mental state changes they will deliver, escape from unbearable psychic pain, and yes, sometimes pleasurable experiences, even if costly. We ignore or deny these realities at our peril, but the counter-position to this "scaffolding" work, is to know when to stop, and how! Risk management in these settings almost inevitably implies a more intrusive, or assertive stance, and there is absolutely no room for the blurring of boundaries. However, an intervention that is *solely* driven with risk management in mind runs the risk of driving a young person away, or conversely creating an unsustainable dependency that increases vulnerability when the worker or professional network leaves.

When a young person is referred to the care system, often an entire social network has broken down, with parental rejection and the young person finding themselves geographically separated from previous supports, so that they are especially vulnerable to these less–than–helpful "helpers". The work is thus focused on repairing pro–social network supports as soon as possible. There are of course known and broadly evidence-based techniques already available, but sometimes before anything that looks like more formal therapy starts, the most helpful manoeuvre is to help settle an argument with the sports–coach, so that training can resume. In this way, the worker tries to operate within the young person's existing world and to engage with the reality of what they experience as helpful and unhelpful. Where active risk management is required, significant efforts need to go into "marking" the fact of our professional obligations, and our longer–term intentions, as well as our recognition of how intrusive this can seem.

Working within your NETWORKS

– Working within multiple domains
– Keyworker responsible for integration

With complex problems, the required help is rarely limited to mental health care. Struggles and concerns present in all kind of domains ("from the molecular to the political"), all interconnected. AMBIT requires a "wide-angle lens" of workers, to ensure that there is work occurring in all those domains, when and where this is required. Inevitably, this will result in an expanding multi-professional and multi-agency network of help. The downside to these large networks (described above) is that workers will have conflicting ideas about how to define the "problems", what work should take precedence, how to sequence it, and who in the network should be delivering which identified tasks. We have already described the failures in cross-agency mentalizing about this as "dis-integration": no professional attends work with an *intention* to undermine the work of another worker, but it happens extremely often, and in these situations, professionals risk becoming as *non*-mentalizing towards one another as they are mentalizing towards their shared client.

AMBIT workers, within their "ambit", are invited not only to ensure that the appropriate domains are being addressed but also to intervene when necessary to help 'get noses pointing in the same direction'. Thus, an approach consisting only of psychological interventions is not the AMBIT way. Interventions at school, regarding safety, living arrangements, sports and hobbies, and so on, need to be considered. Sometimes getting a young person back into football is better than any therapy.

The keyworker is expected to actively engage with and is responsible for trying to help integrate, the different interventions within these domains – by helping the different workers to mentalize one another as well as the young person or their carers. A range of simple tools has been developed to support this work, which is often about reminding each other that, while *systems of care are inherently mindless* they are still comprised of individual minds that can be influenced to become more or less mentalizing of each other. This is why AMBIT avoids concrete (teleological) recommendations about organisational structures, as local cultures and service delivery contexts will deeply influence these. Our assumption is that failures in mentalizing across complex professional networks are often closely associated with heightened risk.

LEARNING at work

– Respect for local practice and expertise
– Respect for evidence

Working as an AMBIT-influenced team means being transparent about what you do and how you do it. The team seeks consistently to broadcast its intentions, and one of the main instruments to support this (though not universally used – there is a high degree of flexibility in how AMBIT is used, in keeping with its emphasis on adaptability) is by recording their own local learning in their own local version of the AMBIT wiki manual. The AMBIT core is freely available in a wiki (a "user-editable website" accessible at https://manuals.annafreud.org/ambit). Teams who receive training receive local versions of this manual that inherit all of the core content, but which can be edited locally, as a transparent account of *"who we are, what we do and how we do it"*. The AMBIT core is extensive – it has pages on theory, procedures, guidelines, training, treatment methods, all illustrated with helpful images or videos and downloadable resources.

Using AMBIT means realising that it is essential to respect and use evidence-based practices. We do not want to deliver services that 'do nothing'. This is in accordance with the basic mentalizing attitude of a searching and tentative curiosity, avoiding the assumption of knowledge that is unmoored to evidence (pretend mode). On the other hand, realism forces us to acknowledge that there is relatively little robust clinical research on working with these particular clients, whose rates of co-morbidity often lead them to be excluded from randomised controlled trials. Evidence-based practice will be complemented by locally held "practice-based evidence" that will be attuned to local culture, and service contexts. We are no more interested in asserting a "one size fits all" (teleological) set of steps and pro-cedures than we are in inviting teams to "make it up as you go": AMBIT invites teams to set aside some time in their programme to reflect together on how they hold this particular balance. A team, strictly speaking, cannot mentalize, but to collectively and collaboratively "manualise" how they address particular elements of their work might be the nearest equivalent: creating a meaningful shared narrative of 'our collective customs and practice', as it were. Sometimes, a page emerging in a local version of the AMBIT manual is so useful that it will be taken into the core and thus distributed to all other local versions. In this way, AMBIT aspires to support a "Community of Practice" (Lave & Wenger, 1991).

AMBIT: a quick start

AMBIT is designed not as a 'one size fits all' package, but as an approach based on evidence and accumulated clinical experience from training several thousand workers over the past decade. A full team training takes a lot of planning and could represent major changes in how services are adapted to fit the needs of clients, but the AMBIT programme at the Anna Freud National Centre for Children and Families is keen to stress that they are interested in supporting teams to "work under the influence of AMBIT" - adapted to suit the context - rather than in creating "AMBIT teams". There are several quick wins that can be quite easy to implement.

Working out what we need

We see the "well-connected team" as the primary engine for change in large complex systems of care, rather than individual practitioners, or indeed senior executives, although informed and active support from senior management is crucial to successful implementation. Assuming it is true to its intentions in "Working with Networks", one team starting to work under an AMBIT influence may have a surprising influence on other teams in the multi-agency system; in its "bottom-up" approach to culture change, working on the principle of increasing understanding across service boundaries, it has been described as a (benign!) 'guerrilla approach' to system change.

Some understanding of the rationale behind the stance and principles represented in the AMBIT wheel, and an intellectual commitment to these ideas, is a good foundation for developing an AMBIT influence in your team. However, perhaps even more important is that the team as a whole finds opportunities to reflect on *what they would want and need from any shared training*; defining an outcome of a successful training as "practising AMBIT" is not meaningful! Instead, teams considering training are invited and supported to reflect together to identify actual areas of their lived experience that repeatedly challenge them, and which could be improved. There are plenty of online resources to support this (readers could search ambit.tv on YouTube for a series of introductory videos, and preparatory team evaluations are shared online in the wiki manual such as the AMBIT Service Evaluation Questionnaire or ASEQ).

Three "tasters" of AMBIT

AMBIT provides a lot of tools and techniques, all grounded in mentalizing theory/practice, and developed in collaboration with workers. Three are offered here as "tasters".

Dis-integration grids

We have discussed dis-integration across services above. A simple technique to support systematic mentalization across a multi-professional or multi-agency network that appears to be "pulling in different directions" is the Dis-integration grid. On a piece of paper, create a grid, with the main actors (client, Dad, Mum, You, Social worker, Psychiatrist, School mentor, etc.) at the head of the **columns**, and with three **rows**, that invite mentalizing about three levels (where, we contend, most dis-integration occurs) titled thus:

1   **Explanation** ("What is the problem?")
2   **Intervention** ("What needs to be done?")
3   **Responsibility** ("Who should do this?")

The grid can be used in three ways (at least), but all involve attempts to mentalize these "actors", recording a few "bullet points" in each box so that *if the actor read these* they might nod and feel heard, or understood. In other words, the effort is to represent *their* understandings, rather than to impose one's own. Sometimes the "problem" as a young person sees it, is the intrusion of people like us. If this is denied, or ignored, little helpful work will ensue. Professionals tend to get into more conflict in rows 2 and 3, but just identifying the level at which the misunderstandings are located can be a start, and the overarching aim is to remind ("re-mind") professionals of our shared intention, which is to help. Usually, there will be some blank spaces, and these may stimulate curiosity to understand more. In other areas, more fundamental differences or conflicts may stand out that help to explain contradictory behaviours and stimulate practical efforts to strategize about how I might facilitate a 'connecting conversation' to explore and work around different positions, rather than have these differences enflame debate and stifle mentalizing. These grids can be used (a) as "thought experiments" by a worker or in supervision where a case has stalled, (b) they can be used as a means of notating multi-professional meetings, and (c) they can be completed *with* a young person or family member, in ways that emphasise their agency in facing a helping network that may not entirely make sense to them.

Thinking together (and not apart)

This is the main supervision technique in the AMBIT core. The example with which this chapter started is a typical example of Thinking Apart. "Thinking together" structures how all consultation or supervision (help-seeking between team members) is conducted, by defining four steps:

1 **Mark the task:** *any* consultation starts with a clarification of what is asked from the consultant, what is the problem to be addressed? We tend just to start talking, which leaves the helper without a clear focus on why or what they are listening for, and the help-seeker without having made a start by mentalizing themselves (*"why am I approaching H just now? What do I want or need?"*) The range of potential 'tasks' is limitless; from *"help reassure me that my risk plan makes sense"* to *"help me understand why I feel annoyed with X"*.

2 **State the case:** here, the consultant or group is provided with the bones of the case, the information that is needed to resolve the task. The consultant is responsible for monitoring whether we are falling into 'storytelling' (pretend mode), or when enough info seems to be present. These two opening stages can be tough and business-like (boundaried, in fact), but this is acceptable if both parties know the third step awaits.

3 **Mentalizing the moment:** *First* the helping colleague(s) mentalize the *help-seeking colleague* (*not* the client, which is tempting, but *they are not present*); this is the pre-requisite for any help that might be offered being accepted and digested. Once there is attunement, there can be joint mentalizing around the other minds involved in the dilemma.

4 **Return to purpose:** finally, when the worker is mentalized and some mentalizing has occurred around the problem, there is room for considering

new options in the light of the agreed task. Ideally, solutions come from the help-seeking colleague him/herself, helped by the recovery of their mentalizing, but it is the role of the helping colleague to try to ensure that there is a reconnection with the originally defined purpose.

When a team starts using "Thinking Together" to discuss cases, it can feel awkward, as it involves creating a social discipline around an activity that we do anyway, every day. However, when a whole team understands and accepts the value of these steps, it can be transformative in helping a team to focus attention on each other's minds, and a shared responsibility to support each other's (inevitably, and appropriately fragile) mentalizing.

Reflective practice: am I working this case in AMBIT style?

The AMBIT wiki manual has a downloadable self-audit form, the AMBIT Practice Audit Tool (AprAT). This simple questionnaire offers a brief reflective audit of a specific case in relation to an AMBIT framework and the eight elements of its principled stance. Sample questions include:

- Do you have a mentalized understanding of the difficulties of the young person/family (mentalizing)?
- Have you identified resiliencies in existing relationships in your client's informal network (scaffolding existing relationships)?
- Have you done a Disintegration Grid (taking responsibility for integration)?

Used as a pre-supervision reflection, this is less about scoring fidelity, but more about stimulating reflection with a view to opening opportunities for change, particularly when challenging cases become stuck.

Conclusion

In this chapter, we have discussed how the AMBIT approach has been designed collaboratively to help to develop services better able to adapt to the needs of highly complex and often not conventionally "help-seeking" young people with severe problems. Using mentalization and attachment theory as the oil between the cogs, eight guiding principles ("grabholds" for unsteady workers in the field) have been discussed. These cover how such teams work not only with the client, but with their own colleagues, and across often large and complex multi-agency systems. Another important principle is imperative, as a team, to maintain an active learning stance that balances evidence and local expertise.

Implementing the whole core of AMBIT is a significant change, but it is a framework that is by design adaptive, so that starting as an AMBIT-interested team, and working towards an 'AMBIT influence' is more achievable. Four tools have been offered with which an unobtrusive start may be made. Further reading should include the aforementioned manual Adaptive Mentalization-Based Integrative Treatment: A Guide for Teams to Develop Systems of Care (Bevington et al., 2017) and of course, the online AMBIT core (https://manuals.annafreud.org/ambit).

References

Bevington, D., & Fuggle, P. (2012). Supporting and enhancing mentalization in community outreach teams working with hard-to-reach youth: The AMBIT approach. In N. Midgley & I. Vrouva (Eds.), *Minding the Child: Mentalization-Based Interventions with Children, Young People and Their Families* (pp. 163–186). London: Routledge.

Bevington, D., Fuggle, P., Cracknell, L., & Fonagy, P. (2017). *Adaptive Mentalization-Based Integrative Treatment: A Guide for Teams to Develop Systems of Care* (1st ed.). New York, NY: OUP.

Bevington, D., Fuggle, P., & Fonagy, P. (2015). Applying attachment theory to effective practice with hard-to-reach youth: the AMBIT approach. *Attachment and Human Development*, 17(2), 157–174. https://doi.org/10.1080/14616734.2015.1006385.

Bevington, D., Fuggle, P., Fonagy, P., Target, M., & Asen, E. (2013). Innovations in practice: Adolescent mentalization-based integrative therapy (AMBIT) - a new integrated approach to working with the most hard to reach adolescents with severe complex mental health needs. *Child and Adolescent Mental Health*, 18(1), 46–51. https://doi.org/10.1111/j.14753588.2012.00666.x.

Caspi, A., et al. (2014). The p-factor: One general psychopathology factor in the structure of psychiatric disorders? *Clinical Psychological Science*, 2(2), 119–137.

Fonagy, P., Gergely, G., Jurist, E.J., & Target, M. (2004). *Affect Regulation, Mentalization, and the Development of the Self*. London: Karnac Press.

Fonagy, P., & Target, M. (2005). Bridging the transmission gap: An end to an important mystery of attachment research? *Attachment and Human Development*, 7(3), 333–343.

Fuggle, P., Bevington, D., Cracknell, L., Hanley, J., Hare, S., Lincoln, J., & Zlotowitz, S. (2014). The adolescent mentalization-based integrative treatment (AMBIT) approach to outcome evaluation and manualization: Adopting a learning organization approach. *Clinical Child Psychology and Psychiatry*, 20(3), 419–435, https://doi.org/10.1177/1359104514521640.

Lave, J., & Wenger, E. (1991). *Situated Learning: Legitimate Peripheral Participation*. Cambridge University Press. ISBN 0-521-42374-0.

McCrory, E. (2019). How neuroscience is helping to motivate a preventative psychiatry approach (PDF lecture slides, ACAMH lecture), accessed online from www.acamh.org on 06.11.19.

Weisz, J.R., & Simpson Gray J. (2008). Evidence based psychotherapy for children and adoelscents: Data from the present and a model for the future. *Child and Adolescent Mental Health*, 13(2), 54–65.

Index